The Methods of
Breaking Bad

The Methods of *Breaking Bad*

Essays on Narrative, Character and Ethics

Edited by JACOB BLEVINS *and* DAFYDD WOOD

McFarland & Company, Inc., Publishers

Jefferson, North Carolina

LIBRARY OF CONGRESS CATALOGUING-IN-PUBLICATION DATA

The methods of Breaking bad : essays on narrative, character
and ethics / edited by Jacob Blevins and Dafydd Wood.
        p.   cm.
    Includes bibliographical references and index.

    ISBN 978-0-7864-9578-8 (softcover : acid free paper) ∞
    ISBN 978-1-4766-1935-4 (ebook)

    1. Breaking bad (Television program : 2008–)   I. Blevins,
Jacob, 1970– editor.   II. Wood, Dafydd, editor.

PN1992.77.B74M48 2015
791.45'72—dc23   2014042489

BRITISH LIBRARY CATALOGUING DATA ARE AVAILABLE

Front cover images © 2015 iStock/Thinkstock

Printed in the United States of America

McFarland & Company, Inc., Publishers
  Box 611, Jefferson, North Carolina 28640
  www.mcfarlandpub.com

For Carol Wood

Table of Contents

Acknowledgments

Jacob Blevins would like to express specific thanks to his wife Alison and his friend Lisa Tauzin for providing support during the trauma of *Breaking Bad*'s final season. He also owes thanks to three graduate students, Robert Beard, Luci Mireles and Katya Cummins, all of whom wrote research papers on *Breaking Bad* and at least partially planted the seeds for putting together a volume of essays.

Dafydd Wood would like to thank his children for frequently giving him time to work on the volume and watch the series. And, most important, he would like to thank his wife with whom he watched the series, from the pilot episode to "Felina."

Together, the editors would like thank all the contributors for their hard work, insight, and willingness to put up with (and largely adhere to) the deadlines and consider the editorial comments we have made through the process of putting this manuscript together. We really could not be happier. Finally, as coeditors of this volume, we are also both very pleased and feel very fortunate to have had the opportunity to work with one another on this book. It has been a tremendous partnership and an editorial relationship we hope leads to other projects.

Introduction

JACOB BLEVINS

Vince Gilligan's *Breaking Bad* is a crowning achievement in a line of aesthetically and culturally sophisticated television series that have been produced over the last 15 years. Not only has the quality of these series been high, but, consequently, the personal investment audiences have made has been unlike anything seen in television before.[1] With the rapid growth of social media and other outlets for fans to engage actively and participate "in real time" with these programs, the opportunity for fans to take a more active role in the development and dissemination of commentary, interpretation, and predictions has altered the way television is critically examined. In a sense, we all become critics, and as a result of that potential, filmmakers must be much more clever in the manner in which they construct character and narrative. In order to be a part of this new kind of television, creators, writers, actors must all engage in a much more nuanced form. Audiences can pause, rewind, and re-watch every episode of every show. Nuances can be "talked out" by fans; fans *need* to talk out these nuances. It is simply part of what quality television has to be today if it is to have longevity, to have real resonance for audiences.

Gilligan has taken full advantage of this more dialogic medium, even making narrative decisions based on audience response,[2] and the result is a series that is as significant from a literary and artistic standpoint as anything produced in recent history. *Breaking Bad* represents a stratified vision of character, morality, ethics, and the power of aesthetics that is rich and deep in every facet of its makeup. It builds a dialogue with its viewers, among its viewers, and with narrative history itself. There is nothing one-dimensional about *Breaking Bad*, and because of this no one viewer's perspective can draw out all that Gilligan and his cast do. To understand the full significance of Gilligan's creation, our dialogue must be broad. With that realization, this volume of essays brings in multiple voices from multiple perspectives with the hope that through such critical dialogue we can better understand the manner in which this series takes us out of our areas of comfort, identifies the very discord of our culture, and seeks to structure that discord through the medium of television. Our voices are not the only ones,[3] but the editors have attempted to bring together a group of critically relevant voices in dialogue with one another and that will invoke continued critical discussion.

The essays in this volume draw out many of the intricacies of Gilligan's creation, but undoubtedly the show's center is located in the titular character Walter White. White functions as the new manifestation of the tragic hero. We have seen in narrative history the cultural and literary importance of the hero, and we have seen that figure develop within various cultural contexts and dominant ideologies. In the broad heroic tradition of Oedipus, Hamlet, Willy Loman, and Michael Corleone, Walter White solidifies his place in that tradition, and while Gilligan's hero shares many of the generic traits of those others, White is unique: a hero that emerges from the 21st-century contexts of health care concerns, a fallen economy, indefinite gender roles, gun violence, and the confrontation with the ethnic other (primarily in the immigration issues arising from Mexican border violence). Walter White *must* be a different kind of hero, one whose presence is located in a very different cultural context, but a context that is undeniably ours. Unlike representations of the tragic hero we have seen before, White is fallen when the series begins—or at least he unconsciously defines himself as fallen. He has missed his opportunity at the American corporate dream as he watches his former partners Gretchen and Elliot make billions in Graymatter, while he is a schoolteacher, underpaid and underappreciated. The show never really tells us why Walt sold his share of Graymatter for $5,000—Walt and Gretchen seem to have very different stories—but ultimately the reason does not matter. Walter identifies himself as a failure, and when he learns he has cancer and cannot pay for treatment nor feel confident that he can provide for his family after his death, Walt confronts the image of himself as that failure head on, deciding to pursue financial gains through cooking meth. With this, a reconstruction of his identity begins.

To a large degree, for five seasons, we as viewers witness the processes of this identity construction, a constant struggle to project an ideal image of the self amidst a cultural backdrop that constantly works to destroy or at least alter that ideal image. Perhaps an even better way to characterize the journey of Walter White is one of wish fulfillment. Had Gilligan made the poor, yet well-precedented, decision of concluding the series with the revelation that the audience had in fact been viewing an extended dream narrative of a disillusioned school teacher, we could see the entire dream as fulfillment of basic psychical drives: death, aggression, masculine control, and libidinal pleasure.[4] Slajov Žižek has written and lectured much on the "reality" of fantasy, that fantasy manifests itself in our "real" lives and becomes a truer reflection of the self than identity without such fantasy: the fantasy shows us who we really are.[5] Gilligan has given us Walt's fantastical projection of himself—Heisenberg—and through that we see the true Walter White emerge.

Several of the essays in this collection deal with the fragmented identity that Walt exhibits throughout the series, and how the self constantly searches for reconciliation between the disjointed elements of Walt. Jason Landrum in "Say My Name: The Fantasy of Liberated Masculinity" directly addresses the issues of fantasy and masculinity in the Walter White figure. Landrum, using Lacan specifically and psychoanalysis more generally, contends that the split personality of Walt serves as "a new allegory of masculinity in the early twenty-first century," one that centers on the re-emerging nature of masculine loss. Philip Poe in "Patriarchy and the 'Heisenberg Principle'" is also interested in the struggles of masculinity Walt faces as the head of household, the father, the provider. Poe identifies Walt's adherence to traditional patriarchal ideology as the crucial factor that directs Walt's actions; of course, the ideology itself breaks down—he destroys the family for which he should provide—despite his continued desire and attempts to adhere to the ideology itself. Both essays demonstrate how these ideological pressures of manhood exert themselves on the figure of Walt. Both his identity as a father and husband (the provider) and his role as drug kingpin and father-figure to his partner Jesse are situated around a kind of masculine ideal.

Somewhat ironically, Walt's wife Skyler must come to similar terms with the expectations of a wife as unequivocally supportive of her husband, regardless of the terms of her husband's masculine desires. Interestingly, fans have tended to dislike Skyler,[6] but Skyler struggles with the same kind of pressures of identity that Walt does. Rebecca Price-Wood, in "Breaking Bad Stereotypes about Postpartum: A Case for Skyler White," looks at the White family from the perspective of Skyler and the postpartum experience. Price-Wood argues that Skyler's actions—her affair, her "support" of Walt's meth cooking, and her allowing Walt to continue to share her bed[7]—are all consistent with Skyler's postpartum reality, and our perception of Skyler has everything to do with stereotypes about the postpartum experience. Skyler must negotiate being the proper wife and the proper mother, but she is indeed subject to certain physiological and psychological realities that factor into her actions and reactions to her changing life with Walt.

Still, the narrative action revolves around Walt's own re-identification of himself. In "'Round the decay/Of that colossal wreck': Pride and Guilt as Narrative Emotions" Pablo Echart and Alberto N. García discuss Walt from a moral perspective, particularly how Walt deals with what he first considers immoral actions spurred on by a growing sense of hubris and the guilt he feels at those actions themselves. Echart and García assert that Walt's moral decline is the result of pride overpowering the emotion of guilt; however, the final episodes suggest a return to a guilt-driven ego, which results in a "perverse happy ending." And Meron Wondemaghen in "Walter White: The Psychopath to Whom We Can All Relate?" takes the psychopathetic traits identifiable in Walter and attributes the audience's identification with those traits as a primary reason for the show's success. Wondemagen argues that psychopathetic tendencies are present in us all—we are all potential Walter Whites—and Walt provides us with a case study of those tendencies unmitigated by the "existential process" of self-presentation, compartmentalization, dehumanization and lack of empathy that prevent us from acting out.

These essays show Walt as a broken figure in various ways, but what is definitely suggested in all of these works is the fact that we are somehow drawn to that broken nature of Walt. He becomes our drug: the source of our high, our compulsion, the mirror for our own psyche's potential. But, of course, this is what the tragic hero has always done. Our catharsis, according to Aristotle, results from our identification with Oedipus, the fear that we could all fall from excessive pride.[8] As *passive* viewers, we are asked to make *active* ethical judgments, to come to terms with how the discord between our narrative expectations and the actual narrative we experience violates the ethical framework we bring with us to the series; *Breaking Bad* forces us constantly to redefine our own ethics. We at first sympathize with Walt. Even when he murders Krazy-8 in Season One,[9] we want that immoral act to fit into our own ethical and moral acceptance. Walter had to do it; there was no other choice. But as Walt's actions become less and less able to be ethically justified, the audience turns its sympathies to Jesse: a drug addict, dealer, ultimately a murderer. Jesse even deliberately tries to sell drugs to Andrea (Brock's mother) at a rehab meeting just to show his friends that he could do it.[10] He is willing to fake a relationship with her in order to get her back on drugs. Jesse is not a good guy—at least not based on his actions—but we accept Jesse and are approving of him in some ways because of his visible guilt, his "weakness" for children,[11] and his innocent demeanor. But "innocence" suggests either "free from guilt" or a kind of "ignorance," and Jesse acts with neither of those. He knows fully what he is doing and what the implications will be, and his actions themselves are far from "free from guilt." However, Jesse is a tragic hero in his own right. Arguably, he is the true hero of the show: a fallen figure who feels immense guilt, but cannot prevent himself from self-destruction. His lack of strength, his indecisiveness (as opposed to Walt making a decision and always "moving on"), causes Jesse to continually falter, with only brief remissions in his downward spiral.

The audience even shifts its sympathies to Mike, who also is far from innocent, but he operates within his own ethical code that we come to accept and through which we judge him: he is loyal to his criminal boss and to the men he has sworn to care for and he murders, but only with discretion. When he is killed by Walt, we feel pity for him. Why? And, again, the characters whom we *should* be on the side of—Skyler, Hank, Marie—we are never fully, for various reasons: Skyler is a nagging, unsupportive wife; Hank is as arrogant, as pride-driven as Walt; Marie is an intrusive, annoying kleptomaniac (even Walt and Skyler's son Flynn, who acts every bit like the teenager he is, is difficult to like). These characteristics should NOT drive us to the likes of Walt, Mike, Jesse, and even Gus—but they do.

The success of this kind of audience re-positioning has everything to do with Gilligan's vision of narrative structure, or seeming lack thereof. Neil Connelly, in "What Writers Can Learn from *Breaking Bad*: The Risks and Rewards of Deliberate Disorientation," examines Gilligan's narrative practice of disorienting viewers visually and narratively to create suspense and finally to build a kind of trust between the narrative and the audience. Connelly shows this technique has been significant in some of the most important literary narratives, most notably Toni Morrison's *Beloved*. What is implicit in Connelly's discussion of narrative technique is the deliberate disorientation of the audience's ethical and moral framework. In the same manner that Gilligan builds narrative suspense and restructures the narrative through disorientation, the ethical elements of the series are constructed in exactly the same way.

Ultimately, the ethics of *Breaking Bad* is a major component of the series: for the audience and for the social implications of what the show teases out. Ron W. Darbeau, in "Scientific Ethics and *Breaking Bad*," looks at Walter

White and the ethics of science itself. From the perspective of a scientist, Darbeau asserts that we must separate how we view Walt as a scientist and the pure science he practices in the meth lab from the relative moral actions that take place outside of the lab. While Darbeau argues for what the scientist *is*, Cheryl D. Edelson's "Talking 'bout Some Heisenberg: Experimenting with the Mad Scientist" shows how the scientist is perceived and represented. Edelson looks at Walter White as a kind of gothic mad scientist figure who represents the dangers of technology and the decline of culture. What makes Gilligan's version of the mad scientist (Heisenberg) so appealing and effective is that Walt is not a static character but one whose transformation we experience fully. Darbeau and Edelson—though approaching the role of science from different perspectives—illustrate effectively how the ethics of science and its social implications affect how we view not just science itself, but those who practice it. Walt, as well as Gayle, while in the lab view their project as something that is pure (both the product itself and the process of production), but the purity—in every sense of the word—becomes something else outside of the scientist's lab.

The philosophical and ethical elements to *Breaking Bad* abound, and in various ways most of the essays in this volume highlight this. While Edelson and Darbeau focus on science, in "Breaking Health Care" Matthew A. Butkus looks at the series as a case study for the ethical problems inherent in health care and the desperate lengths that people will go to in order to satisfy their basic health care needs. Walter White is a fictitious figure that reflects a real dilemma: what does a society owe to its members? Butkus considers Walt's story as a "proxy" for the current political and ethical debates about the Affordable Care Act and the core medical ethics at its center. Butkus asserts that the series does revolve largely around this health care debate; Walt must find a way to survive financial ruin because of an illness, and later Hank unknowingly must accept large amounts of money from Walt to cover what his own health coverage will not, which is simply the best possible treatment. The broader question of ethics, market-place production, financial realities, and the context of Walt's story is argued by Jeffrey R. Di Leo to be part of a neoliberal illusion that "everyone [has] the opportunity to be a shareholder, an owner, and an entrepreneur." In "Flies in the Marketplace: Nietzsche and Neoliberalism in *Breaking Bad*," Di Leo considers the dialogue between Gilligan's "Fly" episode and Nietzsche's "Of the Flies in the Market-place," concluding that the fly image permeates not just the philosophical discourse in the two works but points towards the failures of neoliberalism from a philosophical perspective.

It would be incorrect to suggest that other artistic representations have not attempted to depict and comment on the psychological, gender, ethical, and philosophical complexities that we face in our culture; in fact, most art aims at exactly that. However, Gilligan has given us one of the most successful and effective representations. Part of that success lies in the mass appeal; he has managed to make the series work on multiple levels where no single intended audience has priority. The effectiveness at reaching multiple audiences at once lies in the diversity of discourse that is present in the series itself. Miguel E.H. Santos-Neves in "Our 'word ... is half someone else's': Walt and the Literary Echoes of Whitman" notes that *Breaking Bad* does something that other acclaimed series, such as *The Sopranos*, does not: rather than existing within a single discursive community as in *The Sopranos* (or even *Mad Men* to a lesser degree), *Breaking Bad* is more all-encompassing, refusing to "portray an insular community speaking a discourse of its own, which every so often clashes with the world at large." *Breaking Bad is* the world at large, and even its allusions to literary and cultural sources work to create multiple dialogic possibilities.

Dafydd Wood in "Flies and One-Eyed Bears: The Maturation of a Genre" takes this a step further and sets the entire conception and production of *Breaking Bad* into the larger generic structure of which it is a part: the dramatic television serial. Wood looks at Adorno's early statements about television and television drama and shows just how far *Breaking Bad* has brought the genre. Also, Wood points out that our consumption of television, with the advent of Netflix and other streaming sources, has altered the way we have experienced serials over the last decade or so, and *Breaking Bad* capitalizes on this new mode of consumption. One might say that locked away in a dark room late at night, needing just one more episode to satisfy our cravings, all we need to do is hit "watch now" and we have our fix; this is television experienced in a way it has never been experienced before. Wood's essay sets the context for this collection as a whole. We are in a new era of television, one where the potential to create high art for the masses is not only possible but has been realized by Gilligan, the actors, and the relationship between audience and artifice that *Breaking Bad* has given us.

Breaking Bad is a work that facilitates, perhaps even makes possible, a dialogue about aesthetic, philosophical, psychological, and ethical elements in our culture in a way we have yet to see in television. For each of those elements, it is a work that centers itself on friction, fragmentation, conflict, and discord, but it seeks to structure such discord in a way that draws the audience into the dialogue itself. *Breaking Bad* is not just a great television show; it is a cultural landmark, and this collection of essays provides a glimpse into the bricolage, the dialogic foundation on which that landmark is laid.

Notes

1. The level of fan interest in these recent television serials has reached levels we have not seen before. However, television has always had this potential, and there have been a few previous series that have had similar interest. *M.A.S.H.*, *Dallas*, *Cheers*, *Seinfeld*, all could arguably be seen as precursors to the audience obsessions with emotional investment with television programming. Vince Gilligan, in fact, has mentioned the finale of *M.A.S.H.* on several occasions when discussing the conclusion of *Breaking Bad*.

2. Most notably, and well-documented, a teenage boy with cancer, Kevin Cordasco, wanted Gretchen and Elliot to be part of the show's finale and Gilligan obliged. See "How a Teenage Cancer Patient Changed the Ending of 'Breaking Bad,'" *Forbes*, September 27, 2014, accessed July 8, 2014, http://www.forbes.com/sites/allenstjohn/2013/09/27/how-a-teenage-cancer-patient-changed-the-ending-of-breaking-bad/.

3. Much credit should be given to David P. Pierson for editing the first volume of essays on *Breaking Bad*, *Breaking Bad: Critical Essays on the Contexts, Politics, Style, and Reception of the Television Series* (Lanham, MD: Lexington Books, 2013). Several of the essays in this current volume are in implicit dialogue with major themes in Pierson's collection: neoliberalism, masculinity, narrative structure, and so on. Enough cannot be said about the importance of Pierson's collection. The current editors hope that the essays included here will continue the critical discourse begun by Pierson and his contributors, specifically adding the perspective of having experienced the series in its entirety, from pilot to conclusion.

4. In the first episode of Season 2, "Seven Thirty-Seven," Walt practically, or nearly, rapes Skyler in the kitchen after a drug deal with Tuco.

5. Žižek discusses this aspect of fantasy in many of his lectures and published works. However, for the most complete treatment, see *The Plague of Fantasies* (New York: Verso, 1997).

6. There are many varying opinions out there on why Skyler is such an unlikable character, but dislike for her certainly exists. All one must do is a general Google search using "breaking bad hate skyler" and more than 100,000 hits come up, and the "I Hate Skyler White" community Facebook page has more than 31,000 "likes." Anna Gunn, the actress who plays Skyler, wrote an article, "I Have a Character Issue," in the *New York Times* (August 24, 2013: A21). Gunn expresses the fact that she never imagined there would be such disdain for Skyler.

7. The degree to which Skyler "supports" Walt is debatable; however, she certainly covers for Walt, launders money for Walt, and continues to "share Walt's bed," something she expresses her inability to stop in "Fifty-One" (Season 5, Episode 4).

8. Aristotle's well-known discussion of the tragedy in the *Poetics* discusses the relationship between the tragic hero's traits and the audience's connection to him. Aristotle uses Sophocles's Oedipus as the perfect representation of the tragic hero, whose *hamartia* (sometimes translated as "flaw") is pride and stubbornness in the face of learning the truth about his own reality.

9. "And the Bag's in the River" (Season 1, Episode 3).

10. "Abiquiu" (Season 3, Episode 11).

11. Jesse demonstrates consistent concern for Tomás, Brock, and Drew Sharp, the boy shot by Todd after the train heist. Walt's poisoning of Brock is what drives the final wedge between them.

Flies and One-Eyed Bears
The Maturation of a Genre

DAFYDD WOOD

Breaking Bad, the most extended character arc ever filmed, crystallizes the accomplishments of the recent golden age of television. In the last decade and a half, years from the 1998 premiere of *The Sopranos* forwards, as everyone agrees, television serials have been in a good way. The long-form television drama has matured as a medium. If the play was the dominant aesthetic genre from the late 17th century well into the 19th, and the novel took over from the mid–19th to the mid–20th, and film dominated from at least the 1970s, so the television serial has quashed its oedipal father, the motion picture, which, in truth, did not put up the biggest resistance as it was preoccupied by a choking death rattle of repeated remakes and sequels; Brett Martin argues that this genre has "become the signature American art form of the first decade of the twenty-first century."[1] Television dramas not only proliferate, but references to them abound in society at large.

Television never had the best artistic pedigree. Film had established itself as an artistic genre, while television remained its poorly-behaved but ever popular younger step-brother. For example, in 1954 Theodor Adorno, never sympathetic to mass culture, discussed television's "overt" and "hidden" messages, the latter of which are beyond "the controls of consciousness," and will "sink into the spectator's mind." His observations regarding television typify how the medium was perceived from the 1950s until about the last decade: "the majority of television shows today aim at producing, or at least reproducing, the very smugness, intellectual passivity and gullibility that seem to fit in with totalitarian creeds even if the explicit surface message of the shows may be anti-totalitarian."[2] While Adorno the crank is here on full display, if we substitute "ideological" for "totalitarian," he is doubtless correct. Seven years later in 1961 FCC chairman Newton N. Minow famously called television a "vast waste-land." But for our purposes, shortly before the famous quip, Minnow declared, "When television is good, nothing—not the theatre, not the magazines or newspapers—is better."[3] While certainly hyperbolic, we can recognize the truth here, now in our "third golden age" of television.[4]

In *Television*, Raymond Williams looks at the different "forms" of television, the different types of programs, many of which are a "combination and development of earlier forms: the newspaper, the public meeting, the educational class, the theatre, the cinema, the sports stadium, the advertising columns and billboards."[5] But he suggests, as early as 1974, that some forms are "not in any obvious way derivative, and which can usefully be seen as the innovating forms of television itself."[6] The television series is a wholly new aesthetic form and it operates in a manner significantly different from either the film or the novel.

Television's previous attempts at seriousness were never on its own terms, meaning they never exploited the form of television. The best to be expected was a one-off special like one of Ken Russell's documentary lives of a composer, the broadcast of another artwork like an opera or an adaptation (such as the BBC's versions of plays or novels), a liminal work from an acclaimed cinema director as in *Alfred Hitchcock Presents*, or a children's show primed by research in early childhood development for a parent who already feels guilty.

Both Brett Martin and Alan Sepinwall in their recent studies of this period in television used the term revolution, right in the titles of their books.[7] The change, this revolution, from the television of the past, even the preceding golden ages, is qualitative. For example, scholars and academics in media studies refer to these series, and the older ones that anticipated these, as "quality television." This is significant and telling. Almost as a rule, we try to avoid privileging one kind of text over another—all are open to analysis, and all are informative about the culture from which they spring. Since the advent of postmodernism and theory, we generally frown on value judgments. We consistently view all texts as equal, despite the greater design often inherent in the literary, the high brow, the elitist. To embrace all of that, in the very name scholars have given it, by the profession the most sensitive to such matters, bespeaks the significant difference between *The Wire*, *Breaking Bad*, or *Louie* and *Jersey Shore*, *Toddlers and Tiaras*, or *Keeping Up with the Kardashians*.

This suggests an avenue for the developments of scholarship: namely, complexity of design as a value judgment can liberate us and take the place of limiting epithets like "literary" or "high brow," because a show like *Breaking Bad* is not only complex and sophisticated but also engaging and widely-loved.

Both Martin and Sepinwall see complex moralities and ambiguities that readily engage the viewer in the series. If *Breaking Bad* is indeed the transformation of "Mr. Chips into Scarface,"[8] as the series' creator Vince Gilligan conceived it, the series consistently engages the audience and demands an assessment of Walter White's morality—which monstrous act marks Walt's transformation? When does the good father and high school teacher disappear? The series asks the individual viewer to stand in judgment and decide for him or herself. But beyond complex moral questions, these television dramas experiment with their inherited forms and genres, develop character and narrative differently, and demand more engagement from the viewer in terms of analysis and comprehension in addition to morality and ethics. Quite simply we watch television differently than how we once did.

Television's dissemination and consumption has radically changed, and this in turn shores up new formal possibilities. The emergence of HBO and other premium cable channels, unfettered by the requirements and standards of basic cable broadcast, is surely important, but it did not start this development, rather HBO and the like were facilitators, creating a cultural space in which new shows could develop.[9]

The first seasons of *The X-Files*, *Sex and the City*, and *The Sopranos* were all originally released on DVD in 2000; these were the first TV shows to be released in such a format. This technological development literally changed the way we watch television, weakening the importance of airing in a particular spot on a particular day. The DVD could contain multiple episodes and could be set to play all episodes in quick succession. This facilitated a radical change in the consumption of television, the most significant development in the history of the medium. Viewers could now sit down and consume a vast amount of a show over an extended period and on their own terms not according to real-time scheduling. The emergence of streaming services which could make multiple seasons of a series available instantaneously only solidified marathon viewing as a common cultural experience; Netflix and Hulu now release entire seasons of their own programming at the same time.

There are other notable formal developments that enabled the emergence of quality television and mark it separate from the norm. The cable stations that provide these series are free of paid advertisements; without commercials, writers could ignore the necessity of making commercial breaks. But beyond such structural concerns, freedom from advertising was liberating; David Milch, the creator of *NYPD Blue* and *Deadwood*, compared the importance of commercials to the authority of the church, i.e., you cannot offend their moral values. Thus with the loss of commercials, as Milch and Martin see it, the narratives could abandon a moral center and embrace antiheroes, narratives that were "antiversions of all forms," and stories that abandoned all "preexisting expectations ... [and] conventions."[10] Certainly the station and audience still had to be pleased, but writers could now be less enthralled to corporate interests and were free to pursue subjects that had never aired on television.

Furthermore, a given season might be only half as long as a traditional network series—usually thirteen episodes but sometimes as short as ten as is the case for HBO's *Game of Thrones*—but the same amount of time dedicated to writing and producing a season. As Martin suggests, this means "more time and care devoted to the writing of each. It mean[s] tighter, more focused serial stories. It mean[s] less financial risk on the part of the network, which translate[s] to more creative risk on-screen."[11]

In turn, this kind of television enabled showrunners and writers to modify their expectations of the audience. The most noticeable structural transformation of recent television lies in the shift from a rigidly episodic structure to a more expansive serial narrative. In trying to explain the television of today, I know that I and other viewers compare it to the serialized 19th century British novel of Dickens or the like. But such an analogy falls short in the context of the genre's history. Rather what the new television represents is the radical transformation of an inherited form, more similar to modernist experimentation in relation to its predecessors.[12] It is worth noting, however, that not only the comparison to 19th century serialized fiction but also the understanding that the television serial is something new were both made again by Raymond Williams.

After making the startling point forty years ago that "most people spend more time watching various kinds of [television] drama than in preparing and eating food,"[13] Williams argues that the television serial has "precedent[s] in the cinema and in radio ... in the serialized fiction of the late eighteenth and nineteenth centuries.... [But] the *series* has fewer precedents, and these are mainly in nineteenth-century and twentieth-century fiction.... Yet there have been interesting serials of other kinds [e.g., not genre shows]: in effect successors to the widely ranging realist and naturalist works of an earlier fictional period."[14] One might add after *Breaking Bad*, successors of modernist works as well. Even before this current era of quality television, Williams recognized the cultural analogues but also the radical newness of the television series.

Television writers could now presume their viewers were reasonably caught up to date with a show, and they knew the audience was willing to dedicate many hours to it. Thus, viewers already invested in a series could be more attune to the series' on-going plot and character developments,[15] were potentially more forgiving or trusting, were willing to go along with a series' more radical developments. Consider the gradual accretions to the mythology and lore of *The X-Files*, an earlier show that ran from 1993 to 2002: the mystery of the government's relationship to the existence of aliens expanded and became so complex that the casual viewer's understanding was lost. *The X-Files* was a liminal series between episodic construction with casual viewers and the extended narrative of *Breaking Bad* and the like. Quality television has certainly lost that casual viewer who tunes in for the odd episode, but it has gained tremendously.

While Adorno was quoted earlier to encapsulate an older attitude to older programming, his analysis of why those shows failed sounds remarkably perceptive.

> Those who produce the material follow, often grumblingly, innumerable requirements, rules of thumb, set patterns, and mechanisms of control which by necessity reduce to a minimum the range of any kind of artistic self-expression. The fact that most producers of mass media are not produced by one individual but by ... collective collaboration ... is only one contributing factor to this generally prevailing condition.[16]

Adorno registers the multi-billion dollar industry's strong control over its products. And as seems to be the case, he correctly imagined the amount of interference and approval that the larger parent corporation exercised over its television series. A corporation as large as a television station, not to mention a Hollywood studio has invested a vast amount of money into a series or a film, and it is understandable that they would want such control over their product to ensure a return on their investment. But what Adorno recognizes is that these "requirements, rules of thumb, set patterns, and mechanisms of control" subjected upon the final product transform it into a "collective collaboration" or a "corporate dramatic enterprise" as Raymond Williams called it.[17] The end-product as Adorno sees it is a weaker cultural product, stripped of artistic self-expression and impersonal; an aesthetic object produced by a board to entertain the largest demographic possible ends, ironically, by perhaps satisfying a majority but really only pleasing a few. In 1960 Dwight MacDonald wryly observed the same phenomena that typifies the majority of television and Hollywood films to this day: "mass 'entertainment' ... imposes a simplistic repetitious pattern so that it is easier to say the public wants this than to say the truth which is that the public gets this and so wants it. The March Hare explained to Alice that 'I like what I get' is not the same thing as 'I get what I like[.]'"[18] What emerges in *Breaking Bad* is unheard of: a challenging, often experimental work of art loved by millions; the finale was watched by 10.3 million people.

The premium cable stations like AMC, HBO, Showtime and the like quickly recognized the success that met the post-*Sopranos* TV series and have generally pursued a hands-off policy with their final products, trusting their showrunners and writers who already created the successful show and gained its audience. Adorno was correct, and in some areas like big-budget Hollywood he is still. But regarding the television of today he is doubly wrong. Artistic self-expression is immediately perceptible in these series. And furthermore a modification of his "collective collaboration" is still in operation—all of these series rely upon a large group of writers, directors, producers, actors, cine-matographers, etc. But this collective without so much corporate interference or bureaucratic approval works together to achieve Adorno's "self-expression" under a unified stylistic and aesthetic goal; the smaller enclave has a unified vision of their final product and is given the freedom to achieve it. In his study of post-*Sopranos* television, Brett Martin echoes Adorno above by arguing for the unified vision of the showrunner who exercises "godlike powers over an ever-expanding universe."[19] For Martin, the television writer is the central authority, analogous to the director in film. His power "would be wedded to the creative freedom that the new rules of TV afforded. And the men who seized that role ... would prove to be characters almost as vivid as the fictional men anchoring their shows ... [and wielding] near total control of a multimil-lion dollar corporate operation."[20] However, Martin of course knows that the work of many go into each of these series, consistently alluding to the auteur but never quite embracing it.

Later in discussing how a group of writers work under a given showrun-ner, Martin uses the analogy of a cathedral: the writer is similar to a draftsman in charge of perfecting a small part of the massive work, like a sconce; however accomplished, it must fit into the architecture of the whole.[21] But later, he quotes Vince Gilligan himself emphasizing the collective nature of making a TV series. Gilligan vehemently rejects auteur theory as "the worst thing ... the

French [ever] gave us" and a "load of horseshit."[22] What emerges from Gilligan's process of writing *Breaking Bad*, discussed in detail by Martin who sat in on the writing of the fourth season's episode "Shotgun," is a collaborative and democratic process of artistic creation; all the writers contribute and conceive a season and what occurs in the episodes together, while the writing of the specific episodes are parceled out to individuals.

Consider *The X-Files* again; it serves another purpose in the genre's development. Another reason that that series' later seasons appeared baroque or decadent lies in an understanding of the scope and lifespan of a series. There was simply never a conclusion in sight within the show because the reality of the TV series format was to continue indefinitely. Such an indefinite duration is perfectly acceptable for a series with the traditional episodic structure— e.g., *Law and Order, Columbo*, the majority of *The X-Files*, ad infinitum. But as *The X-Files* developed, the larger secrets had to be dealt with and took a percentage of the series' entire output.

The final failure of such a show is simple—faulty closure usually due to an inherently open design that allows for an indefinite retardation of the conclusion. David Lynch's pioneering *Twin Peaks* (1990–1991), for example, was canceled after its second season while Lynch never expected the series to continue into a second season at all. Lynch answered the large narrative thread— who killed Amanda Palmer—halfway through the second season but needed to continue making episodes until its end.

In practice many of the television series of our time since *The Sopranos* proceed with such an indefinite ending. Furthermore, echoing the concerns of Adorno quoted above, studio intervention in finales can bring shame upon a well-liked series; Showtime stipulated that the final season of *Dexter*, widely considered the worst conclusion to a television show, would not contain the death of the well-liked titular character. So it ended completely nonsensically with Dexter sailing with the corpse of his sister into a hurricane and then mysteriously appearing as a lumberjack some time later.

For the creators of a television series, cancellation is a reality. Many causes might contribute to a series' end, including fatigue. It is ironic to note, of course, that the most acclaimed series of this golden age are those that have reached their conclusions on their own terms. Lukewarm critical and audience reception, or a rash of horse deaths as in the series *Luck*. Any viewer can immediately enumerate a favorite show or two that was canceled too soon—*Deadwood* or *Firefly* for instance—but also multiple shows that had to patch an ending on too early or too late. The most highly regarded television series, perhaps of them all, *The Wire*, reached its ending organically where its show runner, David Simon, wanted it to end, and for Vince Gilligan, a writer on and producer of *The X-Files*, *Breaking Bad* was conceived with a definite end-date in mind.

In another text from the 1950s based on his experience of American television, Adorno observes the formal constraints exerted upon the genre and the impact this has upon the quality of the work:

> The main difference [between television dramas and film] lies precisely in the brevity of the television dramas: most often they are a quarter-hour, at most a half-hour long. This affects the quality as well. Even the modest development of plot and character permitted in film is impossible: everything must be set up immediately. This supposedly technological necessity, itself dictated by the commercial system, favors the stereotypes and the ideological rigidity the industry in any case justifies on the basis of consideration for a juvenile or infantile public. These television dramas relate to films in a manner similar to the way the detective novellas compare to detective novels: in both cases the formal shallowness serves an intellectual one.[23]

Since that time, the hour-long TV episode has become standard, but more importantly the serialized television drama has emerged as a medium. And *Breaking Bad* shows just how much television has evolved, offering in the face of Adorno's critique perhaps the most extended narrative and character development ever filmed. It seems like our moment is diametrically opposed to what Adorno had seen sixty years ago. Television needs an initial attention-grabbing pilot, but it has entire seasons to set up plot, character, and everything else. After fifteen years of such series, films now seem abrupt with hastily made introductions, stereotypes, and ideological rigidity. The formal richness of *Breaking Bad* serves an intellectual one.

While Adorno might never have been able to accept television, or Jazz for that matter, there are structural innovations and experimentations he would certainly have appreciated as a diligent modernist within *Breaking Bad*. This series consistently manipulates, disorients, and defamiliarizes the viewer in a manner suggestive of Viktor Shklovsky's *ostranenie* (literally, *strange-making*, but usually translated as defamiliarization or enstrangement device). To put it simply, such defamiliarization involves twisting in some way the representation of or perspective on a quotidian object. Some of Shklovsky's famous examples include Tolstoy not naming familiar objects, using a horse as a narrator, or describing religious dogmas as if they had never been encountered before.[24] This is at work in *Breaking Bad* and seems almost a guiding aesthetic—the series, as has been frequently observed, looks like no other television show.

There are many tropes within the series that possess a twinge of the avant-garde and the defamiliarized. The beginning of the first episode asserts the show's difference, establishes patterns that the series will continue, and lays down what the writers will expect from the audience: a radical, completely uncontextualized, but strangely beautiful desert landscape with a pair of khakis fluttering in the wind, before they are run over by an RV. The next shot brings us inside the RV: a driver in a gas mask wearing only his white brief underwear and three bodies sliding around. The end of the teaser opening finds Walter White now missing only his pants aiming a gun ahead towards the road and provides one of the canonical images of *Breaking Bad*. Such disorientation verges on the surreal and will only continue throughout the series. In fact, all of the radical formal innovations of the show, not to mention the very narrative itself, can be read through the guise of defamiliarization; the familiar is made strange: a high school teacher becomes a drug kingpin, a toy bear becomes a symbolic representation of Walt's responsibility in the deaths of 167 airline passengers, a shovel is anthropomorphized and given a point of view however briefly, or a narrative which the audience has been following is adapted into a Mexican music video in a genre with which the audience is likely not to be familiar.

The second season and probably the series' most extreme project of defamiliarization begins in black and white with a shot of a dripping hose then various other garden objects (a hummingbird feeder, a snail, a wind chime, patio furniture, house, and pool). After establishing setting—the Whites' backyard and pool—the camera lingers on an object rotating within a pool—an eyeball, we eventually discover, probably artificial. After it gets sucked into the pool's trap, a pink stuffed bear floats into the camera and pivots showing the audience its charred half and missing eye. After the titles, all hint of this material disappears until the beginning of the fourth episode in which a suited man fishes the bear from the pool and places it in an evidence bag next to other bagged objects. The bear appears again in the season's tenth episode where men in hazardous material suits remove it from the Whites' property. The camera pulls up showing Walt's damaged car and two body bags. Then the season finale shows the entire sequence and finally begins the process of contextualization and revelation: the camera continues pulling up showing similar objects scattered throughout the neighborhood, subsequent body bags, and two columns of black smoke. Before the titles, the sequence rapidly becomes colorized.

These disorienting sequences while contributing vastly to the show's style, look, and aesthetic, achieve larger goals than simply unmooring the audience. A pair of glasses in an evidence bag looks very similar to Walt's. Two body bags near Walt's car could easily contain two central characters. The audience does not know what is happening and tries to figure it out—what has Walt done? Of course, the in-air collision between two planes is a far greater tragedy than could have been gleaned from the clues left by Gilligan and company. Furthermore, Walt's hand in it, obscured at first and gradually revealed, demonstrates the repercussions of what many viewers see as one of his first truly corrupt actions—letting Jane die, the daughter of an air traffic controller. The pink bear further suggests innocence and its destruction. Walt finds the bear's eyeball in his pool's trap and keeps it. Nothing is said of it, and it is met with confusion by other characters like Skyler and one of the assassin Cousins, but Walt keeps it at least through the fourth season, seen in his suitcase, in a drawer in his apartment, and again in a drawer at his home. What it means to him is not clear, a reminder of his role in the airplane crash perhaps, but the eye clearly a synecdoche for the bear itself is highly symbolic and suggestive.

While the second season's teddy bear/airplane collision sequences are the series' most disorienting openings, there are many more.[25] The fifth season opens to Walt with a full-head of hair and a full beard a year into the future of the show, before it is dropped again until the opener of the second half of the fifth season. There, the Walt residence abandoned and wrecked hosts skateboarders in the empty swimming pool. Walt arrives in his new car, enters the house, sees a graffito of the name Heisenberg and retrieves his hidden ricin. It is not until the season finale that the audience can put these scenes into the context of the series' narrative. Similarly "Ozymandias," the antepenultimate episode and climax of the series' entire narrative, begins in flashback to the beginning of the series as it sets up a variety of echoes, foreshadowings, and ironies between Walt and Jesse at their first cook, and Walt and Skyler on the phone discussing their future.

Breaking Bad's experimentation is by no means limited to its opening pre-titles sequences, however. Michael Slovis, the director of photography from the second season forward is largely responsible for picking up the radical look that was pioneered in the first season. Bizarre, point-of-view camera angles consistently punctuate the show amounting to a signature of sorts on each episode. These perspectives are surreal, startling, and disorienting at first, but later the audience anticipates this kind of inventive camera work and wonders at how such shots could even be made or when they will appear. Some of these shots include perspectives from: inside a rolling barrel, a fly, a can of gasoline Jesse is pouring all over the Whites' house, the inside of a spinning dryer full of cash, many trunks of many cars, beneath stove tops, the tank of a toilet, a pyrex tray of freshly cooked meth, the head of a shovel, the bottom of a fryer full of hot grease, a Roomba.

A surrealism emerges in *Breaking Bad*'s desire to linger on the material qualities of things or idiosyncratic details. In "Caballo Sin Nombre," Walt frustrated with Skyler throws a pizza, purchased as an olive branch, which lands on the roof. It gradually decomposes until Walt removes it in "I.F.T." The third season opens with a wildly disconcerting sequence of adults crawling on their bellies along a dirt road. By the end of the trailer the Salamanca Cousins have joined the crawlers and arrived at a crude occult shrine dedicated to Santa Muerte, a folk saint in Mexican Catholicism and often venerated by Cartel members. While this background would not be known to most viewers, the sequence establishes without any further explanation the ritual elements, the crawling in supplication, and the Cousins' votive offering for assistance in their plan to kill Walt. Another startling and genre-defying moment of experimentation comes in the second season episode "Negro y Azul." The beginning of this episode amounts to a music video for a Mexican narcocorrido song about Heisenberg performed by Los Cuates de Sinaloa. Narcocorrido is a genre of Mexican folk music whose lyrics glamorize tales of real-life drug smugglers and criminals. Similarly the episode "Kafkaesque" contains a commercial for Gus Fring's fried chicken chain restaurant, Los Pollos Hermanos.

These idiosyncratic and aesthetically-minded shots and sequences, not to mention the other levels of detail within the series—color palettes representing particular characters and functioning like leitmotivs—act almost like a manifesto against the quotidian nature of most films and television series. Shot on film, Slovis and Gilligan planned on careful realistic lighting, embracing shadows that could never be seen on basic cable. Likewise they alternated between filming on dollies and using handheld techniques. Any episode can be rigorously analyzed for wide landscapes, slow-motion, time-lapse shots, camera-filters that defamiliarize with unreal colors, montage, distorted mirror-images, lingering poetically on quotidian objects, and then the stray surreal object like a tortoise baring a severed head.

Finally, however, *Breaking Bad*'s experimentalism is not some kind of mannerism or late-style, rather it is a vigorous and consistent renewal of the formal possibilities of film, and it always functions in subordination to the larger narrative concerns, never Swinburnian excess or gilding.[26] The transformation from the familiar—Walter White, Chemistry teacher at J.P. Wynne High School—to the strange— Heisenberg, inventor of the highest grade crystal methamphetamine—lends thematic unity the series' defamiliarizing or enstranging thematic. It is worth noting that such formal innovation in television has by no means ended: the fourth season of FX's series *Louie*, created, written, directed, and edited by Louis CK who also stars in it, pushes narrative structure and experimentation even further than *Breaking Bad* with scenes of unadulterated surrealism or mini-narratives within the larger series, that are sometimes interrupted by other episodes or set decades before the series in order to comment upon the series' present.

It is worth turning once again to Raymond Williams to further consider the success of *Breaking Bad*:

> [The television serial's] persistence and popularity is significant, in a period in which, in so much traditionally serious drama and fiction, there has been a widespread withdrawal from general social experience.... [The] cultural importance of the serial, as an essentially new form, ought not to be limited to ... the attempted blending of fictional and dramatic forms [e.g., Masterpiece Theatre–like dramatizations].... Few forms on television have the potential importance of the original serial. If the form has been overlaid, understandably, by the "classic" emphasis [again referring to BBC adaptations], and more generally by the stock formulas of crime and illness, that is a particular cultural mediation, which is necessary to understand and look for ways beyond.[27]

With the television series of today, we have gone beyond as Williams hoped 40 years ago, and *Breaking Bad*'s success is due in large part to its investment in the "general social experience." *Breaking Bad* introduces the audience to Walter White as a species of everyman for an early–21st century recession-era United States. Walter works two jobs to provide for his family, and he is alienated from both of them. At the high school, his students are bored and hardly paying attention; at the carwash, he is forced to wash cars sometimes even in front of his students. His wife is distant and pregnant while he is in middleage. His son has special needs. He develops lung cancer and cannot afford medical care. Walter is oppressed on all sides where any single one of the hardships above could make an audience sympathize.

But Walter violently seizes the symbolic capital of his expertise in chemistry and uses it to transform his life. *Breaking Bad* thus begins as a kind of twisted American cliché—he pulls himself up by his bootstraps, he makes himself, he comes from nothing to success. He manufactures a product, ironically referred to throughout the series as "product," which is a perfect example of a commodity—his blue meth perpetuates its own consumption, its own demand that can only be fulfilled by Walter's supply. Its superiority to all of the other meth on the market, however, singles it out for Hank's attention. If Walter's meth had not been so pure, he would have not made as much money, but he also might have been able to survive longer as a kingpin. The series wholly embraces this social experience. Furthermore, the last few seasons are concerned principally with money, what to do with it and what is enough.

The series offers a final symbol, or rather an immense metonymy, for the character's success, his achievement—Walt's loss and Heisenberg's gain: the enormous square block of bills in the storage unit, most memorably with Huell lying on it. This pile of money makes manifest and literal Walt's earnings, his drug and blood money. Likewise it takes the everyday familiar objects of bills and enstranges them by the vast amount, calling further surreal attention to itself with Huell and Kuby. The metonym literally and physically leads to what Walt saw as his nadir—Hank's death in the desert where the money, now in barrels, was buried. Hank follows Walt to the GPS coordinates, to the site where all of his earnings from making meth are buried. If *Breaking Bad* were not so well written, it would be crass allegory. Not to mention the later scenes of Walt rolling his last barrel, returned patronizingly to him by the white supremacist gang, across the wide desert landscape. *Breaking Bad* is masterfully designed: from the 60-hour narrative and character arc to developing visual metonymies, synecdoches, and metaphors, from narratological experimentation to defamiliarization and color-symbolism. It is beautiful. *Breaking Bad* represents the finest achievement in a genre that we have just watched reach maturity.

Notes

1. Brett Martin, *Difficult Men: Behind the Scenes of a Creative Revolution: From* The Sopranos *and* The Wire *to* Mad Men *and* Breaking Bad (New York: Penguin, 2013), 11.

2. Theodor W. Adorno, "How to Look at Television," *The Culture Industry: Selected Essays on Mass Culture*, ed. J. M. Bernstein (New York: Routledge, 2001), 165–166.

3. Newton N. Minow, "Television and the Public Interest (speech, Washington, D.C. May 9, 1961), American Rhetoric, http://www.americanrhetoric.com/speeches/newtonminow.htm.

4. I doubt this term is very helpful, at least in thinking of the previous two golden ages—their canonical series have generally not aged well. The "first golden age" murkily began in the 1940s and continued to the 1950s or 60s; there is no consensus. It certainly did contain exceptional work: *Alfred Hitchcock Presents*, *The Twilight Zone*, and tele-

casts of Arturo Toscanini, Leonard Bernstein, Shakespearean plays, operas, and ballets. The "second golden age" apparently occurred at some point in the 1980s to early 1990s: its most notable example is David Lynch's *Twin Peaks* which, whether from an age of gold or tin, anticipates our current shiny period. But, putting all of this parsing aside, there is little consensus: the period of *The Sopranos* to *Breaking Bad* is often referred to as the "second golden age" and even "the golden age." The problem is semantic: "golden age" might be a helpful descriptor or marker, but in practice it is of little use; there are after all references to a "golden age of pornography" and another of piracy. Finally, golden age rhetoric intertwined as it is with *translatio imperii* seems best avoided.

5. Raymond Williams, *Television* (London: Routledge, 2003): 39.

6. Ibid.

7. Martin's *Difficult Men: Behind the Scenes of a Creative Revolution: From* The Sopranos *and* The Wire *to* Mad Men *and* Breaking Bad, cited above, and Alan Sepinwall, *The Revolution Was Televised: The Cops, Crooks, Slingers, and Slayers Who Changed TV Drama Forever* (New York: Touchstone, 2012).

8. Gilligan originally pitched the show to AMC with this line, and it has since stuck and proliferated wherever the series is discussed.

9. HBO began in 1972 and *The Sopranos* premiered in 1998; that's a 26-year gap, a gap full of good programming, surely, but nothing so radical. AMC, *Breaking Bad*'s broadcast channel, was founded in 1984 as a station that aired classic films, and at that time called itself American Movie Classics. In 2002, the station rebranded itself AMC and launched its new programming. Thus *Breaking Bad* came into being because of AMC's deliberate imitation of, or navigation into the space created by, HBO—from the initials of the station's name, to its programming, even to its latest catchphrase, "Something Different," hardly different conceptually from "It's not TV. It's HBO."

10. Quoted in Martin, 87.

11. Martin, 6.

12. In addition to the multi-season narrative of shows like *Breaking Bad, The Wire*, and others, there also has emerged a slightly different narrative structure in series like *Dexter* and the rebooted *Doctor Who*, namely a season-long narrative or mystery which is more or less resolved at the end of a season providing significantly more closure than the structurally more innovative series.

13. Williams, 56.

14. Ibid., 56–57.

15. Interestingly, Williams argues that shows more serial in nature construct a different kind of continuity, "not of an action but of one or more characters." See Williams, 57.

16. Adorno, 168.

17. Williams, 57.

18. Dwight MacDonald, "Masscult and Midcult," *Against the American Grain: Essays on the Effects of Mass Culture* (New York: Random House, 1962), 10–11.

19. Martin, 8.

20. Ibid., 8–9.

21. Ibid., 72–73.

22. Ibid., 265.

23. Theodor W. Adorno, "Television as Ideology," *Critical Models: Interventions and Catchwords*, trans. Henry W. Pickford (New York: Columbia University Press, 2005): 60. Originally published in 1953.

24. See for instance Viktor Shklovsky, "Art as Device," *Theory of Prose*, trans. Benjamin Sher (Elmwood Park: Dalkey Archive Press, 1990): 6–14.

25. For further discussion of the series' disorienting openings, see Rossend Sánchez-Baró, "Uncertain Beginnings: *Breaking Bad*'s Episodic Openings," *Breaking Bad: Critical Essays on the Contexts, Politics, and Reception of the Television Series*, ed. David P. Pierson (Lanham, MD: Lexington Books, 2014): 139–153.

26. For a close reading of the episodes "Seven-Thirty-Seven" and "ABQ," see Pierre Barrette and Yves Picard, "Breaking the Waves," *Breaking Bad: Critical Essays on the Contexts, Politics, and Reception of the Television Series*, ed. David P. Pierson (Lanham, MD: Lexington Books, 2014): 121–138.

27. Williams, 58.

Flies in the Marketplace
Nietzsche and Neoliberalism in Breaking Bad

JEFFREY R. DI LEO

"What is your aim in philosophy? —To shew
the fly the way out of the fly-bottle."
—Ludwig Wittgenstein (*PI* §309; 103e)

Walter White does not have long to live. Or, more precisely, he has sixty-two episodes of *Breaking Bad* to live. Dying of terminal lung cancer, Walt (played in the series by Bryan Cranston), an overqualified high school chemistry teacher, decides to start cooking and selling methamphetamine in order to provide his wife and children with a strong financial future after his demise. His pregnant wife Skyler (Anna Gunn) and his teenage son Walter Jr. (RJ Mitte), who has cerebral palsy, are unaware of his criminal undertakings for much of the series because Walt tells lie after lie to protect his secret identity. His wife only learns of his "breaking bad" mid-series and his son not until the final episodes. Adding to the dramatic tension and irony of Walt's deceit is the fact that the people he is closest with outside of his immediate family are Skyler's sister, Maria Schrader (Betsy Brandt), who is a health care worker (and kleptomaniac) and her husband, Hank (Dean Norris), who is a Drug Enforcement Agency (DEA) agent—a federal agent who unbeknownst to him is pursuing his own brother-in-law and close friend.

Walt learns about his cancer and makes his decision to cook and sell meth in the series pilot. He also is introduced to his partner, Jesse Pinkman (Aaron

Paul), in the inaugural episode. Walt rides along with Hank to observe him busting a meth house. Without Hank knowing, Jesse slips out a window during the drug raid and avoids identification and capture by the DEA. Walt though witnesses Jesse's escape, and recognizes him as his former high school chemistry student. They soon decide to become entrepreneurs and go into the meth business, where Walt will "cook" and Jesse will "sell."

By mid-series both Walt and Jesse have amassed millions of dollars, and by the end of the series Walt himself has some $80 million in cash buried in drums in the New Mexico desert. All of this happens over the course of a few months, or at the very most, less than a year. The magical realism of the series is grounded in our suspension of disbelief that this is possible. Or, more progressively, the underlying neoliberal vision of this series (what might be termed *neoliberal magical realism*) is that anyone strapped with debt can become an entrepreneur in the free market if they are willing to ignore their moral and social conscience by engaging in violent criminal activity that destroys lives and society. Walt lives the American neoliberal dream—a dream where self-interest and market forces beget violence and financial reward. In the neoliberal world of Walter White, crime pays and pays well. Or does it?

Though Walt has amassed a fortune, perhaps enough money to provide financial security for his family for many generations, he has in the process lost them—and himself. By the end of the series, his son hates him and refuses to take his money, his wife is broke and barely evading prison for aiding Walt in his criminal enterprise, and his brother-in-law has been murdered while trying to bring Walt to justice. In a last ditch effort to get money to his family after his death, he threatens to have his former grad-school colleague, Elliott Schwartz (Adam Godley), and Elliott's wife (and Walt's former lover), Gretchen (Jessica Hecht), murdered after his death if they do not "donate" the remainder of his meth fortune to his family.

Over the course of the series, Walt transforms from a mild-mannered high school chemistry teacher into a lying, murdering, violent drug-kingpin, who is known and feared by the name "Heisenberg." Interestingly, his cancer is in remission when he is "cooking," but acts up when he stops. Walt tries to lead a dual-life by hiding his Heisenberg-persona from his family including his brother- and sister-in-law. However, by the end of the series, his criminal persona is known not just by his family, but the world over. As public enemy number one, he hides out in a shack in the woods of New Hampshire, trying to evade capture, but decides to return when his son refuses to take his money and he is renounced by Elliott and Gretchen on television as having had no role in the founding of their highly-successful business. No one wants to associate with Walt including his former partner, Jesse, who now wants Walt dead.

As someone who believes that visual narrative (e.g., film) can present epistemological, metaphysical, and moral issues as effectively as verbal narrative (e.g., stories), *Breaking Bad* is a philosophical goldmine. Among the many topics addressed are the nature of evil, the meaning of life, the meaning of death, our freedom to control our actions and choices, social justice, our obligations to others, friendship, and so on. One of the virtues of dark and philosophically rich contemporary visual series like *Breaking Bad*, *Mad Men*, *The Wire*, and *The Sopranos*, is their power to engage a broader public in both the social and political issues of the day along with the moral and philosophical problems of the ages. Series such as these play an important social role in educating a public that is increasingly more visually literate as opposed to verbally literate. For many, television and film are their only exposure to philosophical thinking and critical inquiry.

However, like *The Sopranos*, *Mad Men*, and *The Wire*, there is often much debate and confusion about their message. For some, they are glorifications of violence, greed, lust, murder, and crime; for others they are morality tales warning us of the horrors of violence, greed, lust, murder, and crime. Should we be attracted to their lead characters or repulsed by them? Are they "heroes" or "anti-heroes"? Supermen or villains? Deities or devils? Such matters complicate understanding these narratives in ways that make them more philosophically interesting and socially progressive than mass media series of say the previous century or generation.

In the 60s, a television series like the original *Star Trek* (1966–1969), a perennial philosophical favorite, made it easier for their audience to sort out such matters. Most episodes of *Star Trek* revolved around presenting a distinct philosophical problem and resolving it. Captain Kirk and his crew were the heroes charged with helping the audience sort out the philosophical complexities presented by their voyages. However, the same cannot be said of the recent generation of series. For example, while there are episodes that stand out as more philosophically rich than others, a series like *The Sopranos* has more in common with a novel than an individual television episode. The unconscious of Tony Soprano and its role in the sociopathic violence in which he participates is the driving force of the series. Much the same could be said of *Mad Men* though for Don Draper it is sociopathic *lust*, rather than violence.

In fact, just as David Simon, who created *The Wire*, pitched it as a "60-hour long 'visual novel,'" so too should we regard *Breaking Bad*.[1] Or, more specifically, *Breaking Bad* is more like the serialization of a Dickens or a Dostoevsky novel, than *Star Trek*, where each episode is more like a short story rather than a chapter of a novel.[2] These long-form series are one of the more amazing developments of the Golden Age of television—and are in fact a development that has brought a lot of "thinking" people and socio-political critique back to weekly network and cable programming. *Star Trek* is here used as a foil to *Breaking Bad* not to belittle it, but rather to distinguish it as one of the two major forms of non-cinematic philosophical visual narrative: episodic versus novelistic visual narrative.

In episodic visual narrative, a philosophical problem can be established, pursued, and resolved in thirty to sixty minutes. In novelistic visual narrative, one or more major philosophical problems is established, pursued, and resolved in sixty *hours* or more. Argument and counter-argument can be developed in novelistic visual narratives such as *Breaking Bad* in ways impossible in episodic— or even cinematic narrative. *The Sopranos, Mad Men,* and *The Wire,* are series that are more philosophically rich considered as a whole as compared to individual episodes. *Star Trek,* however, is just the opposite. As a complete series its philosophical message is less powerful than the distinct philosophical messages of individual episodes, some of which are philosophically stronger and more intriguing than others. In this light, cinematic narrative, which usually varies between ninety minutes and three hours, has more in common with episodic narrative than novelistic narrative.

However, *Breaking Bad* eclipses its kindred series by offering an episodic moment that is arguably the philosophical center of the series. In a way, the episode functions similarly to "The Grand Inquisitor" section of Dostoevsky's *The Brothers Karamozov* or "The Battle Royale" section of Ralph Ellison's *Invisible Man.* In other words, just as "The Grand Inquisitor" and "The Battle Royale" sections of these respective novels are their philosophical centers, and are often considered as independent philosophical works in themselves, so too can and should one of the episodes of *Breaking Bad*—an episode simply entitled "Fly."

The central argument of this essay is that the "Fly" episode of *Breaking Bad* is its philosophical center. It is an episode that not only is a self-reflective one for its major character, Walter White, but also for the series itself—and arguably is its most self-reflexive moment. "Fly" reveals both some of the historically Nietzschean strains of *Breaking Bad* as well its contemporary neoliberal dimensions. It also illuminates a semiotic system that provides a wholly non-verbal dimension that beautifully complements the verbal dialogue of the series. The "Fly" episode of *Breaking Bad* is a major work of art and philosophy, and arguably the most philosophically powerful episode in the series, if not also among its kindred series, *The Sopranos*, *Mad Men*, and *The Wire*.

This essay will begin with an introduction to the "Fly" episode, and then follow it with a discussion of its direct connection with the philosophical tradition, most notably the philosophy of Friedrich Nietzsche. It will then show how this episode also reveals major aspects of *Breaking Bad*'s critique of neoliberalism. The essay will conclude that the power of the "Fly" episode comes from it ability to both look backward to the philosophical tradition and forward into the negative dimensions of contemporary social behavior and political thought in a way not often exemplified in contemporary visual media.

Before moving on to an examination of the "Fly" episode, it should be noted that my overarching interests are threefold: (1) to locate *Breaking Bad* as a site of critique and resistance to the terrors of neoliberalism in America[3]; (2) to identify *Breaking Bad* as a major source of philosophical inquiry that is potentially more appealing to a wider public than more traditional modes of philosophical inquiry, viz., articles and books[4]; and (3) to establish that one of the historical lines of philosophical inquiry that *Breaking Bad* engages is Nietszchean in a direct, significant, and interesting sense.

Fly

By the midpoint of the *Breaking Bad* series, things are seriously starting to break apart for Walt. His marriage is falling apart just when his daughter Holly is born. His partner, Jesse, is in the hospital after nearly being beaten to death by Walt's brother-in-law, Hank, who came very close to catching Walt red-handed with Jesse in their mobile meth lab. But this is just the beginning of Walt's troubles: the drug cartel has a hit out on him for the murder of Tuco Salamanca (Raymond Cruz), and, to that end, The Cousins (Daniel and Luis Moncada) are aching to be allowed to take out Walt.

However, Walt is not yet aware that The Cousins are after him. Rather, he cooks for fast food chicken restaurant mogul Gustavo Fring (Giancarlo Esposito) who has provided him with an industrial-quality state-of-the-art meth lab safely tucked away in the bowels of one of his plants. Gus though is being pressured by The Cousins to be allowed to kill Walt.

In order to protect his investment in his meth cook and interstate distribution system, Gus deceives The Cousins into believing that they are allowed to take out Hank, who as a DEA agent is off-limits to the cartel. The Cousins ambush Hank in a parking lot though he manages to survive after killing one of the cousins and nearly killing the other. Hank is now in the hospital slowly recovering, but Marie refuses to take the treatment offered by her insurance company for her husband. For her, the course of treatment afforded by Hank's health care insurance seems inferior, so she opts to pay out of her own pocket for an alternative and presumably better (albeit more expensive) recovery route. It is at this point in the series that an episode entitled "Fly" appears.[5]

From the opening sequence, it is apparent that this episode is going to be different from the others. "Fly" opens with the sound of a woman singing the children's lullaby "Hush little baby don't you cry." Against the lullaby, a baby is heard crying from time to time. The singing woman is never seen, nor is it clear who is singing the lullaby. However, from Walt's comments later in the episode, it becomes fair to assume that it is Skyler singing to the newborn Holly.

An almost surreally horrific tension is built by positioning these opening sounds against highly magnified shots of a common housefly. The early shots are indistinct and fuzzy but soon one can recognize the detail of a wing and then there is a clear, full-screen close-up of the two red eyes of a fly. The lullaby and surreal fly shots go on for about thirty-seconds and then the intro sequence cuts to the *Breaking Bad* theme music and title sequence. After the theme music is played and titles are shown, the episode opens with a full-screen shot of a blinking red light. The circumference of the light's base touches the top and bottom of the screen. It blinks a few times. The camera then pulls back to reveal that the source of the light is the blinking red light of a smoke detector set against vertical shadows that look like prison bars.

It soon becomes apparent that Walt is awake in his bed staring at a flashing smoke detector light on his ceiling. The clock next to his bed reads 2:00am amidst a dark room. The next shot is of his hand turning off his alarm at 6:00am in a fully lit room. He rises from his bed and sits on the side of it to put on his glasses. He is tired and just over his shoulder the blinking red light of the smoke alarm is seen flashing.

So, why, one might ask, does the episode open with a full-screen shot of a blinking red light? What does it mean? On an iconic level, the red of light mirrors the red eye of the fly viewed earlier. On a symbolic level, the red stands for the red phosphorus that is used in the production of methamphetamine. Walt's whole life is consumed by the production and distribution of methamphetamine, and red phosphorus is one of the key elements in its production. In fact, in one of the earlier episodes of the series, Walt sees a stranger buying materials to set up a clandestine meth lab. The stranger however has the wrong matches in his cart. So, Walt, ever the "teacher," says to the stranger, "Those matches, they're the wrong kind. Red phosphorus is found in the striker strips, not the matches themselves. You need to get the big 200-count case of individual matchbooks. More striker strips, you understand? Those only have the one."

In Walt's world, the flashing red light associated with red phosphorus holds a metonymic relationship with the elements of meth production, if not meth production itself. Using it in the opening shots of the episode sets the stage for the intense psychological drama concerning meth production that occupies the remainder of the episode. Revealing the ominous blinking red light of the smoke detector set against vertical shadows that look like prison bars reminds the viewer of the dangers of meth production and distribution, namely, prison. But more directly, the blinking red light of the smoke detector set against vertical shadows symbolizes the "prison house of meth" that now dangerously occupies and controls the life and world of Walter White.

The scene now shifts from the inside of Walt's bedroom to the outside of the laundry that houses Walt's meth lab. The "prison house" imagery is continued in this scene as it opens with rolling vertical images of the fence bars that surround the laundry/meth lab. The vertical fence bars mirror the vertical shadows from the smoke detector shot—and again recall prison bars. They are seen from the perspective of Jesse, who is arriving at the plant dock where Walt and he cook. Walt has already arrived though he is sitting in his car a bit dazed and out of it when Jesse pulls his car next to him. Atmospheric music à la Brian Eno plays while Jesse gets out of his car and walks over to Walt's driver side window. He raps on the window loudly and breaks Walt out of his stupor. So too ends the atmospheric music.

Up to this point of the episode, there has been no dialogue. There has just been fly, red light, and prison bar imagery. Nevertheless, a lot has been communicated in the prelude to "Fly." Most notably that Walt is losing sleep with worry about the meth "prison house" that now controls his life and in which he is now incarcerated.

By working for Gus in his lab, Walt and Jesse now are laborers in a factory type atmosphere. They are required to produce 200 pounds of meth a week, an obligation that Walt, after the near fatal shooting of Hank on Gus's order, now worries about. He knows that if the meth is not produced on schedule or if they steal some of the meth that they are producing, then their lives could be in serious danger as Gus will stop providing them with protection. As they walk into the laundry and pass Gus's workers punching the time clock, Jesse says to Walt, "I'm surprised he doesn't make us do that!" These are the first words of the episode—ones indicative of their level of resentment toward Gus and level of control he has over their lives.

This line of comment continues by Jesse when he and Walt get down into the lab and commence cleaning the equipment. Jesse tells Walt about a television show about hyenas that he saw: "The hyenas have a pecking order. The head hyena, he's the man. All of the other ones have to like kiss his ass. I mean literally it is so gross. They have to lick his junk. I can't even believe they showed it on TV."

Jesse, perhaps even more than Walt, resents that they have to cook for Gus, rather than themselves. He had hoped to cook for himself before Walt convinced him to be his partner in fulfilling Gus's "million dollar" meth order. The hyena story as well as the time-clock comment show Jesse to be not "worried" about what he is doing in the lab and its implications for his life and the life of others, but rather annoyed about the lack of entrepreneurial freedom that cooking for Gus affords him. Working for Gus in this way is "working for the man," rather than being an "entrepreneurial man." Or, more crudely put, working for Gus is akin to having to "lick his junk," that is, degrading. The ignominy of cleaning the meth lab only amplifies his frustration with Gus and the new business situation he shares with Walt. "If this is supposed to be all major league and all," comments Jesse, "we should have equipment maintainer guys and water boys, you know?!"

Up to now, Jesse has been more or less talking to himself. It is a major moment of self-reflectiveness for him in the episode—and one that reveals a lot about his view on things. What has been clearly established is that he is unhappy. However, compared to Walt, he is relatively unworried about his role in the prison house of meth. His main gripe is that he wants to be more like the warden of the prison or even the owner of the prison, rather than just one of the prison house cooks and a prisoner himself. His self-reflection ends when he asks Walt if it is ok to start cooking.

Walt, however, seems to be lost in some heavy calculations. "I don't understand," says Walt. "These numbers, they just don't add up." According to him, they should be producing .14 percent more meth than they have, that is, he and Jesse are about ¼ to a ½ pound shy. Though Jesse wants Walt to pass off the discrepancy to spillage, evaporation, or vestiges (gunk left in the tanks), Walt refuses to explain away the calculational difference in this way and keeps on trying to make the numbers work. Jesse though knows that the numbers don't add up because he has been skimming meth off of their output in amounts roughly equivalent to the amounts found in Walt's calculations. He wants Walt to write off the difference to spillage, evaporation, or vestiges—and put the whole thing behind him. But he won't. Jesse asks Walt if he is ok to which Walt replies, "Why?"

Jesse goes home now thinking that Walt is going to do the same after he wraps up his calculations. But Walt continues to ponder why the numbers are not working out. Soon a fly is heard. It briefly breaks Walt's concentration. It then lands on his calculation sheet. He tries to grab it with his hand but misses.

We are now only six minutes into the entire episode. The majority of the remaining time will involve Walt and Jessie trying to capture a fly. Most of the remaining dialogue is from Walt, for whom the episode provides a major outlet for self-examination. Aside from the unknown workers lining up at the time clock both earlier and later in the episode, Jesse and Walt are the only two characters we see or hear in the entire episode.

In a way, the episode is a sort of dark and absurd two-character play. After the fly lands on Walt's calculation sheet, he becomes obsessed with killing it. At first he chases it around the lab with his calculation sheet rolled up into a fly swatter, but when the fly goes to the ceiling, he throws his shoe at it and breaks a bulb. When he goes to retrieve his shoe from the light fixture, he ends up falling from the upper level lab to the lower level in an effort to swat the fly with a broom. Lying on his back after the fall the fly then lands on his eyeglasses. The episode then cuts to the next morning with the workers punching in.

When Jesse arrives at the lab the next morning, Walt says that the lab is contaminated. Their absurd and comic dialogue goes like this:

> WALT: Something got into the lab.
> JESSE: So it's dangerous?
> W: Not to us, particularly.
> J: So what exactly what kind of contaminate are we dealing with here?
> W: A fly.
> J: What do you mean? A fly like?
> W: A housefly.
> J: Like one fly, singular? What did it do?
> W: It got into the lab and I'm trying to get it out. Understand?
> J: No.

Walt tries to get Jessie to understand, but he never does. He insists,

> This fly or any fly cannot be in our lab. It's a problem. It's a contamination. And that is in no way a misuse of the word. Ok? So in terms of keeping our

cook clean and our product unadulterated we need to take this very seriously. Do you understand? ... I know this seems unusual for you, a layman. A fly it seems insignificant. But trust me in a highly controlled environment such as this any pollutant no matter how small could completely.... No cooking until this fly is dealt with.

Jesse wants to start cooking, but Walt will have nothing of it. The lab has been contaminated and until it is decontaminated, viz., the fly is dead, there will be no cooking. In some of the best lines in the episode, Jesse says to Walt, "We make poison for people who do not care. We probably have the most unpicky customers in the world."

As a former meth-head and -dealer, Jesse knows the market first hand. However, remember that the meth they are producing is not just any old home-cooked meth. Rather, it is a blue meth so pure that it has come to dominate the southwest meth market and landed the two of them a million-dollar corporate production gig. But nevertheless, even in the world of corporate, government-sanctioned, production of brand-name trademarked products, there is some room for contamination. After all, says Jesse, "even the government does not care that much about quality. Know what it is ok to put in hot dogs? Pig lips and assholes. But I say have at it bitches because I love hot dogs."

The political critique here set up by Jesse is outstanding. Whereas the government sanctions the production of contaminated legal goods, Walt (a government outlaw) refuses to sanction the production of contaminated *illegal* ones—even if it is poison (viz., meth).

For Jesse, the notion of contaminated poison is simply absurd as even the government always already sanctions at some level the production of contamination; for Walt, who sets himself and his world outside the control and sphere of the government, and who is governed only by the laws of chemistry and the market that his product dominates, contamination—even if it is only in the poison that he is producing—is unacceptable. This is a hard jab at the state from two individuals who spend the entire series on the run from the government and the state.

So, what about the pesky fly that Walt is so adamant about killing because it has contaminated his lab? What then does it represent? The next sequence of events suggests the fly represents Jesse. Convinced that Walt is losing it, Jesse decides to start cooking without Walt, who is lost in pursuing the fly anyway. In preparation for cooking, Jesse dons a ventilation mask on top of his head. The vents on the mask are red so that when the mask is worn on the top of his head, Jesse looks like a fly. The iconic relationship of the two red vents with the two red eyes of the fly that filled the screen in the opening sequence to the episode is unmistakable and brilliant. If there were any doubt that Jesse is the fly, it is put to rest when he tries to put sodium hydroxide into the vat and Walt swats him with his homemade human-fly-sized swatter.

But if Jesse is the fly that is contaminating the lab and is driving Walt to sleeplessness and distraction, how does Walt hope to resolve the situation? Remember Jesse only comes to work in Walt's corporate lab under extreme circumstances. He was nearly beaten to death by Hank though at the time was no longer in partnership with Walt. He is only brought back into partnership in an attempt to keep him from exposing to the authorities Walt's true identity. Before Jesse drugs him in an effort to get him to cease his manic pursuit of "the fly," Walt says, "This fly is a major problem for us. It will ruin our batch. Now we need to destroy it and every trace of it so we can cook. Failing that we're dead. There is no more room for error. Not with these people."

"These people" are Gus and the cartel that will not take kindly to finding out that Jesse has been stealing some of their meth and dealing it on the side. On one level, this is the "contamination" that Walt is obsessing about. He refuses to confront Jesse about it directly earlier in the episode, but near the end of the episode, when they finally leave the lab and are about to go home, he does. When Jesse then denies skimming meth from the lab, Walt says that he won't be able to protect him from harm if he is skimming it. Responds Jesse, "Who's asking you to?"

In a way, Jesse's response to being the "major problem" and a "contaminant" sets the stage for the rest of the series. Jesse will be Walt's ruin. He was already told this by Gus when he warned him against going into partnership with a junkie. But Walt didn't listen to him and now is worrying about the consequences of "the Jesse contamination." Says Walt to Jessie, "If you are not going to help me, then stay out of my way."

Much of Walt's worry, tinged with guilt, is revealed in this episode, particularly after he is drugged by Jesse, who spikes his coffee with sleeping pills in order to stop his fly-swat mania. As the sleeping pills begin to conquer Walt's wakefulness, he starts to get deeply philosophical about his life to date:

> I missed it. There was some perfect moment that passed me right by. I had to have enough to leave. That was the whole point. None of this makes any sense if I did not have enough. But it had to be before she found out, Skyler....
>
> I'm saying I've lived too long. You want them to actually miss you. You want their memories of you to be ... but she just won't understand. No matter how well I explain it. These days she just has this ... no I truly believe that

their exists some combination of words. There must exist certain words in a certain specific order that explain all of this but with her I can't just ever seem to find them....

I was thinking just before the fugue state I didn't have enough money so not then. And plus my daughter was not born yet. Holly was not born yet. Definitely before the surgery. Ah Christ! Damn second cell phone! How could I possibly? I know the moment. It was the night Jane died. I was at home and we needed diapers so I said I would go but it was just an excuse. Actually it was the night I brought you your money, remember?

Walt goes on to tell Jesse about his chance encounter with Jane Margolis's father, Donald, in a bar the night after he (Walt) watched her die of a heroin overdose as she lay by Jesse's side in their bed. Only after the plane crash did he realize that the guy in the bar was the father of Jesse's girlfriend: the father, that is, of the girl he allowed to die. By not attempting to save her, Walt as good as murdered her. All he needed to do was to push her to the side so that she would not suffocate from her vomiting. But he didn't and she died. While Walt comes close to telling Jesse that he allowed her to die, he doesn't. All he says to Jesse is that he is sorry about Jane. Her death too is part of the contamination that Walt is battling. Murder weighs on his subconscious along with all of the other evil actions he has committed to keep his meth business in operation.

Nonetheless, in Walt's mind it all comes down to numbers and calculations. The numbers and calculations that predict the odds of meeting Donald in the bar that night; the odds of finding Jane dying on the bed that night; of the two planes colliding over Albuquerque; of having terminal lung cancer—and as a result cooking meth to purchase a future for your family. Walt says to Jesse just before he falls to sleep,

Think of the odds. Once I tried to calculate them but they are astronomical. Think of the odds of me going in sitting down that night in that bar next to that man.

This comment on "the odds" is both a highly self-reflexive moment for the series, that is, a commentary on the narrative logic of its neoliberal magical realism, as well as a deep insight into the fundamental way Walt sees life and the world, that is, as a series of numbers and calculations.

Drawing on his alter-ego namesake, the German physicist, Werner Heisenberg (1901–1976), best known for discovering and articulating the uncertainty principle in quantum mechanics, Walt goes on to share with Jesse his fundamental beliefs about the nature of the universe:

The universe is random. It is not inevitable. It is simple chaos. It is subatomic particles and endless collision. That is what science teaches us. What is this saying? What is telling us that on the very night that this man's daughter dies it is me that is having a drink with him. How can that be random? That was the moment, that night, that I should never have left home. Never gone to your house. And maybe things would have.... I was at home watching TV. Some nature program about elephants. And Skyler and Holly were in another room. I could hear them on a baby monitor. She was singing a lullaby. If I have lived up to that moment and not one second more that would have been perfect.

Meanwhile the fly is still flying around and is staring down at them. Walt says that the fly is not going to come down and will stay up there forever. As he finally dozes off—and Jesse finally kills the fly—he tells Jesse that it's time to cook and that everything is contaminated.

The next morning, Walt is in bed, and the sound of a fly is heard. He looks up and sees a flashing red light. There is then a cut to a close-up of the flashing red light similar to the one from the opening sequence. The shot of flashing red light again fills screen and then, for less than a second, there is a shot of the red light with a fly on it. The camera then focuses on Walt's face—fearfully looking up at the fly sitting directly on the flashing red light.[6]

Flies of the Marketplace

The philosophy of Friedrich Nietzsche (1844–1900) has often been cited as an inspiration for the *Breaking Bad* series. To wit, Walt is held in comparison with Nietzsche's Übermensch, which is often translated as "Superman." In his *Thus Spoke Zarathustra,* he writes,

> *I teach you the Superman.* Man is something that should be overcome. What have you done to overcome him?
>
> All creatures hitherto have created something beyond themselves; and do you want to be the ebb of this great tide, and return to the animals rather than overcome man?
>
> ....
>
> The Superman is the meaning of the earth. Let your will say: The Superman *shall be* the meaning of the earth!
>
> I entreat you, my brothers, *remain true to the earth,* and do not believe those who speak to you of superterrestrial hopes! They are the poisoners, whether they know it or not.
>
> ....

In truth, man is a polluted river. One must be a sea, to receive a polluted river and not be defiled.

Behold, I teach you the Superman: he is this sea, in him your great contempt can go under.[7]

To draw Walt into dialogue with Nietszche's Übermensch thus takes very few steps:

(1) The Superman is the meaning of the earth;
(2) Chemistry is the science of the fundamental elements of the earth and as such, more than any other science approaches the meaning of the earth;
(3) Walt as a chemist deals with the meaning of the earth;
(4) Therefore, Walt is the Superman. The work he does in his lab to purify and perfect his meth thus is the work of the Superman. The moment he becomes Heisenberg is the self-same moment that comparisons with the Superman begin. Remember, he dubbed himself Heisenberg in the presence of Tuco and then used fulminated mercury to destroy his stash house. The only thing that would have made this moment more explicitly Nietzschean is if he had quoted this line from Zarathustra to Tuco before he did his chemical-explosion magic: "Behold, I am a prophet of the lightening and a heavy drop from the cloud: but this lightening is called *Superman*."[8]

Consequently, there is a very good textual basis upon which to draw comparisons between Walter White and the philosophy of Nietzsche. However, there are a number of different directions that a Nietzschean reading of the series can take and plenty to disagree about regarding the comparison. For example, Nietzsche also writes in *Zarathustra*, "Man is a rope, fastened between animal and Superman—a rope over an abyss."[9] Some might argue that Walt is "man" struggling over an abyss rather than simply Superman. Others might put him more on the side of "animal" than Superman. Others still might see as "the Ultimate Man":

The earth has become small, and upon it hops the Ultimate Man, who makes everything so small. His race is as inexterminable as the flea; the Ultimate Man lives longest.

'We have discovered happiness,' say the Ultimate Men and blink.

They have left places where living was hard; for one needs warmth. One still loves one's neighbour and rubs oneself against him: for one needs warmth.

Sickness and mistrust count as sins with them: one should go about warily. He is a fool who still stumbles over stones or over men!

A little poison now and then: that produces pleasant dreams. And a lot of poison at last, for a pleasant death.[10]

Isn't Walt after all the man who makes the "poison"?

Regardless of the direction one takes in bringing about a dialogue between the philosophy of Nietzsche and the series, there is an important and suggestive connection between the two. And nowhere is this more apparent than the "Fly" episode of *Breaking Bad*.

One of the "Discourses" of Nietzsche's Zarathustra is entitled "Of the Flies in the Market-place." It opens as follows:

> Flee, my friend, into your solitude! I see you deafened by the uproar of the great men and pricked by the stings of the small ones.
>
> Forest and rock know well to be silent with you. Be like the tree again, the wide-branching tree that you love: calmly and attentively it leans out over the sea.
>
> Where solitude ceases, the market-place begins; and where the market-place begins, there begins the uproar of the great actors and the buzzing of poisonous flies.[11]

The connections between this "Discourse" and the "Fly" episode are uncanny and richly suggestive. The "solitude" that Walt flees into is his meth lab. It is precisely the place where the voices from the marketplace have no place and are not welcome. The lab is Walt's sanctuary of solitude where he is safe from the "buzzing of poisonous flies." But somehow, one manages to get in. What then to do?

Nietzsche's response is clear and emphatic:

> No longer list your arm against them! They are innumerable and it is not your fate to be a fly-swat.
>
> Innumerable are these small and pitiable men; and raindrops and weeds have already brought about the destruction of many a proud building.
>
> You are no stone, but already these many drops have made you hollow. You will yet break and burst apart through these many drops.
>
> I see you wearied by poisonous flies, I see you bloodily torn in a hundred places; and your pride refuses even to be angry.[12]

But Walt, of course, has not taken Nietzsche's advice about the "flies of the market-place." Rather than not listing his arm against them, he tries to swat them—and kill them all.

> Yes, my friend, you are a bad conscience to your neighbours: for they are unworthy of you. Thus they hate you and would dearly like to suck your blood.
>
> Your neighbours will always be poisonous flies: that about you which is great, that itself must make them more poisonous and ever more fly-like.

Flee, my friend, into your solitude and to where the raw rough breeze blows! It is not your fate to be a fly-swat.[13]

So, to call Jesse "the fly" is not quite accurate in light of Nietzsche's discourse. While he is representative of the poisonous voices of the marketplace, he is not the only voice.

In his commentary on Nietzsche's Zarathustra, C. G. Jung comments that "swarms of flies are poison in the air, so it [the flies] might mean the thoughts that are flying about, the rumors, the newspapers, or a slogan of the day."[14] In spite of the children's saying that "sticks and stone will break my bones but words will never hurt me," Nietzsche seems to be saying that words do hurt. Jung goes so far as to say that "it is an almost mortal danger to expose oneself to the flies of the marketplace."[15] Arguably, this is precisely Walt's fate.

In the final episodes of the series, Walt is holed up in solitude and seclusion in the woods of New Hampshire. He is told that he cannot go into the neighboring town for his identity could be revealed. After some time in total solitude, he goes to town anyway to mail a box of cash to his son though finds out in a phone call to him that he does not want his money. Sitting at the bar licking his wounds from the hatred his son now has for him, Walt sees Elliott and Gretchen Schwartz on television spreading false rumors about him. This seems to be the tipping point that takes him out of his solitude—and leads him to his death by gunshot a short while later.

The Neoliberal Man

The parallels between the "Fly" episode and Zarathustra's discourse on "Of the Flies in the Market-place" help draw the series into a rich historical conversation with one of the most important philosophers of the nineteenth century. Arguably, the fly Walt is chasing in this episode is all of those voices in the marketplace that are distracting him from his solitude and his chemistry. Walt's struggle to free his mind from the rumors and thoughts of others is a key dimension of his ability to think and act on a different level, specifically, the level of "Heisenberg"—and the Superman.

Nietzsche's "flies" gives us a historical context in which to situate this somewhat unusual episode of *Breaking Bad*. If followed further into philosophical history, the episode might also be connected with Jean-Paul Sartre's play *The Flies* (*Les Mouches*; 1943) which both draws on Nietzsche as well as the Electra myth of the ancient Greek playwrights Aeschylus, Euripides, and Sophocles. Another, though somewhat distant philosophical reading, could also take it into a Wittgensteinian direction, after all, the aim of philosophy for Ludwig Wittgenstein is "to shew the fly the way out of the fly-bottle" (*PI* 309; 103e). Also, Walt's admission "I truly believe that there exists some combination of words. There must exist certain words in a certain specific order that explain all of this but with her I can't just ever seem to find them" is thoroughly Wittgensteinian in its Tractarian *dream* of a language that mirrors reality, if not also the way it recalls the *reality* of language games of his *Philosophical Investigations*.

No doubt, each of these philosophical directions for Walt's fly are intriguing and illuminating, but ultimately this series is paradigmatically of and about the twenty-first century. Recall, if you will, that the pilot for *Breaking Bad* came out in 2008, the year of the economic collapse. Couple this with Walt's health-care woes, his underemployment and low pay as a high school chemistry teacher, and his approach to his family's financial future, and it is easier to see *Breaking Bad* as a series more about finance, rather than flies—more about neoliberalism than Nietzsche.

Neoliberalism is recalibrating American identity—and *Breaking Bad* is arguably a commentary on the changes it has brought to our way of life. The promise (or illusion) of neoliberalism was that it would allow everyone the opportunity to be a shareholder, an owner, and an entrepreneur.[16] The rise of the information and knowledge society over the past forty years afforded the United States an unprecedented vantage point within this new economy. As knowledge production and information dissemination is an integral part of education, it emerged as a major stakeholder in this new economy. As a graduate student in chemistry who was responsible for knowledge production with Elliott and Gretchen Schwartz, Walt participated in the promise of neoliberalism. However, when Gretchen chose to be with Elliott over Walt, and Walt abandoned being a shareholder in their knowledge production, the promise of neoliberalism was lost for Walt. But in this way, Walt's fate within the worldview of neoliberalism was not unusual because for many in America this new economy quickly faded away and was replaced by a much more vicious one: the debt economy.

Like its predecessor, the knowledge economy, the debt economy is a derivation of neoliberal policies. The "indebted man"[17] that emerges out of the intensification of neoliberalism is a docile subject. Think Walter White strapped with lung cancer and no way to pay for its treatment—let alone provide for the financial future of his family. But the power of the neoliberal vision of *Breaking Bad* is that it provides a commentary on both the fortunes of the "indebted man" (Walter White) and the "entrepreneurial man" (Heisenberg).

Walt is able to break out of the world of neoliberalism's indebted man but becoming again an entrepreneurial one. However, as the knowledge economy is long gone, and the world is strapped with the debt of an economy gone sour, the reemergence of neoliberalism's entrepreneurial man is far from a noble one. Pre-2008 images of the entrepreneurial man were of a creative visionary and an independent worker who was proud of being his own boss and aggressively participating in the marketplace of ideas. This illusion ended when the dot.com bubble burst in 2000, and officially gave way to the debt economy with the financial collapse of 2008. The entrepreneurial man's reemergence as "Heisenberg" is also one of a creative visionary and an independent worker who is proud of being his own boss and aggressively participating in the marketplace, albeit not of ideas. Rather, one of drugs and violence.

Heisenberg shows us the pathway of neoliberalism's sanctioning of a system of values determined only by market-forces. The world of neoliberalism is one structured by equations—and Heisenberg is driven-by these equations. They range from an equation to determine how much meth is not accounted for as in the "Fly" episode, or, more famously, from much earlier in the series, the precise amount of money he needs to provide for his family's financial future after his death:

> A good state college, adjusting for inflation, say $45,000 a year, say two kids, four years of college, $360,000. The remaining mortgage on the home, $107,000, home equity line $30,000, that's $137,000. Cost of living, food, clothing, utilities, say two grand a month—I mean that should put a dent in it anyway. 24k a year, provide for, say, ten years, that's $240,000, plus 360 plus 137. 737. Seven hundred and thirty thousand dollars, that's what I need. You and I both clear about seventy grand a week. That's only ten and a half more weeks. Call it 11. Eleven more drug deals and always in a public space from now on. It's doable. Definitely doable.

At this moment, with this line of contemplation, Walt exemplifies the epitome of neoliberalism's entrepreneurial man. He has calculated the precise amount of money he needs to fulfill his neoliberal fantasies. Moreover, he will use this calculation to justify the lying and violence required to acquire the requisite monies.

What is beautiful about this passage is not just the neoliberal effort to place a financial number on his family's future happiness and welfare, but the comment that their drug deals are "always in a public space from now on." This is the public space of Nietzsche's "market-place"—the space of bloodsucking poisonous flies. It is also the lifeblood of neoliberalism: there is no neoliberalism outside of the marketplace.

Conclusion

Neoliberalism only brings despair. *Breaking Bad* does a fine job of revealing this not only for its indebted man, but also for its entrepreneurial man. Heisenberg as neoliberalism's entrepreneurial man ruthlessly pursues the meth marketplace without regard to the lives he is destroying through the "poison" he distributes or the consequences to the people he allegedly loves and cares about, namely, his family.

The "Fly" episode in dialogue with Nietzsche (and perhaps Sartre too) allows us to both give a philosophical context for its somewhat puzzling scenario (Walt chasing a fly) and to draw it into its more contemporary context, neoliberalism. In many ways, the neoliberal man is the return of the existential man who was both responsible for his freedom and—in turn—guilty for his fate. And Nietzsche of course is widely attributed as being one the first proponents of existentialism.[18] However, unlike the existential man whose "hell" was other people, e.g., the flies of the marketplace, the indebted man's hell are his creditors, or more precisely, his debt—and the entrepreneurial man's hell is located in the depths he will go to pursue the wealth of the market. While the entrepreneurial man's entire social existence is defined by economic and/or social exchange, the indebted man's social existence is demarcated by debt, or, alternately, credit. For neoliberalism's entrepreneurial man, equality of exchange was the groundwork of his identity. Economic and symbolic exchange for him was predicated on some notion of equality. Such, however, is not the case for the indebted man—a type of existence wherein equality (and symmetry) of exchange has given way to the inequalities (and asymmetries) of the debt/credit relationship. Whereas neoliberalism's entrepreneurial man held out the promise of profit, *Breaking Bad* does an excellent job at asking "Yes, but at what cost?" In view of this, the perils of debt suffered by the "indebted man" are but only one half of the human damage of neoliberalism.

Perhaps though, given the role of economics and the marketplace in *Breaking Bad*, it would be better to pursue the series not through the lens of Zarathustra, but through that of Nietzsche's economic thought. Though not a topic where he made major contributions, Nietzsche did have "deep insights into why and how man can be a homo oeconomicus."[19] In particular, in *On the Genealogy of Morals,* where he connected man's ability to keep promises with economic progress. One commentator summarizes his economic work in *Genealogy* as follows:

Man is defined as that animal which can make and keep promises. He sees this as the basic and most important moral achievement attained by mankind, an achievement that is even more surprising in that man also has a strong tendency to forget. This insight is at the heart of the concept of cognitive dissonance. By being able to make believable promises, man is creating a link between the present and the future through a process of the division of labour. The promise entails an exchange which is not constrained to take place simultaneously and at the same time; this form of barter we can also observe in animal societies. Instead, the promise allows for an exchange of goods or services in the present in return for equivalent goods or services in the future. This is the basis for such economic activities as saving, investment, credit and bequest. If any one of these institutions is lacking, economic progress can hardly take place.[20]

Walt too makes a promise that creates a link between the present and the future when he makes the decision to exchange goods and services now (meth production and distribution) for equivalent goods and services in the future (his family's financial future after his death). After all, he is adamant for most of the series that he is cooking meth only to provide a future for his family. It is only when they all reject this form of *economic progress* that he admits that all of his actions were about him—not his family's future. Perhaps the reason he fails to make economic progress in the series (viz., exchange goods or services in the present in return for equivalent goods or services in the future) is that flies of the marketplace became his undoing.

Notes

1. Reported by Michelle Kuo and Albert Wu in their article, "In Hell, 'We Shall Be Free': On *Breaking Bad*," *Los Angeles Review of Books* (12 July 2012). http://lareviewofbooks.org/essay/in-hell-we-shall-be-free-on-breaking-bad#.

2. Fyodor Dostoevky's *The Brothers Karamazov*, for example, was published in sixteen installments in *The Russian Herald* over a period of almost two years, January 1879 to November 1880. The similarities (and differences) of the poetics of novel serial serialization and the poetics of television/cable serialization, particularly for philosophically rich series like *Mad Men* or *The Sopranos,* is a great topic for further inquiry though is well beyond the scope of this essay. For a good introduction to the serial publication and its poetics, see William Mills Todd's "*The Brothers Karamozov* and the Poetics of Serial Publication," *Dostoevsky Studies* 7 (1986). http://www.utoronto.ca/tsq/DS/07/087.shtml.

3. For a more general critique of neoliberalism in the humanities, see my *Corporate Humanities in Higher Education: Moving Beyond the Neoliberal Academy* (New York: Palgrave Macmillan, 2013).

4. For a fuller account of the uses of visual media, particularly film, in philosophy, see my *From Socrates to Cinema: An Introduction to Philosophy* (New York: McGraw-Hill, 2007).

5. Season 3, Episode 10. Overall, "Fly" is the 30th episode of 62 in the series.

6. By a wonderful coincidence, almost a decade earlier, Bryan Cranston acted in a similar episode of another series, *Malcolm in the Middle*. In Season 7, Episode 5 (2005), Hal (played by Cranston) battles an angry bee that is attacking him for destroying a beehive. The episode ends with Hal and the bee engaged in a car chase where Hal is trying to run the bee off the road with his car and the bee is attacking the car causing it to swerve. Hal, seeing the bee land on a concrete wall, then smashes his car into the wall in order to kill the bee. This particular episode was the 134th of the long-running, highly successful, series.

7. Friedrich Nietzsche, *Thus Spoke Zarathustra: A Book For Everyone and No One*, trans. R. J. Hollingdale (New York: Penguin, 1969), Prologue, Section 3; p. 41.

8. Ibid., Prologue, Section 3; p. 45.

9. Ibid., Prologue, Section 4; p. 43.

10. Ibid., Prologue, Section 5; p. 46.

11. Ibid., "Of the Flies of the Market-place," p. 78.

12. Ibid., "Of the Flies of the Market-place," p. 79.

13. Ibid., "Of the Flies of the Market-place," p. 80–81.

14. C. G. Jung, *Nietzsche's Zarathustra: Notes of the Seminar given in 1934–1939*, vol. 1. ed. C. G. Jung and James L. Jarrett (Princeton: Princeton University Press, 1988), p. 607. Jung's lecture on Nietzche's flies was given to the Zurich Psychological Club on 16 October 1935.

15. Ibid., p. 607.

16. See Maurizio Lazzarato, *The Making of the Indebted Man: An Essay on the Neoliberal Condition* (Los Angeles: Semiotext(e), 2012), p. 9.

17. Though the phrase "indebted person" reflects more directly the fact that both men and women are affected by debt culture, I prefer "indebted man" because of its associations with the phrase "existential man." Debt is the current existential condition of both men and women in the neoliberal academy. Using the phrase "indebted man" helps make a semiotic link to philosophical history's "existential man." A similar rationale goes for using "entrepreneurial man" in the next paragraph.

18. Though I am primarily thinking here of the existentialism of Jean-Paul Sartre, there are of course a variety of different philosophical senses of the "existential man"— and others may too be apropos. See Walter Kaufmann's *Existentialism: From Dostoevsky to Sartre* (Cleveland: World, 1956) for an introduction to them.

19. Jürgen G. Backhaus, "The Word of Honour," in *Friedrich Nietzsche (1844–1900): Economy and Society,* ed. Jürgen G. Backhaus and Wolfgang Drechsler (New York: Springer, 2006), p. 87.

20. Ibid., p. 88.

What Writers Can Learn from *Breaking Bad*
The Risks and Rewards of Deliberate Disorientation

NEIL CONNELLY

I came late to the *Breaking Bad* phenomenon. Only after the show had finished its run did I begin to watch the episodes, and like so many before me I've quickly become hooked. While the saga of Walter White's transformation from mild chemistry teacher to methamphetamine cook/drug lord offers delights on a variety of levels, as a novelist and creative writing teacher with more than two decades in the classroom, I've found myself especially fascinated by Vince Gilligan's storytelling techniques. Both fledgling students and accomplished authors could learn a great deal about narrative from this disturbing and innovative series. The brutal and unforgiving New Mexico landscape, on the border of two worlds, epitomizes the use of setting as a reflection of character. The interweaving of multiple storylines—and on occasion timelines—generates intense drama. Similarly, juxtaposing one character's perspective against another's creates tension. (In any one scene, we often know more about the characters than they know of each other; it's not unlike watching a poker hand unfold knowing all the player's cards.) Our judgment of the main character (indeed many of the characters) is constantly undergoing revisions, which demands a high degree of viewer engagement but also results in a deeper sense of complexity and authenticity. Of all the narrative techniques Gilligan employs, the one I've found most compelling though is his masterful use of deliberate disorientation.

To explain this term, I should begin by stating what I see as a fundamental principle on which most fiction operates: the reader begins in ignorance and moves, gradually, to a place of final illumination. Any standard mystery will serve as an example. Before reading the first sentence, the ideal reader knows nothing. (We must allow here for contamination from sources like book jackets, reviews, promotional commercials etc. Hardly any of us make truly unsullied ideal readers.) In our mystery, the reader meets a main character, becomes aware of a setting in place and time, senses the work's overall tone. This gradual recognition is universal to all narrative. At some early point, plot begins to form—in this particular kind of work, oftentimes a dead body is discovered—say a Broadway actress. Over the course of the following essays then, various theories are probed, clues are accumulated, suspects are considered and dismissed. Her co-star? The director? That new boyfriend? A demented fan? The jealous aging actress who was supposed to have the role? Inevitably, there is an expansion and contraction of possibility. We leave behind the dead ends, the false leads, the red herrings, and piece together the essential facts of the crime and the perpetrator. We learn it was her ex-husband/manager after all. In those final pages, we come to have the same absolute understanding of the crime as the author has had all along—since the first word even.

Translating this notion to a broader range of work necessitates expanding the conceptual framework of that absolute understanding. Because, even in the most basic murder-mystery, there's more to it than just who did it. There's a why, a motivation. (The ex-husband killed the actress because he didn't want to share her with the world. Aha.) I've come to think of this broader, rich, and complete awareness as a sphere of understanding.

In many works, this sphere of understanding encompasses a deep realization of a character's essential nature. We begin a novel with no sense of who the characters are. We form an initial impression which is then—through flashback, exposition, further action—tested, teased, revised, modified, turned inside out, etc. But it's only in the final essays when we come to our greatest and most complete understanding.

It's a clumsy and mathematical way of conceptualizing this, but consider three sets of Venn diagrams. In the first, before the reading begins, circle A (representing the reader/viewer's sphere of understanding) and circle B (representing the author's perfect sphere of understanding) are entirely separate with no union. There is space between them even. At the halfway point of the story (be it novel, movie, series), A and B have converged to where they overlap significantly, with their union suggesting knowledge shared now by both. But when the story is finished, A and B should, ideally, have merged entirely. When this happens, the reader "gets it." As extreme examples, consider those narratives that rely on a central withheld fact (from "Rose for Emily" to *Sixth Sense*) where in the closing moments all the tumblers fall into place. When the two spheres don't unite, the reader feels left out, unsatisfied, even ripped off.

In his essay "Distance and Point of View," literary theorist Wayne Booth describes this phenomena this way: "From the author's viewpoint, a successful reading of his book will reduce to zero the distance between the essential norms of his implied author and the norms of the postulated reader."[1] Put another way, we'll share the same set of objective facts and have a similar emotional reaction to them. Without some movement of this sort, from initial ignorance to final enlightenment, there can be no satisfying narrative.

Breaking Bad exemplifies this defining dynamic between writer and reader. I am the writer; I have full knowledge of the narrative and a perfect sphere of understanding. I will guide you. You are the reader; you understand the logic of narrative, but you know nothing of my specific story. You should pay close attention. If you do, I will lead you forward and reward your efforts. Ultimately, you will see all I see and know all I know.

Looked at this way, the relationship has disturbing echoes of the God of Genesis advising Adam about that apple tree, but really, that analogy isn't entirely flawed. As readers, we seek to touch the mind of the creator.

Above all else perhaps, the reader *must trust* the writer, must feel like an intentional master plan is being unveiled, must sense that her efforts are being rewarded with additional knowledge and understanding. If this doesn't happen, the work fails. Superfluous facts and scenes, redundant character impressions, sudden revelations that feel constructed, overt manipulation and withheld random details, all these undermine trust, souring the healthy relationship. Readers put books down. Viewers reach for the remote control.

As a result of all this, one of the few "rules" I offer to beginning writers is this: don't make the reader feel stupid. Or put another way, don't confuse the reader. After all, if one of the writer's key jobs is to make matters clear for the reader, causing her to be baffled or frustrated can only be counterproductive, right? As with most rules in art, this turns out to be more of a guideline. (Thus the need for quotation marks.) It is possible to confuse the reader for a reason, to deliberately disorient her. While *Breaking Bad*'s use of this technique is the focus here, it is a device often employed in literary fiction, where examples abound.

Consider the crucial first line of any novel. It has a great many obligations, but among them it must begin directing the reader towards the ending. The vast majority of sentences are thus discreetly clear, guiding the reader on a straight path towards her final destination, often some hundreds of pages away. Thus a sentence like, "Clarissa Walker fell in love with acting when her mother took her to an off–Broadway play for her tenth birthday." The reader draws much from such a statement. We infer the main character, recognize her passion for acting, suppose she had a loving mother, and realize that we are now in a timeframe when she is at least ten years old, likely a good bit more. We also know our approximate location in time and space. Our first step has been on solid, firm ground.

Select a dozen novels off your shelf and you'll find, I'd wager, a dozen such sentences that inform clearly, that diligently and directly begin the hard work of orientation.

But if you keep selecting books, especially if you have some Faulkner or Joyce, you may come across a sentence like this, "124 was spiteful." This, the opening line of Toni Morrison's *Beloved*, does not make sense. I offer this as observation, not criticism. Considered by itself, it cannot have reliable meaning. Ask a hundred readers and you'd get a hundred different interpretations, none of them correct. The only response can be confusion, possibly frustration, though the degree depends on the individual reader's experience. In any event, the reader is not drawn forward but in fact pushed away, cast into a state of deeper ignorance. She goes from the standard neutral state of knowing nothing—which she occupied before she began to read—to a position where she feels like she's actually missed something. Imagine her taking a step backward on that field, away from the writer, or the two spheres of understanding in the Venn diagram drifting a bit further apart. This is deliberate disorientation.

The novelist George Makana Clark introduced me to a term, "intrigant," which he credited to writer and professor Jerome Sterns. An intrigant is a concept or image which intrigues, briefly creating confusion but simultaneously compelling the reader forward in search of satisfaction. Certainly, any example of deliberate disorientation would qualify. But it's important to distinguish this technique from other more traditional ones that arouse interest.

First off, this isn't just a standard *in medias res*, where manipulating the time stream creates intrigue. (Though this is often used in conjunction with deliberate disorientation.) If the first scene is a man dying from a gun shot wound, we know someone shot him. And we intuit, from the logic of narrative, that we'll soon learn who, why, etc. But that first step is on stable narrative ground, as we know the man has been shot. There is no incongruity.

Even without folding time, many if not most opening lines conjure curiosity. "Chad held the box in his hands, wondering if he should wait for Cindy to open it." Or "Sitting in the hot car with the engine running, I silently prayed." Or "Franklin would give anything for a cold beer." In each, a myriad of questions springs to mind. (What's in that box? What is the relationship between Chad and Cindy?; Why is that "I" praying? Why is the engine running?; What has Franklin been through that he needs a beer? Why are the particulars of his situation that he can't have one?") But alongside the mystery is stability. We do know a great many things. There's a box, a car, the desire for and unavailability of a beer. I can hold on to Chad and Cindy. Some elements are made clear—we are oriented. But others are held back—we are intrigued.

With a true case of deliberate disorientation, the incongruity is definitive, so great that the reader gathers almost no reliable narrative information. Imagine glimpsing a single puzzle piece, one that gives no substantive clue as to what the larger picture will ultimately be.

But even the most radical confusion, we recognize as experienced readers, is a temporary situation. In the same way that I argued earlier that many narratives rely on ever-shifting, evolving impressions of main character to generate plot, we realize that all stories operate by systemic revelation of some kind. Even the youngest child with the minimal exposure to narrative knows this. The pages yet to be read will change what we think of the pages we've already read. Or as Peter Brooks writes, "Perhaps we would do best to speak of *the anticipation of retrospection* as our chief tool in making sense of narrative, that master trope of its strange logic [...] we read in a spirit of confidence, and also a spirit of dependence, that what remains to be read will restructure the provisional meaning of the already read."[2] We know we're not supposed to know.

A few paragraphs into *Beloved*, it is clear to the readers that 124 is the street address of Sethe, the main character, and that her home is haunted by an unruly spirit. We learn it is Sethe's dead daughter, and that she was murdered, her throat cut when she was only two. Since this is the case, then why wouldn't Morrison simply open with "The house at 124 was haunted." Or even "The house at 124 was spiteful." Each of these statements has some greater degree of clarity. But no, Morrison wants you off balance.

The question now becomes, why baffle the reader? The risks here are significant. This strategy, the very first act of a new relationship, violates the essential contract between writer and reader. It does not guide; it misdirects. It calls attention to itself—perhaps to the author—and certainly has the potential to come across as manipulation or gimmickry. To varying degrees, the confusion/frustration may be enough to trigger the literary equivalent of the nuclear option: the reader stop reading.

But the more dogged individual presses on and finds her rewards. At the moment of recognition, when the writer reveals enough to make the incongruity clear, the reader has stepped into the realm of illumination. In regard to that singular idea or image, she touches the mind of the writer, occupies her sphere of understanding. It's a kind of mini-epiphany. By itself, this creates a powerful satisfaction, a more abiding gratification than simply solving a mystery. But more significantly, it reinforces the very narrative contract it initially contradicted. That is, the epiphany that follows deliberate disorientation augments the reader's trust in the writer. As a result, these crucial beliefs—*ah, you do know where you're going*—and—*ah, you will show me the way*—are dramatically reinforced. Especially in the early stages of a narrative, think of it like a promise from the writer, who whispers, "Oh, there's a lot more where that came from."

And to be useful, more there must be. The effect of deliberate disorientation is rarely isolated. More often, as in the case of *Beloved* and *Breaking Bad,* it is cumulative. In the opening pages of Morrison's powerful novel about slavery, the character Paul D comes across Sethe, years after they both are free. When she asks about her long lost husband he says, " 'I don't know any more now than I did then.' Except for the churn, he thought, and you don't need to know that."[3] In the same passage, Sethe recalls her dramatic escape from slavery and how she would have certainly died "if it hadn't been for that girl looking for velvet."[4] Simple images—a churn, velvet—yet entirely confounding. It will be a hundred pages before their significance is made clear. And of course, the reader still has much to learn about the death of Sethe's daughter.

Sometimes the payoff is more quick in coming. During their initial conversation, Sethe tells Paul D "I got a tree on my back and a haint in my house."[5] Like the reader, Paul D can't make sense of this, and even when he presses her for an explanation she refuses. Finally she relents, and we—reader and Paul D—learn together that a ruthless overseer whipped Sethe, scarring her back. Even as more intrigants are offered, generating even greater arousal and curiosity in the reader, the skillful author satisfies some, reassuring the reader of the larger reward waiting in the pages ahead.

And so we are taught the way of this particular narrative. It will not be a straight path to ultimate clarity. It will be crooked, one step forward, two back, then forward again. While there are a great many intrigants in the opening chapter—imagine them like seeds Morrison is planting—they continue throughout the book. Paul D casually refers to "the tobacco tin buried in his chest where his red heart used to be"[6]; one chapter opens with "A fully dressed woman walked out of the water"[7]; another starts with the indecipherable line, "That ain't her mouth."[8] But as each instance moves through its natural progression (introduction, possible repetition/variant, resolution) and the reader undergoes the same movement from disorientation to enlightenment, the relationship between reader and writer is evolving. The writer is storing up a cache of trust. And this is necessary in a book where the past is a haunting presence and a young girl—the titular Beloved—walks from a pond wearing a dress. If the reader is looking for instant explanation, she will miss the novel's main thrust. Instead, trained by the writer, the reader knows to wait patiently.

For Morrison, the true pay off comes approximately three-quarters of the way through the novel. Inserted into the narrative are what can perhaps best be described as four monologues. Throughout the book, the point of view has been roaming, a degree of third person limited for which it's hard to find comparison. But in the monologues, we shift to full on first person. The first, drawing on Sethe's perspective, begins "Beloved. She my daughter. She mine."[9] The second is from the point of view of Denver, Sethe's younger daughter, and starts "Beloved is my sister."[10] Both these sections are relatively straightforward, rendering events from the narrative we know. But in the third, Morrison moves us into the deeper water she's been anticipating since page one. "I am Beloved and she is mine."[11] Even the grammatical tangle reflects the complexity. By this point in the story, readers have come to realize that Beloved is the embodied ghost of Sethe's murdered infant. This section differs from the first two in that it is much more impressionistic, dreamlike, and it rejects conventions of grammar (that first period is the last one we see in the five page section). Beyond this, the content itself is unexpected, jarring, and for many readers incoherent. Consider for example the second paragraph:

"All of it is now it is always now there will never be a time when I am not crouching and watching other who are crouching too I am always crouching the man on my face is dead his face is not mine his mouth smells sweet but his eyes are locked."[12]

Part of the reason why the reader is so initially perplexed is that this section refers to events outside the bounds of the narrative we know. As a ghost, Beloved has become in a way the spirit of all slaves, and she is apparently channeling here the experience of another slave's crossing. To make such a leap, readers must be comfortable in their confusion, and having experienced deliberate disorientation so often already in the narrative, that is the case.

The fourth monologue pushes this conceit even further, merging the perspectives of Beloved the dead child, Beloved as embodiment of all slaves, Sethe, and Denver. It is lyrical and hypnotic, as seen in this passage:

> "She said you wouldn't hurt me.
> She hurt me.
> I will protect you.
> I want her face.
> Don't love too much.
> I am loving her too much.
> Watch out for her; she can give you dreams.
> She chews and swallows.
> Don't fall asleep when she braids your hair.
> She is the laugh; I am the laughter.
> I watch the house; I watch the yard.
> She left me.
> Daddy is coming for us.
> A hot thing."[13]

In order to capture the horrors of Beloved's death and the horrors of slavery, Morrison knows traditional narrative techniques will not suffice. She has to reject convention. But taking it to the extreme she does in the four monologues suddenly, without preparation, would shock the reader to the point where the story might falter. Instead, because of how she has trained the reader through a long series of deliberate disorientations, the strange sensation of not knowing is actually a familiar one now. We recognize this uncertainty, and relying on the trust we've developed for the writer, we read on intensely, confident that illumination is inevitable. Morrison has kept her promises before, and here too, at the novel's emotional climax, she delivers.

This is the narrative power of deliberate disorientation. By subjecting the reader to trials of confusion which result in enlightenment, the writer increases our trust in her, and this allows her to expand her narrative techniques well beyond traditional strategies.

A second effect, and one no less noteworthy, is that thematically speaking this disorientation echoes the deepest reality of the characters themselves. In a foreword to the First Vintage International Edition, Morrison addresses that famous first line, writing, "there would be no 'introduction' [...] into the novel. I wanted the reader to be kidnapped, thrown ruthlessly into an alien environment as the first step into a shared experience with the book's population— just as the characters were snatched from one place to another, from any place to any other, without preparation or defense."[14] In a poetic sense then, to help the reader understand slavery, she makes us slaves.

Like Morrison, Vince Gilligan disorients viewers of *Breaking Bad* for intentional and impressive artistic effect. This technique is especially prevalent and best examined through a study of the first two seasons.

Again echoing Morrison, knowing that he'll be asking readers for a higher than normal degree of trust, Gilligan begins by disorienting them. Consider the opening sequence of the series. To fully appreciate this, you must forget all you have watched and read, return yourself to a state of total innocence/ignorance. You've never heard of Walter White and know nothing about his narrative. The first ten seconds offer three brief establishing shots: a slow fade from black to bizarre-looking branching cacti; a fast forward time-elapsed shadow rolling over a mountain side; a stumpy butte with thin clouds drifting in normal time behind it. Unseen birds cackle and cry. As in any desert scene, there is a sense of beauty and foreboding. The strange landscape does not strike one as hospitable or welcoming to human life. It's hard not think of Morrison's "alien environment" in literal terms.

Next the screen fills with a clear blue sky, and high-pitched music slowly descending. In slow motion, a pair of khaki pants floats from the heavens, billowing with air like a wind sock, drifting downward. They come to rest peacefully on a flattened dirt road, and at that instant real time re-engages. The tires of an RV race over the pants, and the vehicle wildly accelerates down a winding path.

We've had about fifteen seconds of film time now. Between the manipulation of time, the ethereal sounds, the foreign terrain, and the strikingly clear but incomprehensible imagery of the floating pants, I'd argue most viewers are sufficiently disoriented. (What may be worth noting too is that, upon reflection, it's a literally impossible scene. We're about to learn that those pants were hanging on the side view mirror. If they were flung from a speeding vehicle, it's not possible for them to land ahead of the front tires. This scene cannot make sense.)

This intense disorientation continues. Accompanied by rattling drums, we cut to inside the RV, where we find an essentially naked driver wearing a gas mask and white underwear. Next to him in the passenger seat is another masked man, unconscious. A quick shot of the interior of the RV shows glass shattering and what we take as two dead bodies sliding across the floor as the vehicle careens around curves. Obviously panicked, jerking the wheel frenetically, the driver is also frantically trying to clear his vision, as both his glasses and the screen of his mask are fogging up. Increasingly out of control, the RV skids and slams into a ditch.

All of this in less than sixty seconds. I'm hard pressed to think of a more utterly bewildering opening to a narrative. In the remaining material before the title sequence, Walter tumbles from the RV, retrieves his shirt from a hanger on the side view mirror, and leaves a chilling message for his family using a video camera. In it, he identifies himself, gives his address, and speaks directly to his family. He tells them that no matter what they may learn about him in the days to come, he did everything out of love for them. His sincerity is hard to question. Then he neatly arranges his wallet and the video recorder and takes a position in the middle of the dirt road. Wearing a shirt, underwear, and boots, he raises a gun in the direction of approaching sirens. He is clearly no hardened criminal, and the contradiction of that image, a gun-wielding half-naked man, is as absurd as it is powerful.

We have no idea, and no way of speculating, what has happened to bring Walter to this place. No one could guess that he's a chemistry teacher driven to become a meth cook to provide for his family in the face of a deadly cancer diagnosis. But think of what we do know. Thanks to the videotape monologue, we know exactly where we are (Albuquerque, New Mexico). And we know where those floating pants came from (after he slipped his shirt on, Walter scanned the desert floor, looking for them, cueing the reader). In those two ways, we've gained access to the superior sphere of Gilligan's understanding. With the confusion of the opening ten seconds now replaced by knowledge, we have become distinctly oriented; all this serves as a promise from writer to viewer. In essence the opening sequence throws you into a narrative with more mystery than certainty, yes, but the writer has made an implicit promise: *Trust me. Pay attention and you'll be rewarded. All will be revealed.*

Does this initial disorientation and the sensation it creates in a viewer echo Walter White's chaotic and turbulent life? Perhaps. Does it rhyme with the mind-altering effect of the drugs which are at the heart of the series? Quite possibly. In these ways too, Gilligan may be forging a kind of psychic allegiance between his viewers and his subject matter, much as Morrison does in *Beloved*. But he is also laying the groundwork for a vast master plan. Like any novelist, he has a grand vision, one spread out over dozens of episodes. The road ahead will be long, and the writer knows he will need the viewer to trust him, to accept that he will (ultimately) make good on his promise. By the end of the first episode, we have absolute clarity regarding how Walter came to be in the RV. We learn of his cancer, his relationship with his former student/partner, and the identity of those bodies in the back of the RV. We know and understand. But this is only the first installment of Gilligan's ambitious endeavor.

Throughout season one—a mere seven episodes—there are multiple smaller examples of deliberate disorientation, many stemming from the manipulation of time and perspective. Included here must be the signature camera angles where the viewer is seeing the world from an odd perspective or vantage point—the bottom of an industrial vat, the inside of a floor, even from a few feet underground. And these are all effective and noteworthy. However, the way Gilligan employs disorientation across the thirteen episodes of season two can only be described as a tour de force.

The second season of *Breaking Bad* begins benignly, with a close up image of a dripping garden hose. But even this is unsettling, since the image is in black and white. The same is true for the next shots—a hummingbird feeder twisting in the branches of a tree; a snail inching along the top of an adobe wall. So far, the viewer can't even be confident that what we're seeing is from the world of Walter White. (I wonder, of the millions watching, if any reached for the remote to find the right show.) The next image, a poolside chair, a table, and a half-empty glass of water, will be recognized by some, and the setting—the White's backyard—might now be grasped. Following a creaking wind chime, a standard establishing shots confirms this location for all. We see the familiar patio, the back of the house, and the pool. Within this shot is the hose, an adobe wall, branches. Birds are chirping pleasantly.

The next shot is all water, the pool we intuit, reflecting clouds. From the right hand side of the screen, what looks for a moment like a golf ball bobs into view, and the bird song is replaced by distant sirens. The object rotates, revealing itself as an eyeball, and looks squarely at the viewer. The camera cuts to a half-submerged perspective, and we see the eyeball just below the surface. The sirens grow louder and the eyeball gets sucked into the filter.

Then we slip below the water; the sirens become muted, and we come across a floating teddy bear in profile. Because of its vivid color—blaring pink—this image is especially stunning in an otherwise black and white world. The camera rotates around to the toy's front, where the right half of its face is missing. Its entire body on that side is blackened as if by fire. Already one mystery has been quickly resolved—we know where that eyeball came from, but the larger and more ominous ones are impossible to guess: What happened to that bear? Does it belong to Walter's infant daughter? What's with those sirens?

But thanks to the careful lessons of season one, the astute viewer, though indeed disoriented, is not "on the outside." On the contrary, there is recognition, a sense of "ah, I know what Gilligan is up to." We realize that more narrative information will be forthcoming and that this will bring full understanding.

To borrow a famous awkward phrase, this opening sequence represents "a known unknown."

So great is our confidence in Gilligan that, even when this imagery isn't repeated or built upon in the remainder of the first episode, or indeed episodes two and three, we keep the faith.

Along the way, we are reassured perhaps by episode two's opening sequence. Initially, we see a desert landscape and hear a dishwasher sound, a loud rhythmic creaking. As the noise grows louder, a series of shots establish that we are near some kind of human dwelling (beer bottles hanging from a tree as if lynched, a thick caterpillar crawling over a baby rattle), and then in close up, bullet casings—in great volume, scattered in the sand. A rocking shadow on the ground moves in time to the humping noise. More bullet casings, now by the tire of a car which is heaving up and down. Zoomed in, we see the front and rear bumper rising and falling. Shattered glass tumbles from the hood of the trunk. Under the vehicle, we glimpse what could be a body. Then a final shot shows the full car, jerking spasmodically on its shocks, inexplicable. We've learned the mystery of the sound, but are cast into ignorance regarding its origin. What happened here? By episode's end, we have complete knowledge.

Episode four opens by returning to the burned teddy bear scene that began the season. We are in stark black and white, floating in pool water. Recognition here should be instantaneous. To be sure we are oriented, the camera drifts above the waterline for an instant and shows the back of the White home, the coiled garden hose. Then we drift again underwater and encounter for the second time the mutilated pink teddy bear, now upside down, arms splayed. The remaining eye is focused on, and from here the camera angle actually gives us the perspective of the bear for a few seconds. We next see rising air bubbles and, still submerged, we see a man in a protective toxic suit of some sort at the pool's edge, gazing down at us. The next shot is a shadow on the concrete, in motion, dripping water. We follow along as the bear, scooped up in a pool net, is deposited in an evidence bag and laid down in a long row of such bags. A rolling shot scans over them, coming at last to settle on a set of eyeglasses which look very much like the ones belonging to Walter. The black and white mystery has intensified.

Perhaps to reassure us again, episode five follows the pattern of episode two. An initially confounding situation (on the banks of a river, two illegal immigrants come across a set of false teeth encased in a block of glass) is explained by the events in the narrative. The next four episodes make no comment on the burned pink teddy bear, the evidence bags.

But when episode ten's first shot is that iconic pink fluffy head, half-singed, we're quick to recalibrate. We gaze again into the reflective surface of the pool, see shimmering images of men in those toxic suits, striding in slow motion (note again the disorienting effect of Gilligan's subtle manipulation of time). In a large clear tub, they gather the bear, the glasses we saw earlier, and other bags of evidence. Through a shattered windshield, we watch them carry the container to the front of the house. A suited man leans over the windshield with a camera and takes "our" picture. Next we jump to a view outside the car, which is revealed to be Walter's, parked in the driveway. From a slightly elevated vantage point we see the men carrying the tub of evidence. The camera rolls slowly over the roof of the car, and side by side, two body bags come into view. With this last image, Gilligan has raised the narrative stakes dramatically, all the while keeping the audience decidedly in the dark, where she remains for two more episodes.

Episode thirteen, the finale of season two, opens with the identical montage that began the season. As if to reset the viewer, Gilligan returns to the dripping hose, the snail, etc. This merges into the same footage from episode ten, right up to the body bags. But then we see new images: a ruined sneaker, the edges of a singed book, a piece of fabric clinging to a tree branch, an "evidence: do not remove" sign, a metal detector being swept across landscape rocks. Even with all the knowledge we've gathered during the season's episodes, these images are incongruous. We are left to speculate blindly as to their significance.

Following along the clear evidence tub holding the pink teddy bear (here, the jarring camera angle suggests the viewer is a piece of evidence), we pass a third body bag, which is secured in a white crime van. The doors are closed, and the camera pans up, giving us a view of the entire street. We see now five police vehicles, and at least that many men in toxic suits swarming around. As the van drives off and the camera pulls up, color bleeds into the black and white. Behind the White home, a half dozen helicopters buzz about. Twin plumes of black smoke rise into the blue sky.

The scope of this situation has shifted from tragedy to catastrophe, but its specific nature, even its connection to the events of the narrative so far, is impossible to fathom. By teasing us along all season, Gilligan has tantalizingly raised the anticipation to a boiling point. The high degree of this anticipation can only be matched by the degree of satisfaction that comes by episode's end, when the various disparate images we've seen piecemeal all season coalesce into the grimmest of epiphanies. All the mysteries are resolved and we merge with Gilligan's sphere of understanding. With season two's long arc, he's making a powerful comment on the unpredictable and disastrous consequences of the drug trade and human frailty. Thematically, his subject matter is as daunting as Morrison's. To truly do justice to their material, both writers must embrace risky narrative strategies in order to reap rare benefits. My point here about the brilliance of season two's finale might be fortified if I revealed how all these images "make sense" but that would rob some of the joy of experiencing it for themselves.

Indeed, the impact of that intense final realization is arguably the greatest artistic reward of this long series of deliberate disorientations. By expanding the space between reader's knowledge and author's, Gilligan creates the opportunity for a deeper awareness when it does arrive. I hesitate to think in mathematical terms when discussing art, but it seems there is some algorithm that would show a correlation between the level of readerly curiosity and readerly satisfaction, between temporary confusion and ultimate reward.

A second effect is that the unveiling of the specifics of this disastrous act attune us to the mindset of the characters. Our shock and horror are magnified by the fact that these emotions must be shared by Walter White, who plays a significant role in the chain of events culminating in the deadly catastrophe. Like Morrison, Gilligan has aligned us with his fictional characters' emotional reality by recreating their perspective. In Walter's case, we have felt his confusion, the fragmentation of his reality, his panic, and ultimately his soul-crushing realization.

Lastly though, and in terms of the series as a whole this is perhaps most relevant, Gilligan has kept his word. He has withheld (to a dramatic degree, unprecedented in this medium), but he has delivered, making good on his implied promise. By doing so, he has validated the reader's trust and amplified it. This is crucial because the narrative is by no means complete. This is the end, but only of the second of five seasons. Gilligan has yet to reveal the full grandeur of his artistic vision. There will be more disorientation ahead, and more revelations, gradually escalating in scale and magnitude. To accomplish his task, he will need the reader to suspend satisfaction to an unusual degree, to trust him well beyond the normal range, to be comfortable in a state of disarray and confusion, all the while deeply certain that, inevitably, like all good writers, he will offer the faithful the sweet cup of true communion.

Notes

1. Wayne C. Booth, *The Rhetoric of Fiction*, 2d ed. (Chicago: University of Chicago Press, 1983), 157.

2. Peter Brooks, *Reading for Plot: Design and Intention in Narrative* (Cambridge: Harvard University Press, 1992), 23.

3. Toni Morrison, *Beloved* (New York: Vintage, 2004), 9.

4. Ibid., 4.

5. Ibid., 18.

6. Ibid., 86.

7. Ibid., 60.

8. Ibid., 181.

9. Ibid., 236.

10. Ibid., 242.

11. Ibid., 248.

12. Ibid., 248.

13. Ibid., 255.

14. Ibid., xiix.

Our "word ... is half someone else's"

Walt and the Literary Echoes of Whitman

MIGUEL E.H. SANTOS-NEVES

Beginning in 1998 with *The Sopranos,* the "Third Golden Age" of television ushered in, as Brett Martin argues in *Difficult Men* (2013), a far more complex set of formal and aesthetic elements than television serials of the past. Although there are many ways to analyze the aesthetic quality, thematic depth and moral force of these shows, we can attempt to understand all these dimensions by analyzing how these shows dialogue with other artistic works, whether they be television shows, movies, paintings, poems, novels, etc. Not only does the cultural dialogue add intrinsic depth to a work of art, but it also signifies the presence of an artistic discourse, which represents a sustained form of reflection, if not outright critique, on the contemporary moment.

Let us take a look at how one of these shows of the Third Golden Age dialogues with its predecessors. Characters in *The Sopranos* borrow the literal words of the work they are parodying: "Just when I thought I was out, they pull me back in,"[1] are the words uttered in *The Godfather: Part III* by Michael Corleone, whom Silvio Dante impersonates in the three-minute teaser scene that opens the second episode—"46 Long"—of the first scene. Tony's crew is sitting around a table in the back office at the *Bada Bing!* and counting what appears to be a good deal of money. At the same time, they watch and discuss an TV interview given by a federal prosecutor and Vincent Rizzo, a former

Genovese family soldier turned government informant; John Gotti is behind bars for life and the mob is in decline, in part because of "a disregard of the rules that serve the old dogs so well."[2] The hordes of cash on the table suggest otherwise—an incongruence between the words uttered on TV and the dramatic representation at the *Bing!*—for, by all accounts, business appears to be going well for Tony and his crew.

However, the implication of the scene is not one of financial but moral decline. Judging by the language of Tony and his cohort, we can see that the elegance, putative nobility, and Romanticism of the Corleone family are things of the past. For example, we could not imagine Don Corleone or his son Michael speaking these words: "Yeah well, when you're married, you'll understand the importance of fresh produce" as Tony tells Christopher during dinner at the *Nuovo Vesuvio* in the "D–Girl" episode in season two.[3]

The dialogue between *The Sopranos* and its antecedent works is paralleled by Tony's struggle with the tradition of the mafia and his personal past, which comes into relief during his analysis sessions with Dr. Jennifer Melfi. Tony, the perennial analysis patient, constantly feels that the good times have passed him by; he constantly dialogues with his past and that of his family, as well as with an imaginary past where mobsters observed tradition and respected the codes of honor and loyalty, which seem to have fallen by the wayside when Tony looks at his cohort. The ducks that fly away in the pilot episode symbolically establish Tony's personal conflict, one that will develop and ramify through the six and half seasons of the show. For example, in one session, Tony brings up concerns he has about AJ, who has been speaking about the ultimate absurdity of life and the non-existence of God, in part because he has recently read Camus's *The Stranger*. When Tony complains to Dr. Melfi, she says, "Sounds to me like Anthony Jr. may have stumbled onto existentialism"; Tony replies, "Fuckin' internet."[4] These malapropos reinforce and heighten, on the one hand, the satirical, ironic and parodic dimension of *The Sopranos*, because the language of the straight world is juxtaposed with the language of the gangster world. The doubling of these worlds makes it hard to imagine anyone in the Corleone cohort uttering these words or being the butt of laughter, showing thereby just how far the mob genre has traveled.

On the other hand, the literary reference and its misunderstanding, which produce great comic effect, reveal a central theme of *The Sopranos* —the existential alienation of modern suburban life and the absence of a contemporary philosophical language to express this feeling of modern angst. Extending beyond a mere formal parody of *The Godfather* or *Goodfellas*, *The Sopranos* makes a statement about "men alternately setting loose and struggling to cage their wildest natures."[5] The show reworked, according to Martin, "postwar literature's most potent tropes: horror of the suburbs, which in novels from Richard Yates's *Revolutionary Road* to Joseph Heller's *Something Happened* to John Updike's Rabbit series, had come to represent everything crushing and confining to man's existential nature."[6] And Tony sums up and embodies this duality and very theme, albeit in exaggerated form, as a suburban everyman, yet a natural born killer.

Despite its seeming universality and Tony's putative everyman appeal, *The Sopranos* portrays a "hermetic world of the North Jersey mob" that makes few forays into the straight world.[7] We can say, therefore, that the discourse of the show has its origin in the insular world of the mob, and when it clashes with the discourse of the world at large, the ironic effect allows the viewer a special entry into an alien, yet familiar world. After all, the show resonates with an American audience familiar with the existential wasteland of suburbia and its false promises of insouciance: the conflict and drama of the show stem from Tony's attempt to preserve the integrity of this world, as symbolized by his "family."

The notion of dialogue evoked thus far, which occurs at the level of genre and character between a contemporary and antecedent artistic work and time, suggests a diachronic understanding of the concept. Although *Breaking Bad* draws on many of the same conventions as *The Sopranos*—the antihero— as well as many of the same themes—the family—it does not portray an insular community speaking a discourse of its own, which every so often clashes with the world at large. Rather, the setting is suburban Albuquerque, which could be Anywhere, USA. The middle class lives just out of reach of the American Dream. Walter White holds the very middle class job of a high school chemistry teacher; a shell of man, he works a second job as a cashier at a car wash to make ends meet. His brother-in-law Hank, a DEA officer, appears slightly better off financially, perhaps because he does not have kids, but his profession hardly affords him a life of middle class bliss; his wife's kleptomania further deprives him of domestic bliss. Despite these similarities, *Breaking Bad* does not dialogue with or parody a genre per se, like *The Sopranos*. We could say that its antecedents are any of the numerous shows or movies about American suburban life, such as *American Beauty* or *The Simpsons*. The absence of specificity in such an observation renders it complicated to carry out a rigorous analysis at the level of genre.

But if we probe further, we see that a subtle diachronic dialogue occurs in the form of literary allusions. While the literary allusions creep into *The Sopranos*—references to Camus, Mme. de Staël, Melville, Nietzsche—in a fleeting manner, generally to highlight the parochialism of the family, *Breaking Bad* maintains a sustained and rich dialogue with its literary predecessors. Fans are familiar with the red thread of Walt Whitman and *Leaves of Grass* that is weaved through the show starting in season three. Gale Boetticher introduces Walter White to Walt Whitman, when he recites the poem "When I heard the Learn'd Astronomer." Gale gives Walt a copy of Whitman's *Leaves of Grass*, and subsequently we see Walt reading from it, looking at it, and demonstrating a significant affinity for the book. The "Learn'd Astronomer" resounds through the show, and the poems "Song of Myself" and "Gliding O'er All" are alluded to in several episodes.

When a literary allusion occurs once, it is amusing; when it occurs several times and in a sustained manner, it calls for analysis and interpretation. It becomes fair to ask what purpose Whitman and his poetry are serving in their new artistic home, that is the target work. To ground and orient our analysis that will take place henceforth, it is necessary to erect and deploy a theoretic framework. Russian theorist Mikhail Bakhtin develops an excellent heuristic in *The Dialogic Imagination* for understanding the notion of synchronic and diachronic dialogue.[8] He considers an allusion or a fully recited poem in the target language and its new context, to be a "reprocessing, reformulation and artistic transformation that is free and oriented toward art."[9] The cited work gains a new artistic home in the target work and language:

> Departures from the empirical reality of the represented language may under these circumstances be highly significant, not only in the sense of their being biased choices or exaggerations of certain aspects peculiar to the given language, but even in the sense that they are a free creation of new elements— which, while true to the spirit of the given language, are utterly foreign to the actual language's empirical evidence.[10]

Finally, according to Bakhtin, the act of transmission is fraught with semantic consequences and ramifications: "the speech of another, once enclosed in a context, is—no matter how accurately transmitted—always subject to certain semantic changes."[11]

In light of Bakhtin, this essay will argue that the literary allusions in *Breaking Bad* function to effect and signal important transitions in theme and plot, in addition to foreshadowing critical moments in the development of the characters and the relations among them. At the same time, this essay will read *Breaking Bad* against these references and offer an interpretation of this intertextuality, by arriving at an understanding of the semantic and contextual implication of this literary dialogue. It will attempt to answer two questions: How does reading the works of Whitman (i.e., "When I heard the Learn'd Astronomer," "Song of Myself," and "Gliding O'er All") into *Breaking Bad* increase the semantic depth of the show? What does the poetics and historical context that shaped Whitman's literary work reveal about the moment when the show evokes the work of the American Bard?

Let us begin. Walt Whitman is evoked for the first time in *Breaking Bad* halfway through season three. It is worth recapping the lead up to the recitation of Whitman's "When I heard the Learn'd Astronomer." Walter White has received an offer from Gus Fring to scale up the cooking of his blue crystal meth in a super lab located on the outskirts of Albuquerque. While hesitant at first, Walt eventually accepts the offer after he learns that Jesse has struck out on his own and is cooking and selling his version of blue meth. Gus provides Walt with a lab assistant, the endearingly idiosyncratic nerd Gale Boetticher, who holds a Master's degree in organic chemistry from the University of Colorado. The two of them bond over their shared love for chemistry and X-ray crystallography—Gale's specialization in graduate school and a subject that Walt claims he could spend hours discussing. The pairing seems like a match made in heaven, a meeting of the minds: We see them cooking meth in perfect synchrony to the rhythms of Bossa Nova, while taking breaks to play chess. After they have wrapped up their inaugural cook, Gale and Walt celebrate by sharing a glass of wine and talking shop. By Walt's assessment, Gale has proved himself a worthy chemist; perplexed, Walt asks how Gale ended up as a rouge chemist employed in a criminal enterprise. Gale explains that his lack of affinity for the political side of academia, the extra-scholarly groveling requirements, disenchanted him from the pursuit of an academic life. While kissing the proper behinds disillusioned him, he loved the lab by comparison, where it was "all still magic—you know, chemistry."[12] Walt could not agree more, that chemistry is still magic. Gale says that during his errant academic pursuits, he "all the while, ... kept thinking about that great old Whitman poem, 'When I heard the Learn'd Astronomer.'"[13] Walt, who does not know the poem, asks Gale to recite it, which he does in spite of his embarrassment:

> When I heard the learn'd astronomer,
> When the proofs, the figures, were ranged in columns before me,
> When I was shown the charts and the diagrams, to add, divide,
>   and measure them,

When I, sitting, heard the astronomer, where he lectured with much
    applause in the lecture-room,
How soon unaccountable I became tired and sick,
Till rising and gliding out I wander'd off by myself,
In the mystical moist night-air, and from time to time,
Look'd up in perfect silence at the stars[14] [1865].

Without engaging in an exhaustive reading of Whitman's "Learn'd Astronomer,"
which goes beyond the scope of this essay, it is worthwhile to make a couple
of observations on its salient features, for such an analysis will help us understand how Whitman's oeuvre functions in *Breaking Bad*.[15] If we assume that
Gale offers an interpretation of the poem—that the science of chemistry is
like magic—before he recites it, then we can say that he is wide of the mark: at
first reading, the poem is a statement against the strictures of scientific thought,
in favor of a poetic (and ostensibly more authentic) understanding of the world.

    The poem essentially consists of two parts, with two different structural
features, and two distinct moments of dramatic action. In the first four lines,
the ironic tone creates a distance between the lyrical I and "the learn'd astronomer ... the proofs, the figures ... the charts and the diagrams, to add, divide,
and measure them." This distance is reflected in the rhetoric of the poem,
where the anaphora of the first four lines gives the poem a cadence of repetition. In effect, the rhetorical device implies that the lyrical I views the astronomer's explanation of his subject as repetitive and limited. After all, the
astronomer's purview extends as far as the charts he is discussing; in the first
four lines, the cosmos, his ostensible object of study, are not even mentioned.
By the last four lines, the anaphora has been dispensed in favor of a less regular
structure to reflect the lyrical I's own whimsical and Romantic encounter with
the cosmos: he becomes unaccountable (in other words, unable to count) and
glides and wanders outside to observe "the stars" in wonderment. The poet's
interaction with the cosmos during the night is magical and mysterious, sen-
sual, more authentic, and thereby closer to the actual stars—more importantly,
enjoyed without the encumbrance of words.

    Whitman's poem defends a Romantic interaction with the world, an ethic
which has its grounding in the Transcendentalist movement spearheaded by
Emerson and Thoreau in 19th-century New England: the adherents espoused
an idealistic philosophy that valued insight and personal experience over logic
and bookish learning for a revelation of the deepest truths. As Whitman biog-
rapher Jerome Loving states in *Walt Whitman: The Song of Himself*, "the first
Leaves was a blend of dream-vision and autobiography. Its 'Yankee Transcen-

dentalism' came right out of Concord."[16] Loving adds a caveat, though, to this putative line of influence: Whitman was reviving Transcendentalism, which had already ended by 1855, with the publication of *Leaves of Grass*, but also penning his own version of it. Rather than soaring too high, Whitman offered a "brand of Transcendentalism, with its equality of Soul *and* Body.... Natural facts were evidence of a spiritual fact, or God's Love, Emerson had written in *Nature*, but Whitman's natural facts emphasized the human body and even its private parts."[17] "Transcendence is curiously 'inverted' because the soul now 'transcends' to the body, or meets it halfway," in other words; or the material of the world becomes a gateway for transcendence.

It is fair to ask, therefore, how an interpretation of the text and knowledge of the context of the "Learn'd Astronomer" can explain its function in its new artistic home and offer a more layered understanding of *Breaking Bad*. To attempt to understand why Whitman's poem resonates with Gale and Walt, we must lay aside the dichotomy of science versus poetry, which fails to account adequately for how Whitman himself viewed science and therefore how its reference to science appeals to the two crystal meth-making nerds. Loving's assessment of Whitman's transcendental materiality invites us to look at other works, where it becomes clear that the poet held the pursuit of science in great respect, for he in fact incorporated many contemporary scientific ideas in his poetry. Alice Lovelace Cooke shows, in her article entitled *Whitman's Indebtedness to the Scientific Thought of His Day* (1934), that Whitman was in constant dialogue with contemporary theories of astronomy, geology and evolution. Citing extensively from the poet's oeuvre, Cooke shows that Whitman believed science was indispensable to his poetry, for the scientists "are the lawgivers of poets and this construction underlies the structure of every prefect poem."[18] The poet and scientist walk hand-in-hand in the pursuit of truth, according to Whitman, with a common aim of understanding how humans relate to this vast universe that ranges from the infinitesimal to the macrocosmic. Yet, while he maintained an indebtedness to science, he at the same time recognized that logic and demonstration did not suffice, that beyond their explanation lay a vast mysterious universe: "there remains ever recognized still a higher flight, a higher fact, the eternal soul of man."[19]

Does not the "Learn'd Astronomer" dramatize this very idea? Unlike Emerson and Thoreau—the Manicheans who seemingly brushed aside science in favor of Romantic self-reliance and solipsism—Whitman embraces the scientific mode of apprehending the world, that is when it is underpinned by a Romantic drive for curiosity. The bard, according to contemporary scientists such as the psychologist Dr Maurice Richards Burke, was in possession of "cosmic consciousness"; the mathematician W.K. Clifford "in his essay 'Cosmic Emotion' ... paid tribute to Whitman as a poet who sang with rhapsody of the relations between the microcosm and macrocosm—between man and the inconceivable spatial universe which surrounds him."[20] Precision, accuracy, enchantment and wonderment are all part and parcel of the same pursuit for the American bard, are all part of his universe. Given Walt's personality and disposition, we can infer, therefore, that he does ascribe to Transcendentalism's belief in self-realization, but to Whitman's version of it where self-realization happens precisely through engagement with the material world and not by running away from it. Suffice it to say that throughout the show Walt's self-realization occurs as he wields the elements of chemistry and realizes his value in the world at large.

If we recall Bakhtin's words—that "the speech of another, once enclosed in a context, is—no matter how accurately transmitted—always subject to certain semantic changes"—then the presence of Whitman's poetry in *Breaking Bad* raises an interesting question: if we assume that Whitman's work undergoes semantic alterations in its new artistic home, then how does its new meaning help us understand Walt and his world? Perhaps, the Whitman poem that best resonates with Walt and reflects his state of mind is the triumphalist "Song of Myself," where the poet chants of individual freedom unencumbered by convention and morality: in section 22, for example, we read the lines,

> I am not the poet of goodness only, I do not decline to be the
>   poet of wickedness also.
> What blurt is this about virtue and about vice?
> Evil propels me and reform of evil propels me, I stand indifferent,
> My gait is no fault-finder's or rejecter's gait,
> I moisten the roots of all that has grown[21] [463–467].

Everything transcends with the benevolent soul; before everything, the poet cannot condemn, only glorify.

Whitman's work also pervades the show, appearing to signify important developments in theme and character, even though his work is never recited in full again as in the scene mentioned above. Soon after Gale's recitation, we see Walt reading from *Leaves of Grass* at his new apartment. Even though the camera angle only permits viewers to see the cover of the book, it allows them to understand that *Leaves of Grass* resonates with Walt, that it becomes an important conduit for Walt's own rumination and a reflection of himself. It, therefore, appears that Walt Whitmans' poetry *in toto* resonates with Walter White. As the author Michael Shields notes in the blog *Across the Margin*, Whitman's poetry appears in the show at the very moment when Walt is basking in his newfound power; Shields conjectures, "he is full of an immeasurable amount of pride much like Whitman expresses in the acclaimed section of *Leaves of Grass* entitled 'Song of Myself': 'I celebrate myself, and sing myself / and what I shall assume you shall assume/ for every atom belonging to me as good belongs to you.'"[22] Whitman's celebration of individuality and self-realization resonates with Walt, an interpretation supported by Walt's actions as he leaves behind his meek middle class life of quiet desperation, for a life of unleashed inner drives in pursuit of self fulfillment—consequences be what they may.

In this exaltation, as we examined above, Whitman answered Emerson's call for a poet to set America to meter: "banks and tariffs, the newspaper and caucus, methodism and unitarianism, ... logrolling, our stumps and their politics, our fisheries, our Negroes, and Indians, our boats, and our repudiations, the wrath of rogues, and the pusillanimity of honest men, the northern trade, the southern planting, the western clearing, Oregon, and Texas."[23] In the mid-nineteenth century, Whitman sang the virtues of individuality, liberty and equality in an upstart country that personified these democratic principles. A burgeoning America, asserting itself in the world of nations and espousing territorial expansion as its birthright, projected a Romantic view of itself and left in its wake institutions and traditions that restricted personal liberty and hindered its national, radical experiment in democracy. To realize this sense of conflated individual and national destiny all became permissible. Notwithstanding the moralization of his Transcendentalist counterpart Thoreau, Whitman became the legislator of democratic virtues and economic expansion; Whitman holds a benevolent view of common human beings, a view supported by the assumption that their souls and nature are inherently good. Evil is overlooked in antebellum America.

How, then, does the world of Whitman, which is evoked into the present day in *Breaking Bad,* compare to the world of Walter White? Let's first answer the question: Does Walt live in a world that welcomes and even encourages self-realization? In point of fact, yes! In the essay "Breaking Neoliberal? Contemporary Neoliberal Discourses and Policies in AMC's *Breaking Bad,*" David N. Pierson shows that neoliberalism is the orienting discourse of *Breaking Bad*, which arranges all the interactions among characters. In this ideology, "the market should be the organizing agent for nearly all social, political, economic and personal decisions"; the government is deplored as inefficient and stifling to individuality."[24] As the show progresses, Walt fulfills and eventually personifies several neoliberal exigencies placed upon the individual: he acts only out of self-interest, asserts his individuality and his masculinity, even though he constantly claims to be acting out of necessity and to fulfill the ideal of providing for his family. Moreover, according to Pierson, the town of Albuquerque, as represented in *Breaking Bad,* reflects a good deal of neo-liberal ideology: social services, such as public schools, are in disarray (recall Walt's somnambulant students), while those who ascribe to a market ideology thrive. The show chronicles how Walt himself leaves behind his teaching job as a high school chemistry teacher (public schools are the favorite targets of neoliberal apologists who view it as a center of failed government ideas and inefficiency), and applies his considerable skills toward a moneymaking enterprise to meet the vast demands of the crystal meth market. In the neo-liberal world, the dominant equation is that self-realization is equal to individual acquisition. But does he live in a world, like Whitman's, where the good of self-realization renders sin into foibles and peccadilloes? And does the thriving individual mirror a thriving nation?

Despite sharing a vocabulary of democratic ideals with Whitman, *Breaking Bad* carefully reveals the moral shortcomings of a world oriented by market forces and unfettered individuality. It dramatizes the moral consequences of a neo-liberal ideology taken to its logical conclusion through a *reductio ad absurdum* method of exposition. Walt's actions in themselves are morally deplorable, which becomes abundantly clear as the show progresses and the logical justification for his actions become unconvincing. However, Walt is part of a larger system of widespread evil. As the show unfolds, his small time meth operation with Jesse becomes incorporated into Gus Fring's seemingly legitimate business, which itself has ties with a large multinational corporation—the parent company of Los Pollos Hermanos, Madrigal Electromotive—that allows Gus, Walt and Jesse to produce meth at an industrial level and market it to the world at large (in economic parlance this phenomenon would be called "scaling up the business"). Deception pervades: Gus's legitimate business is in fact an international meth empire hiding in plain sight. Since a legitimate and an illegal business are economic bedfellows, we are left to think that line between legal and illegal, between beneficial and destructive, is a fine one and quite arbitrary. This is a world that lacks truthfulness and prizes hypocrisy (or better yet, deception) all in the name of profit, the amassing of wealth regardless of economic malevolence; in other words, it is hardly the world of Romantic authenticity, the world of Whitman.

The polyphony of voices in the show further reveals the extent of this neo-liberal ideology and the evil of it. At the beginning of *Breaking Bad*, Walt and Hank lead seemingly similar middle class lives. The White and Schrader center of gravity introduces us to a slice of American diversity and a broad spectrum of characters, all of whom possess unique voices. Through Hank, we learn about decent and hardworking DEA agents, American middle class men, who believe in good guys versus bad guys and dedicate their lives to fighting crime. As they face the incredible evil of the drug cartels, which know no limits to their greed and ruthlessness, these agents tend to walk a straight moral line, but in this complex world, they are a "day late and dollar short"[25] in their attempt to win the War on Drugs.

As Walt "breaks bad" and the narrative arc develops, we encounter a more nefarious cast of characters. Take, for example, Walt's partner in crime, the mercurial, uneducated yet smart Jesse Pinkman. Through his playful slang he is the mouthpiece for youth culture, and its disregard for anything conventional in favor of the obsessive performance of mindless, destructive activities. Gustavo Fring, the sociopathic crystal meth kingpin, "hides in plain sight" as the owner of the fast-food chain Pollos Hermanos. He goes through all the motions of being a decent member of society: he produces a quality product pleasing to his customers, while garnering goodwill in his community through his pleasant demeanor and charitable services. This same business mindset, language, and concepts—"quality product"—are used and applied to develop his drug empire. In contrast to Walt's scientific thinking and mode of expression and Jesse's uneducated language, Gus speaks as the shrewd businessman who negotiates to gain the upper hand. At the same time, he deftly negotiates his way through the twin worlds of legitimate and unlawful business, revealing in his words and actions that the line between the two is quite thin and entirely arbitrary—after all, both the labs at Madrigal Electromotive and underneath a laundry facility in Albuquerque join forces to produce a product demanded by the consumer. All the characters live in the world of Gus Fring, who embodies the spirit of capitalism in the 21st century. For these characters to succeed and be afforded a slice of the American Dream, he must be displaced, but the values he embodies are inexorable. To succeed, they must become him.

Thus, the world of suburban Albuquerque in *Breaking Bad* is a locus where characters from all walks of life meet and become entangled, speaking (one could say "exchanging") a variety of languages; thought of in an abstract way, it is a locus for a confluence of ideologies, where ideology in this instance is understood in a Bakhtinian sense—that is without the political, Marxist overtones so in vogue in the academy of today. Rather and more precisely, in Bakhtin the speaking character is an "ideologue" who gives voice to a world-view (ideology) and exchanges his ideology in dialogue with other characters through a system of signs common to all.[26] Applied to *Breaking Bad*, we can say that the system of signs is global capitalism in its legal and illegal forms, as it is reified in the town of Albuquerque during a period of American history, where the American dream is only within reach of those ruthless enough to strive for it—hardly the benevolent world of Whitman. In the market-oriented world of neo-liberalism, ideologies are exchanged and fight for market share.

All of the ideologies, as articulated through the sum total of all spoken utterances, "combine to form a structured artistic system, and are subordinated to the higher stylistic unity of the work as a whole, a unity that cannot be identified with any single one of the unities subordinated to it."[27] In other words, Bakhtin's concept of heteroglossia, although originally used to describe the semantic workings of the novel, can be applied to understanding the dynamics in *Breaking Bad*, for it sheds light on the meaning of the words uttered by the characters in the context of the artistic whole of the work. Into this universe— the "structured artistic system"—enters the literary allusion as the voices and ideologies of speakers past. These echoes add semantic depth to *Breaking Bad* for they create a counterpoint between the show and its fraternal antecedent, one that undergirds the critique of the ethic of individuality that the structured artistic system of *Breaking Bad*.

Allusions to Whitman become more functional as the show progresses,. They connote death and become harbingers of destruction and death. Take, for example, the moment in the "Bullet Points" episode when the White family comes over to Marie and Hanks's house for dinner to sell them on the lie of Walt's gambling addiction—his "hidden talent."[28] Hank, who is recovering from a murder attempt and is wheelchair bound as a consequence, is helping the Albuquerque Police Department solve the murder of Gale Boetticher (killed by Jesse under Walt's orders). He believes that Gale might be Heisenberg— the mastermind behind the blue meth epidemic and Albuquerque's Public Enemy #1—, and he asks Walt to review Gale's notebooks, which include molecular diagrams, sketches for a meth lab, a recipe for vegan s'mores and a reference to the "Learn'd Astronomer." Hank reads out the inscription, "To W.W.: My Star, My Perfect Silence," that has puzzled him and asks who "W.W." might be: "Woodrow Wilson? Willy Wonka? Walter White?" Walt responds "you got me," before flipping the pages of Gale's notebook to find the whole poem written out, thereby deflecting Hank's ironic accusation onto Walt Whitman. But this exchange, which is replete with irony, foreshadows an important moment of recognition later in the series, in which Walt Whitman and his poetry play a central role.

Hank's accusation loses its irony in episode eight of season five, when he finally realizes that Walt is Heisenberg. In the episode entitled "Gliding Over All" (itself the title of a Whitman poem), Hank is using the bathroom at the White house; he picks up a copy of *Leaves of Grass* laying behind the toilet, and reads the inscription "To my *other* favorite W.W. It's an honor working with you. Fondly, G.B." While Hank has the book in hand, his voiceover utters the lines, "To W.W. My Star, My Perfect Silence," before flashing back to the scene in the "Bullet Points" episode discussed above. It becomes clear that allusions to Walt Whitman and his poetry, aside from adding semantic depth to the show and a counterpoint for reflection, structure the plot through the device of foreshadowing: the discussion between Walt and Hank during season four is pregnant with irony, but by season five the veil of dramatic irony falls during Hank's moment of recognition. In addition, Whitman, who is first introduced into the show with a full recitation of his poem "When I Heard the Learn'd Astronomer," has been elevated to the level of motif for the remainder of the show, signaling the acute presence of death and evil, and not the triumphalist self-realization, freedom and individuality so often associated with his work. Invoking "Gliding Over All" makes the point clear: "Gliding o'er all, through all, / through Nature, Time, and Space, / As a ship on the waters advancing, / The voyage of the soul—not life alone, / Death, many death I'll sing" (1871).[29] Written after Whitman himself beheld the wounded soldiers of the Civil War, the poem is lugubrious in tone and subject; in the episode of the same title, a prison massacre ordered by Walt takes place and the death of Hank is foreshadowed, as implied by the fact that he is reading Walt's copy of *Leaves of Grass*.

Walt White strives to fulfill Walt Whitman's proclaimed ideals, but he turns them on their head, and he becomes "a grotesque magnification of the American ethos of self actualization."[30] The Romanticism and epic aspiration that run through Whitman, which would ostensibly portend a utopian world where they are fully realized, are instead rendered ironic in the 21st century. Walt accepts Whitman's ideal on the surface but the individuality he prizes and the free will he exercises occur at the expense of others—a sort of selfish individuality that cannot accept the right of another to self-determination. After exhausting every possible argument to justify his actions, Walt becomes unconvincing even to his own family. The last time Walt and Sklyer meet is a case and point:

Skyler: If I have to hear, one more time, that you did this for the family–

Walter: I did it for me. I liked it. I was good at it. And ... I was ... really ... I was alive.[31]

We hear echoes from the opening lines of "Song of Myself": "I celebrate myself, and sing myself, / And what I assume you shall assume, / For every atom belonging to me as good belongs to you." But when we hear echoes of another's words, it is wise to recall and heed Bakhtin's words: "the speech of another, once enclosed in a context, is—no matter how accurately transmitted—always subject to certain semantic changes."

While the words may sound the same, the meaning is different, and tracing this semantic change is a critical endeavor with profound ethical implications. For, if our words are half someone else's, we cannot claim full authority over them: we are to a certain extent the mouthpieces of our ancestors, much like they voiced the words and ideas of their forbearers. We act as the vessels for these past words and ideas during our lives, fulfilling their potential during our moment in time with the autonomy to refract them at best. If these implications of Bakhtin are actually the case, then Walt is no more responsible than Whitman for the evils of 21st century capitalism in America. The question of responsibility is frankly beyond the scope of this essay, so we will satisfy ourselves with a humbler claim. Like Whitman, Walt is an embodiment of the spirit of his time. He exists in the cultural landscape of 21st century America not as a rarefied archetype, but in the terrestrial and material plane, as a grotesque realization of the American bard's chant and an eponym of Anywhere, USA.[32]

Notes

1. "46 Long," *The Sopranos*, first broadcast January 17, 1999, by HBO, directed by Daniel Attias and written by David Chase.

2. "46 Long."

3. "D–Girl," *The Sopranos*, first broadcast February 7, 2000, by HBO, directed by Allen Coulter and written by David Chase and Todd A. Kessler.

4. "D–Girl."

5. Brett Martin, *Difficult Men: Behind the Scenes of a Creative Revolution: From* The Sopranos *and* The Wire *to* Mad Men *and* Breaking Bad (New York: Penguin, 2013), 84.

6. Martin, *Difficult Men*, 84.

7. Martin, *Difficult Men*, 90.

8. The concept of dialogue is couched within Bakhtin's notion of heteroglossia—

understood as multiplicity of voices at work in the novel. It describes how the exchange of words among characters represents, not only a battle for authority, but a semantic struggle as well, where each character attempts to impose his understanding of the world—that is his "ideology" as Bakhtin conceives of it.

9. M.M. Bakhtin, *The Dialogic Imagination: Four Essays,* ed. Michael Holquist, trans. Caryl Emerson and Michael Holquist (Austin: University of Texas Press), 336.

10. Bakhtin, *The Dialogic Imagination: Four Essays*, 336–7. Although Bakhtin is writing specifically about the novel, he theorizes that the "dialogic imagination" is an essence of human speech and language: "The transmission and assessment of the speech of others, the discourse of another, is one of the most widespread and fundamental topics of human speech. In all areas of life and ideological activity, our speech is filled to overflowing with other people's words, which are transmitted with highly varied degrees of accuracy and impartiality. The more intensive, differentiated and highly developed the social life of a speaking collective, the greater is the importance attaching, among other possible subjects of talk, to another's word, another's utterance, since another's word will be the subject of passionate communications, an object of interpretation, discussion, evaluation, rebuttal, support, further development and so on."

11. Bakhtin, *The Dialogic Imagination: Four Essays*, 340.

12. "Sunset," *Breaking Bad*, first broadcast April 25, 2010, by AMC, directed by John Shiban and written by Vince Gilligan and John Shiban.

13. "Sunset."

14. Walt Whitman, "When I heard the Learn'd Astronomer" in *Leaves of Grass*, ed. Harold W. Blodget and Sculley Bradley (New York: W.W. Norton, 1968), 271.

15. There are but a handful of blog entries and articles on the relationship between Walter White and Walt Whitman: Michael Shields, "Walter White v. Walt Whitman," *Across the Margin* (blog), August 4, 2012, http://acrossthemargin.com/walter-white-vs-walt-whitman/; Kera Bolonik, "Leaves of Glass Breaking Bad's Walt Whitman Fixation," *Poetry Foundation,* August 6, 2013, http://www.poetryfoundation.org/article/246218#article; Danny Heitman, "'Breaking Bad' brings Walt Whitman back to the forefront of pop culture," *The Christian Science Monitor,* August 20, 2013, http://www.csmonitor.com/Books/chapter-and-verse/2013/0820/Breaking-Bad-brings-Walt-Whitman-back-to-the-forefront-of-pop-culture.

16. Jerome Loving, *Walt Whitman: The Song of Himself* (Berkeley: University of California Press, 1999), 180.

17. Loving, *Walt Whitman: The Song of Himself*, 186.

18. Walt Whitman, "Preface," *Leaves of Grass* (1927): 497 quoted in Alice Lovelace Cooke, "Whitman's Indebtedness to the Scientific Thought of His Day," *Studies in English*, no. 14 (July 8, 1934): 93. February 17, 2014. JSTOR.

19. Walt Whitman, *Whitman's Works* (1902): 200ff. quoted in Cooke: 112.

20. Alice Lovelace Cooke, "Whitman's Indebtedness to the Scientific Thought of His Day," *Studies in English*, no. 14 (July 8, 1934): 92. February 17, 2014. JSTOR.

21. Whitman, "Song of Myself" in *Leaves of Grass*, 50.

22. Shields, "Walter White v. Walt Whitman."

23. Ralph Waldo Emerson, "The Poet," *The Essential Writings of Ralph Waldo Emerson*, ed. Brooks Atkinson (New York: The Modern Library, 2000), 304.

24. David Pierson, "Breaking Neoliberal? Contemporary Neoliberal Discourses and Policies in AMC's *Breaking Bad*," in Breaking Bad: *Critical Essays on the Contexts, Politics, Style, and Reception of the Television Series*, ed. David Pierson (Lanham, MD: Lexington Books), 15–32.

25. Hank repeats this cliché a couple of times: "Kafkaesque," *Breaking Bad*, first broadcast May 16, 2010 by AMC, directed by Michael Slovis and written by Peter Gould and George Mastras; "Bullet Points," *Breaking Bad*, first broadcast August 7, 2011, by AMC, directed by Colin Bucksey and written by Vince Gilligan and Moira Walley-Beckett.

26. Bakhtin, *The Dialogic Imagination: Four Essays*, 333–35; cf 429.

27. Bakhtin, *The Dialogic Imagination: Four Essays*, 262.

28. "Bullet Points."

29. Whitman, *Leaves of Grass*, 276.

30. Martin, *Difficult Men*, 268.

31. "Felina," *Breaking Bad*, first broadcast September 29, 2013, by AMC, directed by Vince Gilligan and written by Vince Gilligan.

32. It bears mentioning that references to Kafka in *Breaking Bad* would have yielded a fascinating analysis. Early in the "Gliding Over All" episode, Walt obsessively stares at a fly, recalling the "Fly" episode from season three—the "bottle episode," one of the most critically acclaimed in the series. The symbolic density of the fly leaves much to interpretation, but one possible reading could conjecture that it is an allusion to Kafka's story "The Metamorphosis." As such, it would symbolize Walt's metamorphosis into a sub-human state. Although this episode on its own could not support such a reading, the previous episode is entitled "Kafkaesque" and so perhaps a concatenation exists. Kafka, although not a sustained allusion or motif in the series, offers nevertheless another angle to interpret and understand *Breaking Bad*.

"Round the decay/ Of that colossal wreck"
Pride and Guilt[1]

PABLO ECHART AND ALBERTO N. GARCÍA

"I met a traveler from an antique land"

"Ozymandias," the poem by Percy Bysshe Shelley, tells the story of the irremediable political decadence of leaders and the fragility of their empires, and it contrasts this with the indelible power of artistic works. The verses of the Romantic poet are central to the final season of *Breaking Bad*, both textually and paratextually. The most intense and devastating episode, 5.14, is named after the sonnet, and in the teaser for the final eight episodes Bryan Cranston recites Shelley's poem to the backdrop of images of the New Mexico desert. This reinforces the parallels between Walter White/Heisenberg and the "King of kings" in the poem. Both characters are somewhat mythical, and are stimulated by an extreme sense of pride, for which they ultimately pay a high price.

Breaking Bad is a moral tale that describes the forging of an empire and an ordinary man's loss of his scruples. The discovery of Walter White's cancer serves as a catalyst (a particularly appropriate chemical term) for him to reveal his true *inner self*. His "lung cancer is both plot device and metaphor,"[2] for a moral disease that affects a man (Walter), who sees himself enveloped by a diabolical cloak (his alter ego, Heisenberg).

The progressive moral and criminal decline of Walter White is spurred on by the contradictory tension between two radical emotions that become

78

rationalized in order to justify his actions, which become increasingly less defensible: an intensifying pride and the guilt that fades as the narrative unfolds. These two emotions play a crucial role defining Walter White's last and deeply tragic actions, when "nothing beside remains." This emotional dynamic is not completely linear but rather, like a pendulum, it is constantly in motion, with these two emotions acting as opposing vectors that drive the transformations of *Walternberg*.

In the first part of this essay we will discuss pride as a force that drives the ever bolder actions of the *reborn* Walter and we will contrast this emotion with the parallel emotion of shame. In addition, we will analyze the self-delusions that differentiate Walter from his sidekick Jesse Pinkman, his obsessions, his false alibis and his narcissistic progression up to "Gliding Over All" (5.8). In the agonizing final eight episodes Walter White's actions continue to be driven by pride, and we observe the emergence of the darker facets of his identity, together with a weakness that serves to rehumanize him.

In the second part of the essay we will tackle the theme of guilt in *Breaking Bad*, and we will compare Walter with both Skyler and Jesse Pinkman, two characters who despite supporting Walter in his criminal trajectory, deal with their own guilt in different ways. We will trace the amoral progression of Walter, from the frightened teacher of the pilot episode to the "sneer of cold command" with which he orders the murder of 10 witnesses in prison. However, as discussed in the final sub-section, the events of the final episodes of the series represent a return of the sense of guilt, leading to a perverse *happy ending* for the characters who revolve "Round the decay / Of that colossal wreck."

Pride as an Engine and a Tombstone: *"My name is Ozymandias, King of kings"*

In the academic literature on emotions, pride is considered an emotion with certain positive connotations, as it foments social action and self-improvement. For the timid Walter White presented in the pilot, repressed pride serves as the motor that incites him to turn his life around. As the episodes progress, this pride grows and begins to dominate Walter's motivations, turning into hubris. As Lewis defines it, hubris is a "transient but addictive emotion" where people "seek out and invent situations likely to repeat this emotional state."[3] As we discuss below, the downward spiral in which Walter White finds himself seems to be propelled by an addictive, insatiable ego that creates excuses in order to grow continually. At the end of the story, the engine that drove his actions eventually becomes the tombstone that buries him. As in the myth of Icarus, Walter White flies too close to the sun ("Hazard Pay," 5.3).

Pride and the Family Alibi: "Look on my words, ye Mighty"

Throughout the series, Walter attempts to justify his descent into the world of drugs and his reprehensible actions with a mantra: the need to provide for the family. However, the viewer soon appreciates that this objective, which is in principle genuine, is actually consistent with the drive of Walter's pride, which led him to reject the charity and to seek recognition.

The first season emphasizes the former. In addition to rejecting the economic aid offered by his in-laws to pay for his treatment ("Cancer Man," 1.4), his refusal to accept the succulent offer of employment made by his ex-partners, which would have enabled him to avoid any illegal activity to begin with, is fundamental: it is here that it becomes clear that his pride is more important than his love for his family. Walter appears to follow the famous quote of George Sand to the letter: "Charity degrades those who receive it and hardens those who dispense it."

Likewise, Walter experiences the pleasure of an ever-increasing narcissism. His virtuosity in chemistry and his intelligence earn him the reverential respect—on occasion accompanied by fear—of his rivals. From being a figure lambasted by the rest and by destiny, Walter begins to feel the pleasurable sensation of taking hold of the reins of his life, of "being in control," as he states in front of another patient that is weakened by cancer ("Brothers," 4.8). Although money no longer becomes a need, Walter remains addicted to the business in which he can demonstrate to the rest of the world that his *artistry* is unsurpassable.

So, the ever more pathological personality of Walter demands public recognition, he needs others to be aware of his talent. This is what finally allows him to *become someone*. It is sufficient to compare the scene in the pilot where he hides from his students in the car wash with the excessive reassertion when confronted with some thugs at the end of the first part of the fifth season: "Now: say my name! ['Heisenberg,' says the man] You're goddam right!!" ("Say My Name," 5.7). This sentence shows how Walter has acquired an exaggerated pride—i.e., hubris.

It is the same arrogance that leads him to nearly give himself away in a police murder case (the assassination of Gale), as he can't tolerate that his genius and cooking craftsmanship is attributed to another chemist: "This ...

genius of yours. Maybe he's still out there," he insinuates to Hank ("Shotgun," 4.5). Even Mike makes reference to Walter's pathological pride, situating it as the source of all his ills:

> We had a good thing, you stupid son of a bitch, we had Fring (....) You could have shut your mouth and cooked and made as much money as you would have ever needed. But no, you just had to blow it up! You and your pride and your ego, you just had to be the man! If you'd done your job, known your place, we'd all be fine right now ["Say My Name," 5.7].

This same excessive pride conditions his relationships with the characters that surround him. Walter's relationship with Jesse is one of superiority in his position as a business partner, putative father and master chemist. This superiority results in a toxic, overbearing and belittling dynamic, with accusations such as "you are a pathetic junkie, too stupid to understand and follow simple rudimentary instructions" ("Down," 2.4). It is in situations like this, when his pride is dramatically damaged, that Pinkman's rage emerges, to the point that the couple come to blows on several occasions, most notably the violent confrontation in "Bug" (4.9).[4]

During the first two seasons, the relationship between Walter and his family is strongly based on the other face of pride: shame. As catalogued by Tangney and Fischer, these are "emotions of opposite polarity." At the outset of the story, Walter perceives how reprehensible his actions are, and consistent with the classical response to shame he "tries to hide or escape from the observation or judgment"[5] of others, in this case that of his wife and son, because "when ashamed [...] we are clear about our sense of identity as a horrible, ugly, bad, or awful person."[6] As it turns out, and as Gilligan admits, Walter is a genius when it comes to deceit: "Walt's superpower is that of being the biggest liar in the world. There is no better liar in the world of *Breaking Bad* and the person that he is most capable of deceiving is in fact himself."[7] Therein lies one of the big differences between Walter and Jesse; the latter maintains his moral compass and accepts evil as part of his identity, without self-deception: "I accept who I am: I am the bad guy," he admits in "No Mas" (3.1).

However, by the end of the second season two events occur that alter Walter's self-image: Skyler discovers his continued farces; and his cancer temporally remits. Both these facts—intertwined with the rest of the story, as is logical—provoke a new psychological twist in Walter, and as is a norm throughout the series, his pride overrides the shame or guilt. As is the emotional leitmotif of *Breaking Bad*, Walter White rationalizes his emotions adapting them to the new scenario, yet always giving preference to his pride over other feelings. He again adopts what Williams and DeSteno call a "hubristic pride": "[It] has no particular target and in essence is an unconditional positive view of one's self as a whole that may lead to negative social consequences."[8] The zenith of this transformation (that in the fifth season will descend into domestic psychological terror) takes place in "Cornered" (4.6) when Skyler doubts the physical integrity of her husband, accusing him implicitly of being weak. An irate Walter responds: "You clearly don't know who you're talking to, so let me clue you in: I am not in danger, Skyler. I am the danger. A guy opens his door and gets shot, and you think that of me? No! I am the one who knocks!"

In this sense, Kuo and Wu defined a suggestive analogy between this character and Satan in *Paradise Lost*,[9] and it is clear that Walter adheres to the phrase of Milton's Demon: "Better to reign in Hell than to serve in Heaven." But to reign in Hell it is necessary to act with malice. Accordingly, the progressive dehumanization of the protagonist is driven by his exaggerated pride that, as the story unfolds, becomes released from all the moral constraints, becoming a remorseless man. However, this evil path is tempered in the last eight episodes.

Tempered pride and Collapse: "Nothing beside remains"

While in "Fly" (3.10) Walter describes a touching family scene as the moment he would have liked to die, two seasons later the highpoint of his life is presented in another domestic setting, this time in the final minutes of "Gliding Over All." On the Whites' patio, the six members of the family share a quiet meal. It could have been a happy ending for Walter: the domestic harmony and the tacit reconciliation with Skyler suggested when their eyes meet represents for Walter a manifestation of completeness; he has left the "business empire," has succeeded in providing for his family and has satiated his narcissistic ambition to be *recognized*. Moreover, at this point in the story he has no more enemies to defeat—the last witnesses were executed in prison—the police do not suspect him, and his partners in crime, Mike and Jesse, are out of the game. The comfort and satisfaction felt by Walter in this moment of success, in which he is presented as a happy father, contrasts with the flash-forward that opens the next episode ("Blood Money," 5.9), in which a gaunt Walter surveys his destroyed home.

Hank's discovery in the bathroom deflates Walter's ecstasy and will push him to use his pride as an effective mechanism of self-defense to avoid taking responsibility for the way in which the events have played out. Thus, the second half of the final season sees a return of the Jekyll and Hyde ambivalence between the open and remorseful Walter and Heisenberg, spurred on by the enemy and once again motivated by extreme pride. As in the verses of Walt Whitman ("Very well, then I contradict myself, I am large, I contain *multitudes*"), the internal schism to which the character is subjected is eloquently reflected in his paradoxical actions within the same episode. Thus, "Rabid Dog" (5.12) begins with Walter threatening Saul when the latter suggests that Jesse should be killed—who, consumed by guilt, could drag them all down—yet it ends with a 180° turn of events, with Heisenberg ordering Jesse's execution. In a moral reversal, in "Ozymandias" (5.14) Heisenberg is capable of kidnapping Holly—the most precious of all things to Skyler, along with Walter Jr.—only to return her when he realizes that she misses her mother, evoking in him pity for both mother and daughter.

Consistent with the rest of the series, pride remains a driving force in the later stages of Walter White's moral journey, reappearing towards the end of the series in response to his wounded ego and his desire to be immortalized. First, his wounded pride makes him a victim, demanding the empathy of the viewer necessary to create the conditions required to repair the damage, and encouraging him to act decisively one last time. Listening to the lies of his former partners (the Schwartzes) on TV, Walter goes back on his decision to surrender to the police, and sick with both pride and cancer, he launches his final plan ("Granite State," 5.15).

Second, his pride also responds to Heisenberg's desire to perpetuate himself as a legendary figure: a criminal as feared as he was respected as a virtuoso drug alchemist. In one of the most exciting moments of the series, there is the physical confrontation between Walter and Hank, when Walter realizes that the police are on his trail and Heisenberg reveals his mythical dark side: "If you don't know who I am, then maybe your best course would be to tread lightly" ("Blood Money," 5.9). In the season's finale, "Felina" (5.16), an offended Walter/Heisenberg finds added motivation[10] for exacting revenge on Todd's gang when Badger and Skinny reveal that someone (Jesse) is cooking better methamphetamine than his. This professional vindication culminates in the smile on Walter's face at the moment of his death in the clandestine laboratory: satisfied that the bloody massacre that has just come to an end will ensure that Heisenberg will go down in history, given that his drug—his work of art—continues to be sought after on the streets while he remains a wanted man.

In the same way as the moments of greatest subjective happiness are domestic scenes, it is in the company of his family that Walter displays the remnants of his humanity, his vulnerability and his limitations, and he appears a meek, humble man who is not driven by pathological pride. Thus, the solitary breakfast with which he *celebrates* his 52nd birthday ("Live Free or Die," 5.1)—so far removed from the celebration with which the story began exactly two years previously—evokes compassion in the viewer, who feels Walter's nostalgia for the family he has lost.

The impotence induced by pride is particularly evident in "Granite State" (5.15), in which a delusional Walter realizes that his pride and his desire for revenge contrast starkly with his limitations. One of the most important characteristics of the screenplay of the final season of *Breaking Bad* is the ongoing theme of reaping that which has been sown. This time it is used to show how dominant hubris has turned into pathetic impotence. In "Live Free or Die" (5.1), an emboldened Walter threatened Saul Goodman: "We're done when I say we're done." In the penultimate episode, he tries to repeat his bullying: "Remember what I told you, it's not over, until...," but in mid-sentence he is overcome with a bout of coughing.... "It's over," insists Saul.

In that same episode, Walter's isolation intensifies in the snow-covered cabin in which he hides, the image itself a metaphor for his solitude. On his birthday, he gives a 100 dollar bill to the waitress who treated him with kindness, and in the cabin he is willing to pay $10,000 to his benefactor for a mere hour of his company: as the poet wrote, "nothing beside remains."

Moving beyond the impositions of external circumstances (illness, exile), the farewell to Skyler and Holly ("Felina," 5.16) illustrates the apparent paradox of the vicissitudes of Walter White: the actions supposedly undertaken for the good of the family have ultimately destroyed the family. However, that last visit home—or to the mirage of home, to be precise—allows Walter White, after months of solitude, to embark upon the final stage of his transformation. This represents a point of anagnorisis, of self-recognition. Walter finally accepts that his excessive pride and not the welfare of his family has been the real impetus for his actions: "I did it for me. I was good in it. And I ... I was really ... I was alive." To achieve a state of feeling *alive*, Walter White, as we examine below, had to gradually renounce that which lies at the heart of moral conscience: the feeling of guilt.

Guilt, from Mr. White to Mr. Lambert: "Stamped on this lifeless things"

From the outset, Walter White accepts the damage caused by his immoral actions (manufacturing drugs), both personal and social, with the excuse of doing so for the greater good: a prosperous and stable family legacy after his death.

The moral transformation of Walter White is subtle, gradual and not without setbacks. Consistent with the emotional dynamics at play throughout the series, moral conscience is particularly powerful in the earliest stages. Episode 1.3 ("And the Bag's in the River") is particularly significant. The story lingers on the moral dilemma that confronts Walter when faced with committing a crime. On a piece of paper he writes in the left column the reasons why he should not kill Krazy-8: "It's the moral thing to do," "He may listen to reason," "post-traumatic stress," "Won't be able to live with yourself," "Murder is wrong!," "Judeo Christian principles," "You are NOT a murderer," "Sanctity of life." In the right-hand column there is just one reason—"He'll kill you and your entire family if you let him go"—and the shards of a broken plate.

As the descent into hell that is *Breaking Bad* progresses, the left column shrinks. The line between remorse and shame becomes blurred, as Walter is gradually stripped of the two corrective premises on which guilt is founded: rectifying a wrong and preventing its recurrence.[11] Only in the last three episodes, when catastrophe is inevitable, does Walter try to restore the broken order, as we discuss below.

The Birth of a Superman: "A sneer of cold command"

Breaking Bad can be understood as the story of a monster that is fighting to cast off his human mask. The challenge of the series lies precisely in the extent to which the viewer's interest in the fortune of the character, who is ever more repulsive, can be maintained, and with whom the bond of a shared moral code is progressively lost. As the monster begins to take over, Walter's pride begins to crush his sense of guilt. This is clearly evident through the brutal acts that he commits, more and more outrageous, and severe, and yet the chemistry teacher always finds a way to justify them.

The human qualities of Walter evoke certain compassion, such that the spectator can empathize with him: during the first season, the sick Walter is the victim, the loser, the man who has got less than he deserves, the "identifiable suburban dad under enormous pressure."[12] Furthermore, throughout the first two seasons, the murders are portrayed as products of Walter's instinct for survival: kill (in self-defense) or be killed.

The big change comes later, not by chance, once his cancer remits and Walter demonstrates the strength of Heisenberg's personality with that "Stay out of my territory" that he bellows in the hardware store ("Over," 2.10). Soon later, in "Phoenix" (2.12) Walter lets Jane die despite there being no physical threat to his life (as with the earlier deaths). What is also interesting in this event is the contrast in the way it affects other protagonists: while Jesse's sense of guilt becomes ever more apparent, Walter appears to be ever more immune to the moral consequences of his actions. This inertia is only questioned by Hank's death, which, as discussed later, represents the transgression of the one forbidden frontier: the family.

Although progressive, Walter's moral decline stalls at times. On several occasions he shows signs of acceptance of the evil in his actions, and as a consequence, on occasions he expresses strong remorse. This explains his enraged response to such good news as the remission of his illness ("Four Days Out," 2.9). Walter's response is to cause himself pain (furiously smashing his knuckles in the bath) and in that moment, we sense that he cannot support the guilt of all the pain he has caused. No longer can he argue that mitigating circumstances justify that what he does is for a greater good, in the light of his imminent death. This is the feeling that becomes explicit in "Fly" (3.10): "Skyler and Holly were in another room. I can hear them on the baby monitor. She was singing a lullaby. Oh, if I had just lived right up to that moment ... and not one second more. That would have been perfect [...] I'm saying that I lived too long."

At times like this, the more human Walter struggles to break through to the surface and overthrow his alter ego. As illustrated when Walter falls, defeated in his battle against a fly, his sheer physical weakness facilitates the eruption of guilt and recognition of the pain he has caused; the fly can be interpreted as a metaphor for the *contaminated* conscience that can never be fully purified. Something similar happens when, after being beaten, he breaks into tears before his son. However, having regained his composure after sleeping restfully, he admonishes Walter Jr. to erase from his memory the image of the vulnerability he displayed ("Health," 4.10).

That is the last time that Walter White considers any real alternative to his criminal life. However, a new turn at the end of the following episode (regarding the money that Skyler gives to Beneke) forces him to again forge onwards, and as is by that stage becoming the norm, his pride, coupled to his survival instinct, supersedes any other moral consideration; for example, surrendering to the police and seeking witness protection. Another example of this ebb and flow between Walter and Heisenberg is seen towards the end of "Buried" (5.10). Conscious of the dire situation in which he has placed Skyler, Walter agrees to surrender to the police only if she accepts the money he has gained. This time, it is Skyler who encourages her husband to keep going.

Although the character played by Anna Gunn is infected by Walter's moral Machiavellianism (e.g., her cynicism in lying to Marie about the origin of money, her cruelty regarding the DVD with which Walter incriminates Hank, her insistence on taking "full measures" against Jesse in "Rabid Dog"), her moral conscience is more robust and therefore, her guilt is more apparent. However, as much as she condemns her husband's actions, she uses a similar justification for her actions: the family.[13] Skyler is afraid of losing her children and feels ashamed for failing to report Walter's crimes (including the shooting of Hank in "One Minute," 3.7). Only after Hank's death will she be able to confront the tragic actions of her husband ("Ozymandias," 5.14), and accept the feelings of guilt and shame they provoke.

Substantial differences are also seen between Walter and Pinkman, who serves as an inverted mirror of Walter's guilt. Jesse never escapes from the weight of cyclical feelings of guilt. He does not recover from the depressive state triggered by Jane's death until well into the third season. However, the plot puts him back against the ropes when he is forced to kill Gale. This crime drives his actions for much of the fourth season, culminating in his remorseful lament in "Problem Dog" (4.7); unlike Walter, he is unable to forgive himself for the murder: "The thing is, if you just do stuff and nothing happens, what's it all mean? What's the point? Oh right, this whole thing is about self-acceptance. [...] So no matter what I do, hooray for me because I'm a great guy? It's all good? No matter how many dogs I kill, I just, what, do an inventory and accept?"

In fact, Jesse feels what Lacroix describes as "morbid guilt,"[14] something that reaches its zenith in the latter part of the fifth season. Jesse is unable to get over the murder of the child with the tarantula. Walter himself warns: "Son, you need to stop focusing on the darkness behind you. The past is the past. Nothing can change" ("Blood Money," 5.9).

According to Lindsay-Hart, De Rivera and Mascolo, "unresolved guilt may lead to continual attempts to restore the moral balance by 'being good,' punishing the self, giving up rights, performing actions that appear to be symbolic substitutes for making reparations, undoing a wrong, or making order out of disorder."[15] From "Blood Money" (5.9) onwards, the character played by Aaron Paul adjusts his actions in response to this "unresolved guilt": he collaborates with Hank to catch Heisenberg (restore balance), he falls for the umpteenth time into drug use and despair (self-punishment), he throws the money to which he has a *right* out the car window (giving up rights), and he delivers the rest of the money to the family of Drew Sharp (reparation). Moreover, as will happen to Walter, Jesse pays a heavy price for his sins, since he not only sees Andrea murdered, but he also spends months enslaved in a hellish basement. It is no coincidence that his emotional consolation is his dream of the Peruvian wood box that he swapped for an ounce of marijuana ("Kafkaesque," 3.9). It is a symbol of remorse for having done so much wrong that he now regrets, like an original sin from which he cannot escape.

This sense of guilt makes him more human and enhances his empathy with the spectator, unlike Walter who morally becomes increasingly more distanced from the audience. In the third season, Mr. White steps up a level by running over Gus Fring's two henchmen and orchestrating the liquidation of Gale. In the fourth season, he puts in danger a child (poisoning Brock) and an elderly lady (the neighbor that he uses to ensure the path is clear in "Face Off," 4.13). Likewise, in the fifth season, as well as terrifying Skyler, shooting Mike[16] and killing ten witnesses, his reaction to the death of the child on the motorbike is very significant: projecting along with Jesse a compassion that proves to be false when just moments later we see him whistling happily ("Buyout," 5.6).

During the first part of the last season, Walter becomes a merciless and guiltless man, a superman—*Übermensch* in Nietzschean terms[17]—capable of constructing his very own value system. He adopts what Heller labels as a "narcissistic conscience," where acts are differentiated from consequences: "In the case of narcissistic conscience, 'taking full responsibility' means to reject consciously all responsibility with conscience's usual cry: Here I stand and cannot do otherwise."[18] However, the last eight episodes point towards poetic justice where crime has a cost, narrating the fall of this "King of kings."

The Return of Guilt:
"Half sunk, a shattered visage lies"

The narcissist in Walter White is satiated psychologically in "Say My Name" (5.7), and materially in "Gliding Over All" (5.8), when Skyler shows him the gigantic pile of money he has earned. If the family is the only moral boundary that Walter's conscience dares not cross, it is logical that his greatest regrets come after Hank's murder in "Ozymandias" (5.14).

But even at this point, Walter does not take full responsibility for Hank's death but rather, he transfers this responsibility to Jesse in another example of how he engages in self-deception to continue believing that his actions are for noble and justified reasons. A common pattern in *Breaking Bad* is that

Walter's lowest moments—symbolized by that terrified look that begs for mercy over his glasses and the ground-level close-up of a man who has been morally destroyed, as in Shelley's poem from which the title of the episode is taken— are accompanied by a violent resurgence of Heisenberg. In "Ozymandias," this takes a particularly horrifying form, resolving one of the most intriguing situations in the series in a way that reinforces Jesse's guilt, while punishing him further: "Wait. I watched Jane die. I was there. And I watched her die. I watched her overdose and choke to death. I could have saved her. But I didn't." The constant tension between guilt and pride is reflected in the facial expression of *Walternberg* in this short dialogue: from a rictus of pain to absolute hatred. For this reason he does not hand himself in to the police after Hank's death but rather, he flees with a barrel of money, a new excuse to have a "fresh start"—a redemption that absolves all his sins—with his family.

The end of that crucial episode (5.14) again emphasizes the emotional dichotomy that runs through the entire series. The final call is an attempt by Walter to exculpate Skyler. Walter knows that the police are listening to the conversation and thus, through his excessive rhetoric he seeks her complicity (Skyler, who in contrast to the opening sequence of the episode, has now learned to recognize her husband's lies). After a few seconds, Skyler falls silent and plays along, coming across—in the eyes of the police—as a victim of her husband's domestic violence. It is possible that Walter's disdain and anger contains traces of Heisenberg's pride (especially when he blurts out that she never thanked him for everything he has done "for this family"), yet in the end, Walter's tears reveal his feelings of guilt and the realization of the terrible damage he has inflicted upon those he loves most.

The events of the final two episodes confirm the marked resurgence of guilt, and the consequent remedial practices that accompany it. From his desperation and physical impotence in "Granite State" (5.15), Walter ruminates on guilt for months, while at the same time designing a strategy to compensate for the damage caused to his family, and to avenge Hank; two ways to "repair the failure." Accordingly, Walter seeks to restore the balance that he has upset, a common element of guilt: "The psychological situation of guilt involves a violation of the moral order, for which we take responsibility. The primary motivational instruction of guilt is the felt desire to 'set things right,' to restore the balance in moral order."[19]

Walter White's internal tension leads him to seek forgiveness by calling his son. Flynn's absolute contempt for him ("Why don't you just die already? Just die!!"), leaves Walter more broken than ever, to the point that he takes a step that he had not previously dared to take: calling the police to surrender. This reflects his acceptance of the consequences of his guilt, taking full responsibility for his actions; not only legally but with all the disgrace that this entails. And this is where, for the last time, the proud Heisenberg comes to the rescue of Mr. White, and in an example of circular narrative, Grey Matter again acts as the catalyst for the latest action driven by his wounded pride.

Thus, the series' finale ("Felina," 5.16) shows us a protagonist in search of forgiveness *sui generis*: "The wish to alleviate the burden of guilt," writes Griswold, "is surely the most common and pressing motive for requesting forgiveness."[20] In an attempt to "set things straight," Mr. Lambert (the new alias symbolizing the failure of both Mr. White and Heisenberg) returns to Albuquerque, his actions guided by a mixture of justifications derived from both guilt and pride, and hence his unusual apology.

Once again during the celebrated conversation with Skyler the contradictory personality of the protagonist is displayed. Walter White accepts his wickedness, his hubris, his alter ego (Heisenberg): "I did it for me. I liked it. I was good at it. And I was really ... I was alive." The phrase, which in some way defends his criminal self, also contains features that Griswold[21] attributes to a genuine apology (born of guilt). Walter takes responsibility: he no longer uses the family as an excuse; he recognizes the evil of his acts, revealing the whereabouts of the bodies of Hank and Gomez; he changes his attitude and condemns his actions, since he recognizes his enormous ego as the engine driving his actions; and he agrees not to repeat the offense, as he has returned to say goodbye and to disappear from their lives forever.

To close the circle of guilt, Walter still accepts the ultimate price of his crimes: that of his own life. As before,[22] Walter punishes himself and sacrifices himself to save Jesse, even asking Jesse to pull the trigger. The paradox of the ending—a perverse *happy ending*—is that it satisfies the aspirations of the two emotions that since the outset have battled within him, and that characterize the psyche of Walter Hartwell White.

Conclusion: "Round the decay / Of that colossal wreck"

The ending of *Breaking Bad* stresses the parallelism with Shelley's "Ozymandias": the colossal personal, familiar and moral shipwreck of the protagonist co-exists with the legend of the blue meth. The teardrop that Walter sheds before dying accompanies a smile of satisfaction with his *Baby Blue*. It is this ambiguity that makes the ending (*traditional* and generally predictable) so satisfying. *Breaking Bad* restores order ... a moral order at least. Good, although somewhat battered, still stands tall, and the line that separates it from Evil is clear. The criminal has confessed his sins and now assumes his guilt, ultimately trying to amend the evil done.

Similarly, Jesse has paid his penance for all the pain he has caused. He achieves physical release by choking Todd, yet inner freedom requires that he forgives. Thus, by not shooting Walter White, Jesse fulfils two goals. From the emotional point of view it allows him to escape from the toxic relationship, dominated by Walter, because this time, unlike with Gale, he ignores Walter's command to "do it." In addition, from the moral point of view, Jesse shows compassion by not shooting Walter, thereby, to some extent, forgiving him.

Furthermore, if *Breaking Bad* is the titanic struggle of a man against himself, the ending manages to square the circle by reconciling the bloody vengeance of Heisenberg with the Christian sense of guilt of Walter White: he pays the price for all the evil done (he will not see his daughter grow, his wife and son hate him, his brother-in-law is dead and even he will perish) while attempting to amend the same evil. Walter accepts his penance, however painful it may be. There is no home to return to, all that remains is to die doing one last good deed to find peace with himself ("I just needed a proper goodbye," he explains to Skyler). Skyler actually minimally accepts his apology, as illustrated by the way she stays her hand as Walter leaves the frame ... but Walter Jr. will never forgive him.

And this is where the proverbial ambiguity of the series allows a final *tour de force*: the defeat of Walter, his death, constitutes the final victory of his *alter ego*. The legend of Heisenberg, who so lovingly contemplates the laboratory of his dreams, will grow ever greater with the discovery that he was cooking in Albuquerque while he was the most wanted criminal in America. He will die. But his name, and his sated ego, will live forever in memory.

Notes

1. This essay is based on a previously pubished one: Pablo Echart and Alberto N. García, "Crime and Punishment: Greed, Pride and Guilt in *Breaking Bad*," in *A Critical Approach to the Apocalypse*, eds. Alexandra Simon-López and Heidi Yeandle (Oxford: Inter-Disciplinary Press, 2013), 205–217.

2. Ray Bossert, "MacBeth *on Ice*," in *Breaking Bad and Philosophy: Badder Living through Chemistry*, eds. David R. Koepsell and Robert Arp (Chicago: Open Court, 2012), 77.

3. Michael Lewis, "Self Conscious Emotions: Embarrassment, Pride, Shame, and

Guilt," in *Handbook of Emotions*, eds. Michael Lewis, Jeannette M. Haviland-Jones, and Lisa Feldman Barrett (New York: Guilford Press, 2010), 749.

4. These sudden, violent impulses, which also characterize Walter, show that rage is the product of his shame. As Lindsay-Hartz, De Rivera and Mascolo write, "by putting another down, one [ashamed person] may attempt defensively to repair and in comparison raise up one's shattered sense of self-worth." Janice Lindsay-Hartz, Joseph de Rivera, and Michael F. Mascolo, "Differentiating Guilt and Shame and Their Effects on Motivation," in *Self-Conscious Emotions: The Psychology of Shame, Guilt, Embarrassment and Pride*, eds. June Price Tangney and Kurt W. Fischer (New York: Guilford Press, 1995), 296.

5. June Price Tangney and Kurt W. Fischer, "Self-Conscious Emotions and the Affect Revolution: Framework and Overview," in *Self-Conscious Emotions: The Psychology of Shame, Guilt, Embarrassment and Pride*, eds. June Price Tangney and Kurt W. Fischer (New York: Guilford Press, 1995), 10.

6. Lindsay-Hartz, De Rivera, and Mascolo, "Differentiating Guilt and Shame," 295.

7. Emmanuel Burdeau, "En las entrañas de *Breaking Bad*," *So Film* 1 (2013): 52. Translated by Mark Sefton.

8. Lisa A. Williams and David DeSteno, "Pride and Perseverance: The Motivational Role of Pride," *Journal of Personality and Social Psychology* 94.6 (2008): 1008.

9. Michelle Kuo and Albert Wu, "In Hell, 'We Shall Be Free': On *Breaking Bad*," *Los Angeles Review of Books*, July 13, 2012, accessed April 5, 2013, http://lareviewof books.org/article.php?id=761&fulltext=1.

10. This rivalry was first established in the fourth season, when Walter sees his leadership threatened and he begins to feel *expendable*. On that ocassion, Walter – thanks to the cigarette spiked with ricin—succeeds in temporarily recovering Jesse's loyalty, until his guilt for the death of Andrew Sharp separates them again.

11. Lewis, "Self-Conscious Emotions," 748.

12. Alan Sepinwall, *The Revolution Was Televised: The Cops, Crooks, Slingers and Slayers Who Changed TV Drama Forever* (New York: Touchstone 2013), 356–357.

13. One of the differences between the moral limits set by Skyler and Walter concerns Jesse. For Walter, this character is like a "son" and as such, he is always "off-limits"; he forms part of the family that cannot be touched. By contrast, Skyler has always seen Jesse as a stranger and thus, it seems reasonable to her to liquidate him in order to save her family ("Rabid Dog," 5.12). Finally, the ambush that Jesse and Hank set up for Walter at the end of the same episode leads Heisenberg to declare Jesse to be "dispensable." Only in the final minutes of the series (in "Felina") is a reconciliation they allowed, dramatized in a duel of close-ups that portray their last goodbye.

14. Jean Lacroix, *Philosophie de la culpabilité* (Paris: PUF, 1977), 24.

15. Lindsay-Hartz, De Rivera and Mascolo, "Differentiating Guilt and Shame," 289.

16. Again, the dichotomy between pride and guilt appears after this assassination:

Walter realizes that he has allowed himself to be overcome by rage and begs forgiveness, yet it's already too late.

17. Friedrich Nietzsche, *Thus Spoke Zarathustra: A Book for All and None* (New York: Oxford University Press, 2008), xviii.

18. Agnes Heller, *The Power of Shame: A Rational Perspective* (London: Routledge & Kegan Paul, 1985), 38.

19. Lindsay-Hartz, De Rivera and Mascolo, "Differentiating Guilt and Shame," 289.

20. Charles Griswold, *Forgiveness: A Philosophical Exploration* (Cambridge: Cambridge University Press, 2007), 52.

21. Griswold, *Forgiveness: a Philosophical Exploration*, 56.

22. In the pilot he tries to shoot himself, but there is no bullet in the chamber of the gun; in "Four Days Out" (2.9) he smashes up the bathroom of the hospital; and in "Fly" (3.10) he feels remorse for not having already died.

Say My Name
The Fantasy of
Liberated Masculinity

Jason Landrum

The opening image of Vince Gilligan's *Breaking Bad* crystallizes the depiction of masculinity crucial to the show's success. A pair of pants—khakis to be exact—fall from the sky. The audience has no idea to whom the pants belong, but the imagery is unmistakable. From the beginning of the series, *Breaking Bad* has concerned itself with questions about who wears the pants. The show persistently pursues questions of paternal authority by introducing audiences to Walter White, not through a depiction of what he does for work or how he lives with his family, but through a pair of empty pants, floating helplessly in the breeze, briefly puffed up to appear full, but ultimately flattened and lying helplessly on the ground where a recreational vehicle runs over them. The pre-credit imagery not only conjures questions of who wears or owns the pants, but more significantly, who *deserves* to wear and own the pants. The remaining portion of the scene introduces the man at the heart of the show, frantically recording a goodbye message to his wife and son, wearing only his underwear and shirt, and waiting for the police to arrest him. He confesses to his wife and son that his law breaking activities have been all for them. Gilligan, *Breaking Bad*'s showrunner, has famously stated that he wanted to make a show that depicted the transformation of Mr. Chips into Scarface, a feat he successfully achieved, but he also achieved something else. By positioning Walter White on the continuum between the iconic images of the beloved schoolteacher and ruthless gangster, Gilligan places White within a singular debate about masculinity in the early twenty-first century. While it is not the first show to interrogate fatherly roles or male criminal behavior, *Breaking Bad*'s fusion of the two into one character contributes to its enduring innovative status, and I contend that this fusion establishes a new allegory of masculinity in the early twenty-first century.

Anti-hero narratives have been a crucial stage for Golden Age television and its fantasies of masculinity as a state of emergency. Shows like HBO's *The Sopranos, Deadwood, The Wire*, and *Game of Thrones*, Showtime's *Dexter, Homeland*, and *Californication*, FX's *The Shield, Rescue Me*, and *Sons of Anarchy*, TNT's *Southland*, and AMC's *Mad Men* and *The Walking Dead*, all revolve around, in one way or another, this type of complicated masculinity, a complex mixture of hyper-masculine disregard for the law, family, and the public good. On the one hand, these male characters live in the public sphere of their jobs and family, and on the other hand, they exist in the seamy underworld of violent crime and/or cultural transgression. The dramatic conflict of these shows revolves around the threat that the underworld life poses to the man's public face and name and the resulting state of emergency where the male characters seek to remain. Walter White epitomizes this depiction, the tenuous line between his public face as a high school chemistry teacher, husband, and father and his private identity as the criminal Heisenberg—identities that blur into one another as the show progresses each season. Each episode operates at a fever-pitch, as Walter tells lie after lie (to his wife, son, brother-in-law, partner, and enemies) in order to maintain the intense masculine excitation of being, what he calls, "the danger." *Breaking Bad*, therefore, allegorically represents a broken relationship between masculinity and the social bond of American culture, a broken connection hastened by the constant state of emergency in which Americans have lived after multiple post-millennial catastrophes (9/11, Katrina, Great Recession, Sandy Hook and so on). Moreover, I want to pursue my contention about early millennial masculinity as both a modest theoretical examination of *Breaking Bad* and as a kind of unifying theory of Golden Age television. *Breaking Bad*, specifically, and Golden Age television, more generally, thrive on fantasies of fathers who fail to be satisfied with their satisfaction and who prefer to chase one self-imposed crisis after another. Putting it more simply, these new men are always standing on the side of the road in their underwear, holding a gun and caring nothing about finding their pants.

Breaking Dad

The state of emergency faced by contemporary men has emerged as a response to the perceived loss of patriarchal prestige. The traditional story of patriarchal decline often focuses on postmodernity's gradual erosion of the power that men, especially fathers, enjoyed in the early-to-mid twentieth century. Privileged cultural practices like heteronormative marriage, the masculine burden of financial responsibility, the fatherly right to disregard day-to-day parental guidance, and workplace superiority, as the story goes, have all been assaulted in so many ways by feminists, liberals, and Hollywood that the resulting post-patriarchy of the twenty-first century has left men adrift and ridiculed. Being a man in post-patriarchy is a high-wire performance act in which men must continually prove their necessity while also demonstrating self-awareness about their loss of privilege. In other words, men are caught in a game without a goal. They must appear aggressively interested in recovering their patriarchal power but imbue their pursuit with a kind of cynical disregard for regaining this imaginary wholeness. Mid-century masculinity defined by its restraint, confidence, and detachment, performed effortlessly by cultural icons like John Wayne, has given way to something more manic.

While psychoanalysis does not offer the only theoretical models for understanding of paternal authority, it provides the richest explanation of why and how subjects respond to it. Therefore, my analysis of *Breaking Bad* leans heavily on the work of Jacques Lacan and other neo–Lacanians, such as Slavoj Žižek and Todd McGowan. Lacan conceives of paternal authority as being divided into two categories, breaking the fatherly role into two parts: the–Name-of-the-Father and the primal father. The first, the Name-of-the-Father, operates symbolically.[1] The symbolic father is a figure of prohibition who works to ensure the smooth functioning of reality by eradicating private enjoyment. In other words, the symbolic father prohibits the subject's private enjoyment from the public sphere, requiring the subject to sacrifice his enjoyment in order to gain access to the Symbolic order. A symbolic father's prohibitive role underpins the laws that govern the social bond by offering several inducements for following the codes that restrict public displays of enjoyment. The interaction of public laws governing the social order and the Name-of-the-Father produces both disappointment and relief simultaneously for the subject. On the one hand, the subject is dissatisfied with the rules governing his behavior, and on the other hand, he feels relieved by the protection the symbolic father provides from the enjoyment of others. The symbolism of his authority, however, does not hide the fact that this authority *is* just a symbol, something that real fathers do not actually have, and something that can often be the reason for rebellion and ridicule. It is only symbolic, after all. That said, the social bond's guarantee—that sacrifice of private enjoyment ensures access to the public order—is built upon paternal authority. Or paraphrasing Lacan's description of love, the social bond is a system in which fathers give subjects something they do not have and subjects do not want in exchange for obedience.[2] Television history is replete with symbolic father figures. Consider fatherly characters, then, who wield authority through the phrase "because I said so" as an example of a powerful presence, but who actually stand on nothing: Mike Brady managing the awkward merger of his sons with Carol Brady's daughters in *The Brady Bunch*; Archie Bunker decrying the immaturity of Meathead's politics in *All in the Family*; Cliff Huxtable of *The Cosby Show* officiating an impromptu funeral for Rudy's dead goldfish; Widower Ben Cartwright handling disputes between Adam, Hoss, and Little Joe in *Bonanza*; and, to make my point even finer, the title *Father Knows Best* alone sums up the traditional depiction of dads on television. Above all, the symbolic father guards against slanders to his "good name" more so than threats of injury to his body because, in the end, it is the symbol of the father's name that is most important. Symbolic fathers operate as reminders of the power of symbolism while also highlighting the ephemeral nature of objects, which, like the father's body, are less important than the subject's name.

The second paternal figure is an outgrowth of the superego, a more primal figure far more interested in obtaining objects than maintaining symbolism. Whereas the symbolic father prohibits enjoyment and emphasizes the importance of a "good name," the primal father commands enjoyment and cares little for symbolism.[3] The primal father is male sexual identity at its most idealized. Todd McGowan argues that the primal father figure is unlike other men because he is

> not subject to castration. This nonlacking figure provides a model for male subjects that they cannot possibly emulate—though they endeavor to do so ceaselessly—because he exists only as an exception. Nonetheless, this exceptional figure allows male subjects to constitute their identity by showing them what they aren't.[4]

The primal father operates as an exceptional masculine identity that male subjects desperately try to emulate but cannot access. Its exceptionality provides the idea of enjoyment for the male subject and animates his activity, but this enjoyment remains elusive and out of reach. The male subject, typically, sacrifices the illusory enjoyment promised by the idealized primal father or gives in to its allure, relentlessly chasing its false promise. In other words, men accept the incomplete masculinity of their "good name" or reject it in favor of a more transgressive subjectivity. All male subjects weigh the dissatisfying impact of prohibition against the alluring promise of enjoyment when deciding how to lead their lives. But the beginning of the twenty-first century has shifted the ground under the feet of men. What separates the culture of the mid-to-late twentieth century and the twenty-first century is a shift that deemphasizes the power of public prohibition and elevates the impact of private enjoyment. McGowan argues in *The End of Dissatisfaction?* that late-capitalist culture has radically expanded the significance of enjoyment, which he links to the rise of the superego, while cynically dismissing the crucial role prohibition plays in the social bond. He explains,

> The superego and its command to enjoy have burdened the subject through-out history, but global capitalism allows the logic of the superego to gain pre-dominance. In the epoch of global capitalism, the rise of the superego and of the society of enjoyment finds its apotheosis, allowing the transition toward a duty to enjoy to occur with incredible rapidity. Rather than living in a society that prohibits enjoyment, we are increasingly living in one that commands it. We live under the reign of a tyrant for the next millennium—the superego.[5]

McGowan's conception of the shift from the society of prohibition, ruled by the symbolic father, to the society of enjoyment, ruled by the tyrannical primal father, is the world depicted by *Breaking Bad*. Walter's transformation into Heisenberg demonstrates in microcosm McGowan's larger point about late-capitalist culture. However, Walter does not eschew one male subject position for the other; he neither fully renounces his role as a father/husband nor fully renounces his criminal alter ego Heisenberg. Instead, he prefers to exist in con-stant oscillation between each masculine role and never fully accepts the power of either name. As the show unfolds, Walter no longer needs to chase the sym-bolic masculine image he believes he has lost. Instead, Walter is singularly focused on chasing the feeling of loss itself. He neither needs his pants nor the recognition that he deserves to own and wear the pants. He prefers the rush of losing his pants in public.

Breaking Bad's depiction of masculinity as a crisis state in between two masculine subject positions provides the basis for the dramatic tension of each episode. From the pilot to the finale, Walter navigates the minefield between his position at home and his position in the criminal world, inventing more and more elaborate explanations for his increasingly bizarre behavior. Walter's sense of loss catalyzed by his cancer mobilizes each episode, and he struggles to fill that loss with the sense of accomplishment, money, and power that comes with cooking meth. The more he succeeds at perfecting his meth operation or running his criminal enterprise, the less Walter can enjoy his transgression. McGowan asserts that while we do not feel "the bite" the symbolic traditionally takes out of our enjoyment, we nonetheless feel that enjoyment is increasingly more and more difficult to experience.[6] Therefore, the abundance of enjoyment and its concomitant scarcity in *Breaking Bad* reinforces Walter's state of emergency. Walter's life is one emergency after another because no single enjoyment is better than the excitement of each emergency. On the one hand, Walter is a father, husband, and school teacher who, like the waning reign of the symbolic father, suffers many sleights against his masculinity from his family, his students, his doctor, and his boss at the carwash. On the other hand, he transforms into a powerful figure after his cancer diagnosis—Heisenberg—who cooks methamphetamine, runs a lucrative illegal enterprise, and reigns over his world using the ruthless tactics of lying, fear, and violence. Yet no matter how many objects he attains, none of them satisfies him because to Walter they represent accumulation and do not re-enact loss. Skyler, his wife, neatly sums up this phenomenon of the game without goals when she asks him how much money is enough while they stand in their storage shed looking at $80 million. The answer is, of course, that the money is beside the point. For Walter it is about the danger, the excess danger induced by the crisis in his masculine identity.

Walter's oscillation between symbolic father and primal father begins in the pilot episode, when Walter is diagnosed with cancer, and his emasculations unfold for the rest of the episode. No scene is more crucial to the unmasking of his symbolic authority than his birthday party. Gilligan uses this scene to establish the contrast between Walter and his brother-in-law Hank Schroeder, an agent for the Drug Enforcement Agency.[7] Hank is the very picture of idealized, primal masculinity as he discusses the excitement of his job and allows Walter's son Flynn to hold his gun. Hank gives the appearance of masculinity liberated from a world of wishy-washy compromises. To tap into Hank's masculine power, Walter goes on a ride-along with Hank where he watches Hank break-up a meth operation run by Walter's future criminal partner, Jesse Pinkman, who falls out of a window at a neighboring house and scrambles to redress himself after a sexual tryst with the woman who lives there.[8] Later in the episode, Walter enacts a version of the masculinity displayed by Hank and Jesse when he stands up for his son at the clothing store. Initially, Walter appears to avoid confrontation with the boys who bully his disabled son, but after sneaking out the back door, he returns through the front to attack and assault the bullies. This move by Walter is the viewer's first inclination of the change that closes the episode. The pilot episode also establishes the frantic pacing of the series, especially once Jesse and Walter put their plan into action by purchasing a recreational vehicle and cooking meth in the desert. Cooking is a moment that allows Walter to demonstrate his expertise and scientific prowess, and the surprising events that follow—the showdown with drug dealers and the potential arrest—confirm Walter's new appetite for the excited state these new events produce. The state of emergency created by the decision to cook meth in the pilot episode drives home the mechanism of future shows and seasons, and Walter's crisis surfing appears to be rewarded fully with his return home at the end of the pilot. He climbs into bed next to Skyler and proceeds to ravish her like the man who could not earlier in the show. Skyler is surprised by his aggression, to which she can only ask in a bewildered tone, "Oh Walter, is that you?"

Walter becomes so fascinated with the excited state caused by bouncing between his old symbolic identity (his good name) and his new primal masculinity (Heisenberg) that he describes the feeling as finally being awake when Jesse asks him why he is "breaking bad." The show's continuing appeal depends a great deal on the fantasy of Walter's full transformation into a liberated, powerful man, but the show always forestalls his full transition from one fatherly type to the other. Instead, *Breaking Bad*'s narrative and aesthetic appeal prefers to keep Walter in the emergency of failing to live up to the ideal of either masculine position. This position in between, otherwise known as the state of emergency, is, from the Lacanian perspective, the subject's dialectic of desire. Jon Smith describes this feeling of emergency as a state of being more significant than the one brought on by the accumulation of objects:

> we don't really derive pleasure from obtaining the object of our desire, we derive pleasure from getting all worked up about our desire, from the anxiety of not having the object, and what we fear is not "missing" the object but losing the excitation in us that circling it without ever attaining it provokes. The real goal is to feel something, even something unpleasant as anger or melancholy, rather than nothing.[9]

Walter's desire to break bad and the show's depiction of masculinity as a crisis are much like the high that Walter provides to meth junkies. Masculinity is like the rare blue meth that Walter makes—a high that provides everything and nothing at the same time, brought on by a crisis of need that must be constantly refueled but never satisfied.

Between Two Deaths

Breaking Bad is a part of a larger cultural trend of presenting transgressive activity as being between the prohibitions demanded by law or social custom and the open rebellion against those same laws and customs. As McGowan explains, the place in between is the society of enjoyment, a society in which private enjoyment in the public sphere is no longer prohibited but encouraged, a shift specific to late-capitalism that is characterized by "an ideology associated with the superego rather than with the public Law."[10] In the society of the twenty-first century, therefore, we see all kinds of examples of encouraged enjoyment, but at the center of this commanded enjoyment is the combined feeling of transgression and conformity. But in the world of *Breaking Bad*, Walter's rebellion from his traditional roles of father and teacher is not a transformation that comes with feelings of guilt and shame. Instead, Walter's rebirth as Heisenberg is fully in accordance with the culture's encouragement to enjoy. The only attached feelings are those of a craving for more enjoyment, but like a junky, Walter's tolerance increases, creating a need for more and more transgression in a world of diminishing returns.

The viewer enamored with the traditional story of patriarchy's loss of power can see Walter as a romantic figure refusing to give in to his powerlessness against the cancer and the cultural tide. The viewer who fails to believe in the patriarchy's phony claim to power can enjoy *Breaking Bad* for exposing its pathological cultural grip. Both viewers share, at the level of the show's narrative, Walter's loss, whether it is his loss of power or his loss of everything that should be important to him, like his family and good name. The question, which mimics Skyler's thoughts about Walter's relentless quest for more money, is why does Walter enjoy chasing something so clearly harmful to him and his family. The answer is the narrative decision to have Walter's transformation take place between his cancer diagnosis and his death. Walter is positioned, literally, between two deaths, the effect of which greatly influences his desire to do away with the dissatisfactions of his life before cancer.

Desire, as explained in the previous section, is about feeling something—even if the feelings are terrible—more than attaining objects, so ultimately, desire is a desire for restraint. Restraint keeps us purposefully oriented toward our excited sense of feeling, but it is hardly a sense of emergency. Desire represents a belief that something essential about us has been lost and that it is possible for us to regain this essential lost object, but ultimately discover no satisfaction with this object, only another object to desire.[11] In order to achieve the sense of emergency necessary to Walter's identity crises, his desire must convert into drive, which is the ceaseless energy that cannot be satisfied with any object. Rather, drive concerns itself with the repetition of loss and finds satisfaction in failure.[12] Walter's first death is symbolic and starts his shift from desire to drive. Once he is diagnosed with cancer, he realizes that his life as he has known it has a fairly definitive expiration date. Walter's second death is his real death at the end of the series, which comes after his ambush of his white supremacist collaborators and his rescue of Jesse. The episodes between the pilot and finale are caught in between these two deaths, thus becoming a time where Walter believes he can do away with the dissatisfactions of desire. Slavoj Žižek describes this position between two deaths as the moment when one loses the "life" that comes with symbolic recognition and the real death of the subject's life, a kind of no man's land of losing symbolic status and then real life.[13] Walter's remaining days become a task of proving to his family that he became a criminal for them, even though it is clear he becomes a criminal for selfish reasons. From the outset of his crisis state, he persists in one satisfying failure after another regardless of the risks to his life, with his cancer acting as a kind of fail-safe. His persistence in cooking meth and making money can best be understood as a compulsion to repeat the failure of the Heisenberg lifestyle. Žižek further describes the fictional representation of the state between two deaths as often being depicted as a drive that is "mechanical" in its persistence:

> A drive is precisely a demand that is not caught up in the dialectic of desire, that resists dialecticization. Demand almost always implies a certain dialectical mediation: we demand something, but what we are really aiming at through this demand is something else [....] Drive, on the contrary, persists in a certain demand, it is a "mechanical" insistence that cannot be caught up in dialectical trickery: I demand something and I persist in it to the end.[14]

Žižek's favorite examples of figures caught within various stages of symbolic and actual death range from literary figures like Antigone to cinematic characters like the Terminator. They are undead fictional creations similar to zombies, vampires, and Robocop. What unites these undead fictional creations with Walter White is their constant drive to reproduce the feeling of loss. In the symbolic order, or what we call reality, subjects are guided by desire, a want for something that is only satisfied by wanting something else, which leads to persistent (but pleasurable) dissatisfaction. Shifting into a place between two deaths allows Walter to believe in the fantasy that he no longer falls for the traps set by desire. Instead, he believes himself to be much more akin to the Terminator, a cyborg sent from the future intent on eliminating pre-programmed targets. Žižek's description of the Terminator might as well be a description of Walter as he gets better and better at being a criminal:

> The horror of this figure consists precisely in the fact that it functions as a programmed automaton who, even when all that remains of him is a metallic, legless, skeleton, that persists in his demand and pursues his victim with no trace of compromise or hesitation. The terminator is the embodiment of the drive, devoid of desire.[15]

Walter is a scientist and is characterized by machines and his power to manipulate them. He is also kept alive by machines and medicine, both of which allow him to live long enough to realize his power as Heisenberg. Finally, he enacts his methods of revenge through a mechanical precision, whether it is the coordinated prison hits, the bombing of Gus Fring, or the robotic machine gun used to kill the white supremacists. Each of these examples show Walter's unwillingness to let desire—like sacrificing for the sake of his good name—distract from his drive or his demand to succeed at failure.

Representations of pure drive are attractive and produce fantasies of mastery. In many ways, these representations are sublime examples of human activity unbound by the compromises of reality. Characters depicted with an extra ability to avoid the traps and trickery of desire often appear to have a serene sense of self in their cause that we in reality do not have. Consider the romantic portrayal of the hitman, who lives by a personal code of honor, or the freedom fighter devoted to his or her cause. These figures are solitary individuals who do not accede to their desire, preferring to persist in their satisfaction with not being satisfied. In other ways, these characters can be horrible, especially when their drive is aimed at innocents who cannot figure out why they have been targeted by their destructive aim. Whatever form drive takes, these representations are attractive, but they are often only attractive because their ceaseless drive is eventually contained, bringing their ruthless drive into the realm of the symbolic, whether it is through an actual death and burial or capture with due process of the law. However, Walter's depiction as the pure drive trapped between two deaths does not achieve a symbolic reckoning. He neither restrains himself nor is he contained by others throughout the entire series. Instead, Walter is a purely sympathetic figure who viewers want to see successfully avoid capture and prosecution by the law, which would be, in effect, a third death for Walter, a death at the hands of the police and legal system.[16]

Walter's death, coming as a result of a machine he built, is the only option available that maintains the logic of *Breaking Bad*'s fundamental fantasy.

Drive, moreover, is essentially wasteful. None of what Walter achieves in *Breaking Bad* is necessary or useful. Walter's ceaseless drive to succeed as a criminal is a fantasy of masculinity liberated from symbolic dissatisfaction that mobilizes the hidden enjoyments lurking behind our post-millennial culture. Regardless of how negatively Walter's criminal behavior is depicted in *Breaking Bad*, his behavior enacts the state of emergency that is central to the show's appeal. Walter's wasteful criminality leads to the ruin of his reputation, the break-up of his family, the death of Hank, and the psychological scarring of Jesse. But not once does *Breaking Bad* condemn Walter for the damage he inflicts on others. The sacrifice he makes for his family by becoming a criminal is one we experience as exceptional, an exception to the compromises that are often depicted as weakening men. We experience Walter's losses in the same way we experience drive, as being both horrible and sublime, and Walter's exceptional sacrifices demonstrate the hidden enjoyment attached to the fantasy of a liberated masculinity. The exceptional status of liberated masculinity is a fantasy that exists in between desire and drive, an imaginary position of pure loss in which the subject believes he can see through the futility of the former and the dead end of the latter. No scene more perfectly captures this dynamic than when Walter calls Skyler in the final season when he uses the police listening to absolve Skyler of any collusion with his criminal enterprise. This scene centers on the concept most central to masculinity—the man's name—by effectively capturing the two names between which Walter exists. During this conversation, Walter talks to Skyler as Heisenberg, calling her names and blaming her for disrupting his criminal enterprise. But Walter is also absolving Skyler of any guilt, even though she is guilty of covering up his crimes and laundering his money. Walter performs his verbal assault for the audience of the police in order to make them believe, all the while Skyler knows that he is saying his final goodbye as Walter and releasing her from her collaboration with his failures as a father and a husband. Rather than fully inhabiting either name, Walter exists in the middleground of the manic emergency brought on by the crisis of his identity and talks to Skyler—honestly, really for the first time—as both men at once. Post-millennial American culture is replete with representations of this kind of masculinity, a combined sense of loss about the missing John Wayne masculine detachment with a cynicism about that style of masculinity ever existing in the first place. The combination of loss and cynicism produces a paradoxical feeling that we are liberated from outdated modes of masculinity while being trapped by an over-whelming sense of loss. The paradox, depicted perfectly in *Breaking Bad*, suggests that masculine ultimate enjoyment is now caught in the ceaseless activity between the failure of the symbolic name and the unattainable status of the primal name. The new masculinity exists only in the emergency.

Anti-Hero Television

Stories, whether in literature, television, or cinema, abound with men shedding their traditional roles in favor of a life more transgressive. Anti-heroes are nothing new to fiction and film. Both mediums have long depended on the allure of men who feel compelled to sabotage themselves. What is obvious, however, is that these male characters are not villains or rebels who might otherwise find a new kind of mastery in their rejection of social norms. Instead, these men are heroes, but they are heroes defined specifically against what a hero used to be and without a notion of what they should be. They appear to feel a duty toward dissatisfaction. Television shows, especially those that appear during the prestige time slot of after eight in the evening on weeknights, have been slow to believe that viewers would invite such scoundrels into the intimate setting of their living rooms. But with the success of HBO's *The Sopranos*, the anti-hero trend has become the obvious signifier of a television show that desires the critical recognition typically afforded literature and Hollywood movies. Moreover, anti-hero television is also very popular with viewers across the spectrum, thus hitting the coveted sweet spot of having both critical acclaim and ratings success. Television critic Brett Martin describes this new era as being what he, and many other critics, calls the Golden Age of television by connecting it to the surprise success of pay-cable dramatic shows and the influential popularity of *The Sopranos*. Martin further explains that the resulting Golden Age depended on a new type of character:

> These were characters whom, conventional wisdom had once insisted, Americans would never allow into their living rooms: unhappy, morally compromised, deeply human. They played a seductive game with the viewer, daring them to emotionally invest in even root for, even love [....] From the time Tony Soprano waded into his pool to welcome his flock of wayward ducks, it had been clear that viewers were willing to be seduced.[17]

The television shows mentioned in the introduction, and many others like them, present a similarly complicated mixture of masculine decline and empowerment that is seen in *Breaking Bad*. By way of conclusion, I want to emphasize that what links *Breaking Bad* and other anti-hero television shows is not an aberration or some kind of new creation in the entertainment landscape of post–9/11—the state of emergency for men represented by these shows fits entirely within the culture that produces them. As Adam Kotsko argues, post-millennial television, or what he calls late capitalist television, "points toward a feeling of dissatisfaction with a broken society" and suggests that in this broken society "only a broken person can succeed."[18] In other words, society during the post–9/11 period has produced a feeling that the time before has been lost, leaving us adrift without recourse to recovery. Loss, in and of itself, has paradoxically become a desirable object and not just something to repress.

Anti-heroes at the center of the new television Golden Age revolve around a duty to enjoy that takes on the aimless movement of the drive, a drive that seeks to reproduce the feeling of loss over and over again. I have likened Walter's drive to being a lot like the high that addicts achieve from his special blue meth, but I think it is a different chemical stimulant, which also happens to be blue, that might better distill the symbolic link between representations of men in post-millennial television. The scientific breakthrough of Viagra offers men the chance to continue having sex well into old age, not because men want to continue having sex at the same frequency they did when they were young, but because they must continue to want to want to have sex as long as they possibly can. Stripping all of the psychological or biological problems away from impotency, men are guaranteed an erection whether they actually want one or not. In effect, Viagra suggests that men must continue to pursue sex well into old age because they are now chemically able.[19] Žižek argues that "now that Viagra takes care of the erection, there is no excuse: you should enjoy sex; if you don't it's your fault."[20] Anti-heroes in post-millennial television work under the same kind of command; men must enjoy their liberation from tired, outdated modes of masculinity, and if they do not, it is their fault. Therefore, masculinity cannot help but be depicted as being in a state of emergency as the old models of behavior are no longer permissible in the broken society of the twenty-first century and the promise of primal potency is an unreachable fantasy. In other words, men like Tony Soprano, Dexter Morgan, Nicholas Brody, Tommy Gavin, and Walter White feel compelled to liberate themselves from old forms of masculinity, and this liberation promises a future of unfettered, and increasingly unavailable, enjoyment. They must cast aside a detached aloofness for an aggressive pursuit of crisis and emergency. Put more simply, they are always in a ready state, neither going back nor going forward. Just ready, because they can.

Notes

1. Dylan Evans, *An Introductory Dictionary of Lacanian Psychoanalysis* (New York: Routledge, 1996), 119.
2. Ibid., 103–04.
3. Ibid., 200–01.
4. Todd McGowan, *Enjoying What We Don't Have: The Political Project of Psychoanalysis* (Lincoln: University of Nebraska Press, 2013), 154–55.
5. Todd McGowan, *The End of Dissatisfaction? Jacques Lacan and the Emerging Society of Enjoyment* (Albany: SUNY Press, 2004), 34.
6. Ibid., 40.
7. Hank goes through a similar transition from symbolic to primal as he loses the prestige of his position after he is shot and injured. He shifts into the same kind of man as Walter, obsessive, secretive, and violent. His quest to discover the identity of Heisenberg is also a game without a goal once we see him die ignominiously in the desert.
8. In the uncensored DVDs, Jesse falls out of a window during this scene while a topless woman watches. Walter's distance from powerful masculinity is further emphasized by Jesse's free sexual prowess.
9. Jon Smith, *Finding Purple America: The South and the Future of American Cultural Studies* (Athens: University of Georgia Press, 2013), 3.
10. Todd McGowan, *The End of Dissatisfaction?: Jacques Lacan and the Emerging Society of Enjoyment* (Albany: SUNY Press, 2004) , 31.
11. Todd McGowan, *Out of Time: Desire in Atemporal Cinema* (Minneapolis: University of Minnesota Press, 2011), 11.
12. Ibid., 11.
13. Slavoj Žižek, *Looking Awry: An Introduction to Jacques Lacan Through Popular Culture* (Cambridge: MIT Press, 1991), 21–3.
14. Ibid., 21.
15. Ibid., 22.
16. See Anna Gunn, "I Have a Character Issue," *The New York Times*, August 23, 2013, http://www.nytimes.com/2013/08/24/opinion/i-have-a-character-issue.html?_r=0. Good evidence of this can be seen in Anna Gunn's defense of her character in an op-ed for *The New York Times*. Gunn was often horrified by how many viewers hated her for her depiction of Walter's wife Skyler. Most negative comments focused on her nagging insistence on getting in the way of what Walter wants.
17. Brett Martin, *Difficult Men: Behind the Scenes of a Creative Revolution: From* The Sopranos *and* The Wire *to* Mad Men *and* Breaking Bad (New York: Penguin, 2013), 4–5.

18. Adam Kotsko, *Why We Love Sociopaths: A Guide to Late Capitalist Television* (Winchester, UK: Zero Books, 2012), 94, 14. Kotsko argues that the figure of the sociopath links television shows during the same period that I am discussing.

19. Slavoj Žižek, *The Fragile Absolute* (New York: Verso, 2000), 133–34. My connection between Viagra and post-millenial masculinity is constructed from Žižek's observation about the drug's promise of enjoyment on demand. He argues that Viagra is akin to the command to enjoy that comes from the superego, examples of which he finds everywhere in, what he calls, postmodern, permissive behaviour.

20. Ibid., 133–34.

Patriarchy and the
"Heisenberg Principle"

PHILIP POE

"Your dad must be quite a guy"

During "ABQ," the 13th episode of the second season of *Breaking Bad*, Walter White, Jr. (RJ Mitte), is shown giving a television interview about his fundraising website, SaveWalterWhite.com, and more generally, about his father, Walt (Bryan Cranston). During the interview, Walter Jr. touches on a topic that is both central to his relationship with his father, and in direct proportion to the relationship many viewers had with Walt.[1] Walter Jr. tells a TV correspondent (Kieran Sequoia) why he developed the website to solicit donations for his father's chemotherapy treatments, and also reflects patriarchal ideology of what it means to be a "good man."

> CORRESPONDENT: Judging from the things you and other folks have written about him, your dad must be quite a guy.
> WALTER JR.: Yeah, he is. He's the best.
> CORRESPONDENT: You don't want to lose him, do you, Walter?
> Walter Jr.: None of us do. We love him.
> CORRESPONDENT : He's a good man, isn't he?
> WALTER JR.: Absolutely. Ask anyone, anybody. He's a great father, a great teacher. He knows like everything there is to know about chemistry. He's patient with you, he's always there for you. He's just decent. And he always does the right thing and that's how he teaches me to be.

CORRESPONDENT: Would you say he's your hero?
WALTER JR.: Oh yeah, yes ma'am, totally. My dad is my hero [2. 13].[2]

During this scene, viewers are confronted with a prominent issue that becomes the source of much conflict throughout the rest of the series—Walter White's initial desire to be a "good man" and provide for his family in the event of his death, versus his more personal—visceral—conception of what a man does to ensure his own survival. Understanding these conflicting conceptions, Walter's motivations for breaking the law to provide for his family can be seen in terms of patriarchal ideology, "that ideological mode which defines the system of male domination and female·subjugation in any society."[3] Walt's acceptance and adherence to patriarchal ideology becomes a central theme throughout the series.

Patriarchy in Breaking Bad: *By Any Horrific Means Necessary*

"Patriarchy" means the government of the family, as household, by its head—normally the father—as householder.[4] *Breaking Bad* explores the impact of patriarchy on the White's interfamilial unit, namely his wife Skyler (Anna Gunn), Walter Jr., his infant daughter Holly, and his protégé Jesse Pinkman (Aaron Paul), as each character alternately rebels against or accepts the inevitability of Walter White's dominance within their "family" unit.

While some social scientists differentiate between patriarchy and male dominance, associating the former with suprafamilial levels of organization and the latter with authority in familial relationships, both are universal conceptions.[5] Using this ideology, a man holding the door for a woman expresses masculine strength, not female dominance; a man walking closer to the curb acknowledges the female's "need" for protection.[6] In essence, Walt's primary role in a patriarchal society is to provide for his family's well being, "protecting" them financially and physically, yet as the series progresses, his actions are motivated by his own personal desire to survive, often to the detriment of his family's well being. This incongruity sets the tone for the rest of the series as Walt seeks revenge against the society that screwed him over, undervalued his worth, and overlooked his potential. From the moment of his diagnosis forward, Walt will take what he wants and destroy any resistance to prove that he's man enough for anything, by any horrific means necessary.

Walter White as Patriarch: *"That's pretty much the size of it"*

Walt's move from law-abiding citizen to master criminal happens gradually over the course of the first four seasons. The seeds of this transformation, however, are planted early in the first season, when Walt learns of his cancer diagnosis, realizes his inability to pay for treatments, and seeks out an alternative method for making money. Initially unwilling to undergo costly treatments that would likely negatively affect his remaining quality of life, Walt begrudgingly pursues treatment at his wife Skyler's behest. His desires to keep his family together and remain the "provider" also influence his decision to accept chemotherapy treatments. Having decided to pursue treatments, Walt's next step is to make money to pay for them. He refuses an offer to help from Elliott and Gretchen Schwartz, his former colleagues, as he is resistant to taking a "handout." He explains his reasons for doing so during a Season Two episode, "Peekaboo."

> GRETCHEN: Let me just get this straight: Elliott and I offered to pay for your treatment, no strings attached—an offer which still stands by the way—and you turn us down out of pride, whatever. And then you tell your wife that in fact we are paying for your treatment. Without our knowledge, against our will, you involve us in your lie, and you sit here and tell me that that is none of my business?
>
> [Long pause]
>
> WALTER: Yeah. That's pretty much the size of it.
>
> GRETCHEN: What happened to you? Really, Walt? What happened? Because this isn't you.
>
> WALTER: What would you know about me, Gretchen? What would your presumption about me be exactly? That I should go begging for your charity, and you waving your checkbook around like some magic wand is going to make me forget how you and Elliott—how you and Elliott—cut me out?
>
> GRETCHEN: What? That can't be how you see it [2. 6].

Walt's rejection of the Schwartz's "handout" is symptomatic of his adherence to traditional patriarchal ideology.[7] He will not accept outside assistance because he feels it is patriarchal role as head of household to provide from within. Hank, who is portrayed as a stereotypical masculine figure, a depiction that fits nicely with his role in patriarchal society, is also resistant to accepting a handout. Marie understands this reticence, and chooses not to tell him how

Walt and Skyler paid his physical therapy and rehabilitation bills. Hank's ignorance of the White's financial assistance becomes a turning point in Season 5, as his discovery of the payments, which Walt details during his "confession" DVD, means he can no longer protect his reputation as a DEA agent or pursue his investigation of Heisenberg through normal legal channels. Thus, Hank's embodiment of the patriarchal archetype seals his fate.

While patriarchal ideology is one of many themes present in *Breaking Bad*, it's one that should be of particular interest to viewers still reeling from the series' conclusion and aftermath, because the influences of patriarchal systems inside and outside of the White family essentially dictate the fate of the principle characters.

Patriarchy and the Family: "What does a man do?"

Walt's alienation from his wife and children as a result of his criminal enterprise is one of the show's tragic ironies, since his family plays such a crucial role in Walt's conception of what it means to be a "man." Even when Skyler, having learned of his secret life, pursues a divorce, Walt remains devoted to her and committed to their marriage. In Season Three, Walt decides to get out of the meth business for good in an effort to keep his family together, he explains to Gus Fring (Giancarlo Esposito), who is trying to put Walt in charge of a new, secret, state-of-the-art meth lab, why he doesn't want to go back to "cooking" again. He made some "very bad decisions," he tells Gus, and he now wants to correct them. "Why did you make these decisions?" Gus asks. For his family, Walt replies. "Then they weren't bad decisions." But Walt objects, telling Gus that these decisions have cost him his wife. But Walt still has his children, doesn't he, including a newborn daughter? Gus responds. Gus then gets to the heart of the matter, a matter that involves one of the series' central premises:

> "What does a man do, Walt? A man provides for his family. ... When you have children, you always have family—they will always be your priority, your responsibility. And a man—a man provides. And he does it even when he's not appreciated, or respected, or even loved. He simply bears up and he does it. Because he's a man" [3. 5].

Here Gus, who appears to have no family of his own, makes explicit what has been implicit in the series from the beginning: that there is a point at which even ordinarily decent civilized men can be made to revert to their traditional role in patriarchal society, where duty and honor are principle concerns. Duty, then, is to provide for one's family as well as to overcome the dangers posed to that family by one's enemies and rivals regardless of legality or what's morally right.

Becoming a meth manufacturer is morally wrong and certainly illegal, but the audience can rationalize Walt's choice, given the circumstances of his life. He *has* been dealt a terrible set of circumstances, and he is virtually powerless to change them by legitimate means. During a Season Two episode, "Better Call Saul," Walt urges his brother-in-law Hank Schrader (Dean Norris) to return to his DEA job, and move past the horrific events he witnessed during his time with the El Paso office. Still reeling from the sight of the decapitated head of his informant, and having narrowly escaped the carnage of a Cartel IED, Hank is convinced that he and Walt lack "experiential overlap." He does not yet realize that he and Walt are on opposite sides of the same dangerous game, the results of which have affected him greatly. Walt tells Hank who the "real enemy" is, and in doing so, espouses an ideology based firmly in his patriarchal conception of society:

> WALTER: "I have spent my whole life scared. Frightened of things that could happen; might happen; might not happen. 50 years I've spent like that. Finding myself awake at 3 a.m. But you know what? Ever since my diagnosis, I sleep just fine. I came to realize it's that fear is the worst of it, that's the real enemy. So, get up, get out in the real world and you kick that bastard as hard as you can, right in the teeth" [2. 8].

Though he's still a member of the comparatively better-off middle class, the anger Walt feels having to scrounge for every dollar while being trapped in an monotonous cycle, his life passing by without any joy or fulfillment, is legitimate, and it's compounded by the importance placed on the "traditional" patriarchal family unit, as well the historical pressure and expectation put on men to provide for their families. A man, who can't provide for his family, isn't really a man, goes the thinking.[8]

Insomuch as "family" is a major theme in *Breaking Bad*, it cannot be overstated how important Walt's conception of the "traditional" patriarchal family is to his actions throughout the series. He refers several times to the "sacrifices" he's made for the family.[9] Walt is living an ideal that by design teaches individuals to value the well being of their relatives over those of everyone else in society.[10] This may not seem like a big problem at first glance, but the net result is a society where everyone does what's best for his or her family, often at the expense of everyone else. Society, then, becomes about competition, rather than collaboration, and people often abandon their moral principles when faced with a choice that might negatively impact their family, just as Walt does.

Patriarchy and Duty: "When we do what we do for good reasons"

"Duty" is another important thread that runs through Walt's story—his duty to his family, to his criminal enterprise, and to society. Walt's conception of duty to his family (to provide for them physically and financially) mirrors modern, practical conceptions of patriarchy.[11] He wants to provide for their well being, because that is the "right" thing to do—it is his responsibility as patriarch. Walt's conception of what it means to be a man, then, entails doing what's right, even if the methods for doing so involve acts society considers "wrong," like meth production and murder.

Walt frequently uses his conception of duty toward his family as a justification for his actions. "When we do what we do for good reasons, there's nothing to worry about, and what better reason is there than family?" (5. 2). Walt tells Skyler, who is struggling with the collateral damage from an incident with her former boss and lover, Ted Beneke (Christopher Cousins). Ted is paralyzed while trying to flee from a pair of enforcers Skyler dispatched to force him to pay off his debt to the IRS, preventing the government from finding a trace of the Whites' illegal drug money. Skyler and Walt do what is best for their family, but the result is devastating to other people.[12] *Breaking Bad* brings this issue to the forefront, and the fact that Walt is so frighteningly at peace with this justification forces the audience to call into question its own worldview. The show deftly positions viewers as Walt's final judges—we decide how far is too far. Some may have lost all sympathy for Walt when he began to produce meth and lied to his family. For others, it may have been his murder of Krazy-8. Still, others may have stuck with Walt through his showdown with Gus and the use of explosives in a nursing home. Throughout the series, viewers are left to grapple with a question: How much damage can one inflict upon society in order to protect his or her loved ones?

The damage Walt inflicts is not relegated to those outside his family. Over the course of building his "empire," he destroys the lives of his wife and children, along with those of Hank and Marie (Betsy Brandt), his brother and sister-in-law, and his protégé Jesse. Walt justifies his actions in the name of protecting and providing—his patriarchal duties—yet he fears that his immoral actions will outweigh any "good" he did for his family in the final analysis. Thus, he begins to rationalize his choices. In Season Three, Walt reflects on how he has been unable to make Skyler "understand" his actions, recognizing that the wealth he is amassing only made sense as a way to provide security for his family. He wants to be remembered well by his wife and children. More specifically, he wants them to miss him when he is gone. During a conversation with Jesse in the episode "Fly," Walt even imagines he could put his scientific approach to problem solving to great use in dealing with his family. He does not seem to recognize that there is no scientific formula for respect and understanding between people, and no chemical compounds one can synthesize to produce love.[13]

> WALTER WHITE: I've been to my oncologist, Jesse. Just last week. I'm still in remission. I'm healthy.
> JESSE PINKMAN: That's good. Great.
> WALTER : No end in sight.
> JESSE : That's great.
> WALTER : No. I missed it. There was some perfect moment that passed me right by, but I had to have enough to leave them. That was the whole point. None of this makes any sense if I didn't have enough. And it had to be before she found out. Skyler. It had to be before that.
> JESSE : Perfect moment? For what? To drop dead? Are you saying you want to die?
> WALTER: I'm saying that I lived too long. You want them to actually miss you. You want their memories of you to be ... but she just won't ... she just won't understand. I mean, no matter how well I explain it, these days she just has this ... this ... I mean, I truly believe there exists some combination of words. There must exist certain words in a certain specific order that can explain all of this, but with her I just can't ever seem to find them [3. 10].

Despite Walt's misgivings about whether his patriarchal honor is worth losing the love and respect of his wife for, it seems for a short time that bringing Skyler in on his criminal enterprise might restore unity in his household. Yet in Season Five, we see Skyler begin to treat Walt with fear as, increasingly, he seems willing to dole out lethal punishment to anyone who crosses him, even family members. In Season Five, Skyler finds Walt and the kids watching Brian de Palma's *Scarface* on television, and it immediately suggests to her a potential outcome for Walt's criminal career. As James Bowman wrote in *The New Atlantis*, the idea seems to be that there is no middle way, no easy compromise between ordinary, law-abiding suburban dad and drug kingpin: "When you

stop being the one, then you must start being the other."[14] Walt remains convinced that Skyler's understandable misgivings related to his growing criminal
enterprise will give way to acceptance and she will see through the deception—
and the bloodshed—and understand his "true" motivations for the havoc he's
wrought on his family and on society.

> WALTER : I've done a terrible thing. But I've done it for a good reason.
> I did it for us. That [points to the duffel bag of money] is college tuition
> for Walter Jr. And Holly, eighteen years down the road. And it's health
> insurance for you and the kids. For Junior's physical therapy. His SAT tutor.
> It's money for groceries, gas, for birthdays and graduation parties. Skyler,
> that money is for this roof over your head. The mortgage that you are not
> going to be able to afford on a part-time bookkeeper's salary when I'm
> gone.
> SKYLER: Walt, I–
> WALTER: Please. Please. This money, I didn't steal it. It doesn't belong
> to anyone else. I earned it. The things I've ... done to earn it ... they ... the
> things I've had to do ... I've got to live with them. Skyler, all that I've done,
> all the sacrifices that I've made for this family, all of it, will be for nothing
> if you don't accept what I've earned. Please. I'll be here when you get home
> from work. You can give me your answer then.

We soon learn, as the show careens toward its conclusion, that acceptance
from Skyler is no longer a possibility for Walt.

Walt and Jesse: "I've got this ... nephew"

When Walt partners up with Jesse Pinkman to make meth, Walt's stated
motivation is his family. He wants to take care of his loved ones to provide
practical things. He wants to pay off the mortgage, to pay for college educa-
tions for Walter, Jr. and Holly, and to cover any future medical bills for the
whole family. At one point in Season 1, he even calculates exactly how much
money he needs to make in order to provide for his family over the next 20
years ($737,000). He can quit producing and selling meth when he reaches
that number. So, why doesn't he?

Jesse is portrayed as an archetype of the "bumbling criminal."[15] We first
meet Jesse as he is tumbling down a roof, nearly naked, from a second-story
window, to avoid a DEA raid. Jesse is told by society, even by his own parents,
that he is unworthy. But he is no villain. He does terrible things, some without
remorse, but also experiences great loss as a result. Though their relationship

is initially comical, and mostly antagonistic, Walt learns to accept Jesse as a surrogate son (or nephew, as he refers to Jesse in "Phoenix"). By bringing him in to his family unit, Walt begins to feel the same patriarchal pangs in his relationship with Jesse, expressing a need to protect him, and to help guide him through life. This need is illuminated by a conversation Walt has with Donald Margolis (John de Lancie), an air-traffic controller and the father of Jesse's girlfriend, Jane (Krysten Ritter).

> DONALD MARGOLIS: I have a daughter.
> WALTER WHITE: Yeah. How old?
> DONALD: Old enough to know better. Twenty-seven next month.
> WALTER: Oh. You have other kids?
> DONALD: Just the one.
> WALTER: I've got a 16-year-old boy. Well, he's almost 16. Jeez. There's a spread, huh? But he helps out, though. He's even changing some diapers now, so. It's more than I managed to do when I was his age.
> DONALD: Kids today grow up faster. I think.
> WALTER: Yeah, maybe so. So, any advice? Having a daughter. Any advice?
> DONALD: Oh. No, not really. Just love them. Just ... I mean, they ... they are who they are.
> WALTER: Yeah. I've got this ... nephew. This nephew who is, I mean, he's an adult. But you can't infantilize them; you can't live their life for them. But still, I mean, there is that frustration. You know, that ... God, that frustration that goes along with, you know: "Yes, as a matter of fact, I do know what is best for you, so listen." But of course, they don't. I mean, what do you do with someone like that?
> DONALD: Family.
> WALTER: Yeah. Family....
> DONALD: You can't give up on them. Never. I mean, what else is there? (2: 12).

As the series progresses, Walt does give up on Jesse, despite his initial patriarchal need to protect him like any member of the family. Eventually, Walt's cruelty, driven by self-interest, leaves Jesse a prisoner of white supremacists who only keep him alive because he can "cook" meth.[16] Walt's domineering influence over Jesse renders Jesse helpless to Walt's will; his desire to be "good" is overshadowed by Walt's need to survive.

In the series finale, however, Walt realizes that Jesse's death is one piece of collateral damage he is unwilling to accept. Walt's patriarchal role of "protector" and the depth of his affection for Jesse—a "family" member—lead to a redeeming moment of self-sacrifice. Walt saves Jesse from a stray bullet in the series' penultimate scene, and allows him to escape the carnage. By the end of *Breaking Bad's* run, Walt truly believes what Donald Margolis tells him in the bar.

Patriarchy and the Law: "It's arbitrary"

Hank Schrader, Walt's DEA-agent brother-in-law, spends the first four-and-a-half seasons serving as the voice of "law and order" on *Breaking Bad*. His understanding of "legal" and "illegal" are different from his conceptions of "right" and "wrong." For example, in "A No-Rough-Stuff-Type Deal," Hank explains that he did a "little favor" for an FBI agent who rewarded him with a box of (illegal) Cuban cigars. Walt's conclusion is that the difference between legal and illegal is "arbitrary." Hank disagrees, and points out that Walt's making an argument that many criminals would support. Yet Hank sees nothing wrong with possessing and distributing contraband (Cuban cigars) because as a DEA agent, he's a member of the ruling class.[17] Hank works in law enforcement, but who works to enforce laws as they apply to Hank? His job is to police others and, ostensibly, police himself. Though he is technically beholden to the Constitution and DEA regulations, he consistently ignores legally established policies and procedures that might hinder an investigation, like when he has Walt plant a GPS tracking device on Gus Fring's car. Hank sees his role as upholding the law in situations where breaking the law might negatively effect innocent people. Otherwise, his conceptions of "legal" and "illegal" are his own, and arbitrarily applied. This apparent separation between the ruling class and the ruled (as evident in the conversation between Hank and Walt) relates to the very foundation of law enforcement, which developed as extrafamilal extension of patriarchal ideology.[18]

> Given its derivation from the power of the paterfamilias over his household, police is easily compatible with hierarchical, and in particular patriarchal, regimes that at the same time maintain a strict division between the ruler and ruled, and abstract away distinctions among the ruled, which make up the household as a set of management tools distinguished (only) by functionality.[19]

Using the same ideological frame of reference that permits Walt to do great damage to society in the name of protecting his family, Hank is willing to break the law as long as it benefits him. As a DEA agent, he sees protecting "others" as a patriarchal duty, but one that comes with benefits that outsiders (like Walt) do not receive.

In Season Three, Hank violently confronts Jesse in retaliation for supposedly using Marie to lure him away from the junkyard where the RV/mobile-meth-lab is hidden (it was actually Walt and Saul who devised the ruse). Hank brutally beats Jesse, nearly killing him. As a result, the DEA suspends him, and he considers leaving law enforcement for good, but Walt's behind-the-scenes machinations eventually get him reinstated. Hank's first-hand experiences with the "War on Drugs" leave his nerves shattered and his psyche irrevocably damaged. His brutal reaction to Jesse's "plot" reflects his patriarchal ideology; justice is often "served" in terms of physical retaliation by representatives of the victim toward the victimizer, in this case Hank protecting Marie from Jesse.

In Season Five, Hank's pursuit of Heisenberg, and his realization that Walt is Heisenberg, influence his decision to continue his investigation removed from jurisdictional and constitutional concerns. He breaks laws and ignores regulations that pertain specifically to law enforcement in an effort to catch a drug lord, keep his friends and family safe, and protect his own reputation. This "off the books" pursuit of Heisenberg results in Hank's death. Even casual viewers will notice a recurring theme here, one that directly relates to a patriarchal way of looking at the world—societal laws and norms function as a guide for "other people," but nothing should prevent a man from doing what he considers "right."

Conclusion: "I was alive"

Near the end of "Felina," the final episode of *Breaking Bad*, viewers are presented with a scenario that both sums up one of the show's central premises and brings its main character full circle. Walter White shows up unexpectedly at the cramped apartment of his wife Skyler, who is living in exile while he remains a fugitive from justice. During their conversation, Walt reveals the true motives behind his methamphetamine "empire"; he tells Skyler he did it—produced and sold meth; killed and had people killed; compounded lie on top of lie—for himself, and not to save the family. "I was alive," he tells her (5. 16). This admission reveals a stunning separation from the Walter introduced in Season 1; a mild-mannered high school chemistry teacher diagnosed with life-threatening cancer, with the drug kingpin he becomes throughout the later seasons, Heisenberg. Whereas Walt's stated justification for entering the drug game is to provide for his family in the event of his death, Heisenberg enjoys the danger, violence and adrenaline associated with manufacturing and distributing meth.

While he may say that he just wants to support his family before he dies, what Walt really wants is to finally be a man, a real man, and to get all the privileges that go with being a man in patriarchal society. His family is just the excuse he uses, the lie he tells himself to justify his actions. Walt wants to shed the image of the nerdy chemistry teacher who can't take care of his family. He wants authority and power—he wants respect.[20]

Walt's conception of the patriarchal ideal seems particularly insightful because it is the exact model of manhood that he embraces. By the time the finale rolls around, Walt is so alienated from his family that they reject both his influence and his money, and so he must funnel his drug fortune to them without their knowledge, ensuring he receives no credit—no appreciation, respect or love.[21] In Walt's mind, the measure of a man isn't his relationship to his family, but rather his ability to support them financially. Faced with a terminal cancer diagnosis, and the decision about what sort of legacy he truly wants to leave behind, Walt sacrifices the former for the latter.

Breaking Bad creator Vince Gilligan perfectly summarized Walter White's point of view by the end of the series, during AMC's final *Insider Podcast*. Describing Walt's death in the series finale, Gilligan said, "It felt right and satisfying and proper to us that he went out on his own terms; he went out like a man."[22] Based on Walt's patriarchal conception of what it means to be a man, he certainly did.

Notes

1. Laura Hudson, "Die Like a Man: The Toxic Masculinity of *Breaking Bad*," *Wired*, October 5, 2013, http://www.wired.com/underwire/2013/10/breaking-bad-toxic-masculinity/.

2. Where particular scenes or pieces of dialogue are discussed in this essay, I include the actor's name with parentheses (for first mentions only). Otherwise, only character names are given. All quotations are my transcribed approximations of the spoken dialogue; access to printed scripts was not available. Transcriptions are from DVD box set *Breaking Bad: The Complete Series* (2013). Wherever dialogue is quoted, I note the season and episode numbers; for example, the eighth episode of the first season is rendered here as 1. 8.

3. Roberta Hamilton, *The Liberation of Women: A Study of Patriarchy and Capitalism* (London: George Allen & Unwin, 1978), 12.

4. Markus Dirk Dubber, *The Police Power: Patriarchy and the Foundations of American Government* (New York: Columbia University Press, 2005), 220n16.

5. Steven Goldberg, *The Inevitability of Patriarchy* (New York: William Morrow, 1973), 30–31.

6. Ibid.

7. The World Bank, *The Decline of the Breadwinner: Men in the 21st Century*, World Development Report 2012: Gender Equity and Development, Spread 2, http://go.worldbank.org/6R2KGVEXP.

8. FEDREV, "'The Empire Business': *Breaking Bad*, Capitalism, and the Family," *FEDREV*, July 31, 2013, http://fedrev.net/?p=485.

9. See *Breaking Bad* (3. 3), "IFT."

10. FEDREV, "The Empire Business," 2013.

11. The World Bank, *The Decline of the Breadwinner*, 2012.

12. Ibid.

13. James Bowman, "Criminal Elements," *The New Atlantis*, 38, Winter/Spring 2013, 163–173.

14. Bowman, "Criminal Elements," 170.

15. John F. Preis, "Witch Doctors and Battleship Stalkers: The Edges of Exculpation in Entrapment Cases," *52 Vand Law Review 1869*, 1999.

16. Matthew Jacobs, "Why I've Struggled to Reconcile the Fate of Jesse Pinkman on 'Breaking Bad,'" *Huffington Post*, September 29, 2013, http://www.huffingtonpost.com/jacobs-matthew/the-fate-of-jesse-pinkman-breaking-bad_b_4013526.html.

17. Dubber, *The Police Power*, 2005, 82.

18. Ibid., 220n16.

19. Ibid., 91.

20. FEDREV, "The Empire Business," 2013

21. Readers may also be aware of Skyler and Walter Jr.'s rejection of patriarchal naming traditions, with Skyler taking back her maiden name by the end of Season 5, and Walt Jr. calling himself "Flynn" throughout the last three seasons. The deliberate way in which the series' creators draw attention to this element warrants further discussion, but is outside the scope of this essay. See Amanda Marcotte, "Breaking Bad Recap: S5E15, 'Granite State,'" *The Raw Story*, September 23, 2013, http://www.rawstory.com/rs/2013/09/23/breaking-bad-recap-s5e15-granite-state/.

22. Vince Gilligan, "Breaking Bad Insider Podcast, Episode 516," *AMC*, http://www.amctv.com/shows/breaking-bad/insider-podcast-season-5.

Walter White
The Psychopath to Whom We Can All Relate?

MERON WONDEMAGHEN

Breaking Bad's Walter White has been labeled "evil," "sociopath," "the devil" and "psychopath." Traditionally, psychopaths have been characterized as callous and unemotional individuals who lack in empathy. This term is often used to describe not only serial killers and mass murderers, but also those in positions of power who may not necessarily engage in extreme violence. For example, those in business or politics. Lately, however, there have been a number of scholars who argue that psychopathic traits are not specific to psychopaths at all; we all have them. The difference is that we employ these traits for different end goals. Levin and Fox[1] argue that many behavioral traits that are thought to be specific to psychopathic killers are actually shared with "millions of people" who never kill because we all engage in the "existential process" of self-presentation, compartmentalization, dehumanization and lack of empathy. This essay examines Walter within these four behavioral characteristics and argues that the reasons behind our fascination with the character and the cult-like following this TV series has received reflect our recognition (at least at a subconscious level) that "the psychopath" or "the violent criminal" draws on the same behavioral traits present in all of us.

Series creator and writer Vince Gilligan has famously described the story of Walter White as one about a man who evolves from being "Mr. Chips to Scarface." In Season 1, we learn that Walter is an uninspiring, overqualified chemistry teacher and family man who is financially strained and working at

122

a car wash for additional income. Shortly after his 50th birthday, he learns he has inoperable lung cancer with two years left if he undergoes chemotherapy. This leads to a set of events that transform him from a meek individual who was always afraid of making the wrong decisions, to an intimidating drug lord and mass murderer. He teams up with his former student—Jesse—to manufacture crystal methamphetamine (CM). In his reign of terror, Walter always insisted that it was all for his family's financial security. How was this possible? Was he a "natural" born psychopath or was he "made" by a set of psycho-social circumstances that ultimately resulted in the psychopathic phenotype? Walter used behavioral traits that are part of the human condition in his pursuit of "happiness." Traits we all have and are not particularly specific to psychopaths.

The Presentation of Self or "Mask Wearing"

Self-presentation is a deliberate and goal-directed process in which information about the self is controlled in a manner that influences others' perceptions, impressions and beliefs.[234] Characteristic to psychopaths is their ability to wear the mask of normalcy so successfully. Levin and Fox[1] use the term "impression management" to describe psychopathic killers' ability to appear innocent and beyond suspicion, luring their victims with charm and cunning. But not only do the authors argue that impression management is not specific to these types of killers alone, they suggest that successful people engage in this process because they know how to use their "self-awareness to their personal advantage"—politicians or sales personnel who successfully convince "the people" or clients that they make decisions or suggestions based on others' interests. It is what we do in interviews, dates, business deals and everyday social interactions.

In *Breaking Bad*'s first episode, Walter cooks CM in a desert—using an old RV as a mobile lab—as a means of providing financial security for his family. And he was, initially, genuinely seeking to provide for his family. In the course of his new business however, it is clear his motivation is about something else entirely. The presented self to his wife, his business associates and his lawyer insists that engaging in illegal activities is all for "the family" because he is the provider. The real self revels in the power that comes with the money and "the product" – the purest form on the market. Walter has now taken control of his life. He is in charge, as reflected in his conversation with Skyler in the finale episode "Felina," in which he reveals that he did it all for himself because he "liked it" and it made him feel "really alive." And this is all related to a pervasive sense of failure and inferiority complex that stems from his relationship with his former college partners, Elliott and Gretchen Schwartz. Walter had collaborated on founding a company—Gray Matter Technologies—and was romantically involved with Gretchen, but after the relationship failed, he sold his share for $5,000 and left. She married Elliott. His former partners later develop the business into a multi-billion dollar company and win a Nobel Prize for their research, which Walter claims was his. It is this deep seated sense of failure that allows Walter to justify his criminality. The cancer was simply a catalyst to what was lurking dormant. The need to mean someone. In the pilot episode, he says: "I am awake." And he uses this awakening to present different personae. When the Schwartz offer him a lucrative employment opportunity, he refuses, claiming his insurance will pay for his treatment. Meanwhile his wife believes the Schwartz are paying for his chemotherapy. He has become an elusive criminal, dealing with ruthless drug distributors, demanding money in advance, but to his family, he is the cancer-stricken, under-paid teacher. His brother-in-law Hank's remark (also a DEA agent) illustrates Walter's skill at impression management: "Nothing personal, Walt, but you wouldn't know a criminal if he was close enough to check you for a hernia." It soon becomes clear to the audience that Walter no longer needs to cook CM to provide for his family. He *wants* to continue in the drug-manufacturing business. But he calls it "The Empire Business." He dissociates it from any illegal activity and presents it as a business.

Compartmentalization

Although the term "psychopathy" is often associated with callousness and lack of empathy, psychopaths use a defense mechanism—compartmentalization—to neutralize any guilt they might feel when inflicting pain on their victims rather than completely lacking emotion or concern.[1] This is a psychological process in which conflicting ideas, feelings or beliefs are allowed to co-exist without direct interaction, in separate compartments of the self. Compartmentalizing serves to reduce stress by separating different sets of experiences in separate psychological spaces; for example separating the workplace as a safe place from marital difficulties at home.[5] We employ this coping mechanism in a number of scenarios: when we complete a task at work whilst grieving and dealing with the loss of a loved one; or appear content in the workplace in the midst of an acrimonious divorce; when an otherwise honest individual cheats on tax-returns; when a psychopathic serial killer brutally murders 48 prostitutes but is a loving husband (the "Green River Killer" Gary

Ridgeway); or when a respected president of a church congregation kills entire families including children (the "BTK Killer" Dennis Rader).

Walter also employs this defense mechanism to deal with the cognitive dissonance between his "killer self" and "the family man." He attends his wife's prenatal check-up while contemplating for ways to kill and dispose of Jesse's former associates who had threatened to kill him, Emilio and Krazy-8. Walter ultimately chokes Krazy-8 to death after he realizes the latter was going to kill him. But this is his first kill, in self-defense, and we see him crying as he deals with his two conflicting sets of "self." And progressively, killing (or the thought of it) becomes easier. He makes ricin to kill his distributor—Tucco—believing his family was in danger; he shoots two drug dealers in cold-blood although if he had not, his associate—Jesse—was going to be killed by these men; he arranges for a fellow CM manufacturer—Gale—to be killed because Walter was becoming dispensable and it was a matter of self-preservation; he places a bomb in a nursing home in order to kill his rival and major drug distributor—Gus. But the rationalizations keep going as Walter's business grows, and he evolves from self-defense killings into eliminating those who threaten his status or challenge him in any away. Mike—now Jesse's and Walter's Business partner—is shot dead impulsively because he challenged and dared question the business decisions of the revered Heisenberg. Killing has become second-nature to Walter aided by his ability to dehumanize. He compartmentalizes his activities and emotions—similar to what Nazi physicians did—through a "doubling" process[6] developing two distinct selves, so that any guilt or remorse is trivialized or minimized. And as such, even if he is a murderous drug manufacturer, he is still able to see himself as a carer who is simply providing for his family. He is both Walter, the humble teacher, and Heisenberg, the intimidating drug-lord. He physically and symbolically transforms when he assumes his dominant self, Heisenberg; he walks tall with his chest protruding compared to the hunched down Walter; his voice is more imposing and intimidating; he wears a black hat as though it cues him into the transformation.

Dehumanization and Lack of Empathy

Closely related to compartmentalizing, dehumanization involves the capacity to deny those considered as "the other" a human identity, leading to the conclusion that they are expendable or unworthy. It facilitates mass destruction or mass killings by overriding moral inhibitions against the taking of human life because the victims are reduced to inanimate and dispensable, allowing for the magnitude of the transgression to be committed with indifference.[7] In some cases, dehumanization allows for "effective mastery of many tasks"— during natural disasters, major accidents or epidemics for example, feelings of pity, fear or revulsion are overcome through this defense mechanism allowing for effective rescue operations.[7] This is a psychological process that facilitated any soldiers' view of the enemy or Nazi physicians' view of the Jews as less human. It is apparent in our reactions to various innocent victims of terrorism; we express moral outrage and abhorrence only when those with whom we have cultural and spacial proximity are affected. We place a hierarchy on human life. Empathy is intimately connected with this process and it is required to overcome dehumanization.[8] Empathy—the ability to feel what others may feel—ranges, and is on a continuum with individuals who feel for the plight of the disadvantaged in remote parts of the world; to those who may have sympathy for victims with whom they are close or have cultural and social proximity but have disregard for strangers; and those who completely lack empathy but are not necessarily violent. Levin and Fox[1] argue that men who use women for sex and money and leave them, con artists involved in Ponzi schemes, HIV-positive individuals who engage in unprotected sex, all lack empathy and possess psychopathic traits associated with those who kill for pleasure.

Dehumanization aids Walter in letting Jane die. This is arguably the moment in which the audience realized the true "evil" of Walter White. The moment he truly did "Break Bad." Jane—a recovering heroin addict—was romantically involved with Jesse and had learnt who the elusive Heisenberg was. She had threatened Walter about turning him to the authorities. At Jesse's, Walter finds them both asleep but Jane chokes on her vomit following a heroin overdose. In that moment, he realizes that if he "lets" her die, his problems are solved. He is a "killer" by omission, as many would argue, even if he did not have the intent or the voluntary action of committing the killing. Jane was a nuisance in what had otherwise been a smooth operation, and though he is a father, protective of his family and of Jesse, he draws a line when it comes to those he sees expendable. He shows no empathy or remorse and carries on as usual in his interactions with the grieving Jesse (although in the episode titled "Fly," Walter realizes the magnitude of his evolution and reveals that he wished he had died the day Jane died: "I lived too long" he cries). But self-preservation quickly takes over and he applies his chemistry brilliance to poison a child—Brock, the son of Jesse's girlfriend—fearing the Gus-Jesse allegiance and his ultimate demise. He views Brock merely as a means to an end—he uses him to create a rift between his rivals by making Jesse believe Gus is a child murderer. And Walter's rationalization was: "Yes, I am sorry about Brock, but he's alive, isn't he? He's fine, just as I planned it. Don't you think I knew exactly how much to give him? That I had it all measured out? Come on! Don't you know me by now?" (Season 5, "To'hajiilee"). He becomes increasingly callous towards those he considers outside his family and views them as mere objects he can use for his convenience. So, when afraid that assassins might be waiting for him inside his house, he calls his neighbour, an elderly lady, and expresses concern about leaving the stove on asking her to go inside the house to check. He observes from afar using his neighbour to make sure the path is clear from the assassins. Self-condemnation or guilt is absent because the victims are seen "no longer ... as persons with feelings, hopes and concerns but as subhuman objects."[9] Furthermore, having eliminated all his rivals, and destroyed all evidence that could reveal his identity, he realizes that 10 men in prison know about his involvement in the CM business; the only loose ends who can give evidence. Naturally, as per Heisenberg's style by this stage, he enlists the help of a group of neo–Nazis to eliminate the expendable. In Aristotelian terms, Walter's habituation with criminality further normalizes committing it, enabling him to perfect the conduct without any moral restrictions. Eliminating those who get in the way through violence becomes a matter of habit. At this stage he is the revered Heisenberg; he has made millions although he has a long way to go to reach the heights of the Schwartz; he makes the purest form of CM and is the best at something, having perhaps reached his professional capacity to some extent; he eludes authorities; he makes an accomplice of his wife; he leads; and he got away with multiple murders. He has power. And power intensifies dehumanization so that difficult or painful decisions can be made towards those perceived to be animals or objects.[10]

But Walter is a complex character. He may have no qualms about poisoning a child, ordering a hit or allowing a young woman to choke on her vomit and die, but he will not cross some lines: family. He pleads for Hank's life when the neo–Nazis prepare to kill him, even though Hank's death would mean the end of Walter's problems; no physical evidence, no legitimate investigation, no prosecution. He is appalled at his wife's and lawyer's suggestions about killing Jesse who had become a liability. He expresses concern for those he considers "family," but has disregard for others. Just as we all do.

Why Are We So Fascinated?

Besides the visceral thrill we obtain from watching extreme violence from a distance, Walter intrigues us because he is someone upon whom we can project our deepest desires and sentiments. Building upon the works of Hall et al., (1978), Williamson (1985) and Watney (1987), Garland[11] asserts that specific groups, deviants, or individuals are singled out as "folk devils" because they serve an appropriate platform upon which society can "project sentiments of guilt and ambivalence." Garland further argues that "moral panic targets are not randomly selected: they are cultural scapegoats, whose deviant conduct appalls onlookers so powerfully, precisely because it relates to personal fears and unconscious wishes." In the context of this character, our fascination reflects our unconscious denial and projection that we have it in all of us to be like Walter. We have all employed the same behavioral traits (albeit for different reasons) that have ultimately led to his violent expression following a number of social insults. He is not very different from the rest of us. He experiences financial hardship; he is diagnosed with a terminal illness and has a child with a disability, all of which place an even greater financial strain; he has a pervasive sense of failure, constantly plagued by regret, an inferiority complex and endless "what ifs." He admits that he spent his life "scared, frightened of things that could happen, might happen, might not happen" finding himself "awake at three in the morning." This is a recognizable man, an all too familiar man who ultimately resorted to violence and criminality to nurse his bruised ego and self-esteem while convincing himself that he was doing it all for his family's financial security long after he dies. Laura Hudson[12] from *Wire Magazine* provides a compelling insight about the way masculinity and monetary gains were portrayed in *Breaking Bad*. She argues that money, power and manliness are dangerously intertwined and signify not only Walter's control and self-sufficiency but also his value and identity as a man. He saw himself a (valuable) man not because of his relationship with his family, but because of his ability to provide financially through whatever means necessary. The story is a critical reflection of contemporary society. Granted there may be plot holes in some of the narrative devices used and the show can, at times, seem hyper-realistic but the context and the character arcs and behaviors are realistic. The symbolism and the overall message aim to illustrate how morally unrestricted an individual can be if presented with alluring incentives following a set of psycho-social strains.

We express shock and disbelief as we see him evolve into a brutal killer because people like to express moral indignation and superiority. Labeling those we use as scapegoats reassures us that unpredictability, dangerousness, violence and immorality are characteristic of "psychopaths" like Walter; a reassurance that these behaviors are specific to those who can be labeled and identified rather than accepting the reality that we can all display violent or immoral behaviors if subjected to a set of socio-cultural stresses that undermine our status, value or identity. When socially acceptable means of obtaining power or dominance are not available, some resort to violence. Walter's decision to take control of his life and destiny reflects our deep desires and sentiments to do so, but there is a sense of ambivalence that we sympathize with a familiar man who resorted to extreme violence to obtain "success" when legitimate means failed. In a society that defines success in terms of monetary gains, Walter fell victim to these ideals of contemporary culture and aimed to use his professional capacity in order to "provide" for the family through immoral means. It is a case of *anomie*: criminal conduct that reflects defective and amoral societies; lack of economic regulation and availability of equal resources; and social stressors. As renowned sociologist Robert Merton would argue, individuals are promised success—the "American dream" defined in terms of monetary gains—but do not have equal access to society's resources; and as such, ambition promotes deviant behavior.[13]

One may wonder whether Walter died content or miserable. Did he win or lose? The answer may depend on who is asked. By some standards, Walter seems to have lost everything because he lost the family for whom he desperately sought to financially provide (at least initially) regardless of the immorality of his actions. The fact that this "family man" died alone in a deserted meth-lab may even appear to be a greater failure, particularly when considering the symbolic emphasis that was placed on his almost "ritual" time spent with his family every morning at breakfast. The sense of loss is apparent in his tears when he seems to say a silent "goodbye" to his daughter Holly; when he looks at his son one last time from a distance; and when he begs a "stranger" to stay with him just two more hours for $10K. The loneliness depicted was very powerful.

But by other standards, Walter may be considered to have "won" because he appears to have addressed longstanding feelings of anger and inferiority by confronting his "tormentors" – the Schwartz; he lets them know how he truly felt about them ("this is where you get to make it right") sentencing them to a life of fear about "the assassins" because Walter knows a great deal about fear and its crippling effects. In addition, he was "man enough" to admit to his wife that he engaged in immoral behavior all for himself because it made him feel alive. Indeed, Vince Gilligan explained that he and his writers wanted Walter to "die like a man." The fact that Walter destroyed his Empire Business and all those associated with it, thereby eliminating the drug-trade in the south-west, can be seen as a redemptive action of some sort. Not the least, his forgiveness and salvation of his long-time associate, Jesse. It is curious to also examine these questions from Walter's perspective because he may have seen himself as a "winner." He had fulfilled his professional potential (despite their damaging consequences) to the extent that the likes of Tucco, Gale, Gus, Mike, the neo–Nazis, Lydia and her European clients respected the product and in turn "The Producer" – Heisenberg. He had stood up to everyone who had undermined him, including Hank, with his famous "thread lightly" remark. A significant stance on Walter's part because Hank often belittled Walter: "I'll take you on drug-bust Walt, inject some excitement in your life" and "is the hand gun too heavy for you?" Throughout the show, Walter's remarks are very revealing of how he felt about himself: he was "awake," "the one who knocks," "the danger" and having felt "alive." The smile at the end, lying amongst his precious stainless steel seems to say it all: he may not have felt so alone after all. He had not lost.

In the end, Walter died having made decisions that benefited those he considered "family" whilst eliminating his enemies, the expendables. He saves Jesse, he gives Skyler an opportunity to exonerate herself, he allows Marie to have closure and leaves his son an "inheritance," but instills fear in the lives of the Schwartz, and eliminates the neo–Nazis and Lydia thereby destroying "The Empire Business." He obtains some form of redemption, if it was at all possible for someone like Walter whose abandonment of moral inhibitions seem to have taken him far from any kind of salvation. And a somewhat redeemed Walter may be comforting to some—indeed many continued to sympathize with him regardless of how ruthless he had become—because his story reflects some real-life situations; a financially strained middle aged man in the middle of the Great American Recession, whose feelings of inadequacy and failure lead him to resort to extreme and violent measures to obtain what contemporary society defines as "success." This is a story that has appealed to many because it deals with moral questions about right and wrong, and good and evil, in light of social ideals and strains. What would we do with hardships that undermined our value and identity, if faced with the right incentives to overcome them? It is a compelling sociological inquiry.

Notes

1. Jack Levin and James A. Fox, "Normalcy in Behavioral Characteristics of the Sadistic Serial Killer," in *Serial Murder and the Psychology of Violent Crimes*, ed. Richard N. Kocsis (Totowa, NJ: Humana Press, 2008), 3–14.

2. Roy F. Baumeister, "A self-presentational view of social phenomena," *Psychological Bulletin* 91 (1982): 3–26.

3. Erving Goffman, *The Presentation of Self in Everyday Life* (Garden City, NY: Doubleday, Anchor, 1959).

4. Barry R. Schlenker, *Impression Management: The Self-Concept, Social Identity, and Interpersonal Relations* (Belmont, CA: Brooks/Cole, 1980).

5. Brad Bowins, "Psychological Defense Mechanisms: A New Perspective," *The American Journal of Psychoanalysis* 64 (2004): 1–26.

6. Robert J. Lifton, *The Nazi Doctors: Medical Killing and the Psychology of Genocide* (New York: Basic Books, 1986).

7. Viola W. Bernard, Perry Ottenberg, and Fritz Redl, "Dehumanization: A Composite Psychological Defense in Relation to Modern War," in *Behavioral Science and Human Survival*, ed. Milton Schwebel (Lincoln, NE: iUniverse, 2003): 64–82.

8. Jodi Halpern and Harvey Weinstein, "Rehumanizing the Other: Empathy and Reconciliation," *Human Rights Quarterly* 26 (2004): 561–583.

9. Albert Bandura, "Selective Moral Disengagement in the Exercise of Moral Agency," *Journal of Moral Education*, 31 (2002): 101–119.

10. Joris Lammers, and Diederik A. Stappel, "Power Increases Dehumanization," *Group Processes Intergroup Relations* 14 (2011):113–126.

11. David Garland, "On the Concept of Moral Panic," *Crime Media Culture* 4 (2008): 15

12. Laura Hudson, "Die Like a Man: The Toxic Masculinity of *Breaking Bad*," *Wire Magazine,* October 5, 2013.

13. Robert Merton, *Social Theory and Social Structure* (New York: Free Press, 1957).

Breaking Bad Stereotypes about Postpartum
A Case for Skyler White

REBECCA PRICE-WOOD

As a midwife, the first thing that stood out to me when my husband and I began watching *Breaking Bad* was that Skyler White was in her third trimester of pregnancy. The final thing that stood out to me as we finished the series was how the writers' portrayal of Skyler's psychological progression through pregnancy, birth, and postpartum was so unlike the usual media portrayal of this time in women's lives.

There are two stereotypical portrayals of childbearing women in the media. First, the sweetheart pregnant woman. She doesn't complain about the discomforts of her otherwise blissful pregnancy. She makes no extra demands on her husband, and the only indication that she is pregnant is the growing bump under her shirt. This woman sails through her uncomplicated birth. Postpartum, she is as stable as she was before, if not more so. She has grown in her dedication to being a mother, and she has grown in her love for her husband.

Second, the psycho prego. This woman swells up like a balloon. She hates being pregnant, or at least everyone assumes she does because she won't stop complaining about it. She has high hopes for her birth (which usually go unachieved). During her birth, this woman can be quoted as saying, "You did this to me!" or she physically assaults her surprised husband and/or the medical staff. If this woman's postpartum period is acknowledged at all, she is either back to normal (and sheepish about her behavior), or she is even crazier than before.

In contrast to both of these stereotypes, Skyler's pregnancy, birth, and postpartum period were depicted so believably that it called to mind numerous postpartum cases I have encountered as a midwife and as a postpartum support group leader. Because of this, I found Skyler's character so enjoyable and fascinating to watch. It was astonishing how believable her responses were to the unbelievable traumatic events in her life, and these responses were just about right according to the predictable postpartum emotional signposts.

There are many signs of a postpartum mood disorder, and Skyler often expresses these or something similar: feeling irritated or angry; having no patience; being easily annoyed; feeling resentment toward the baby, the partner, or friends who don't have babies; an out-of-control rage; feeling nothing, emptiness, or numbness—just going through the motions of life; hopelessness, like things will never get better; feeling weak and defective, like a failure; a sense of disconnect, of being strangely apart from everyone; thoughts of running away and leaving the family behind; suicidal thoughts to end the misery. Often a fear manifests that this state or mood is the new reality or the future and that the former self is lost; that if the mother reaches out for help, people will blame her or even take away her baby.

Skyler, throughout the course of this series, experiences many psychological triggers during her pregnancy, birth, and postpartum period. Additionally, she has almost none of her needs met by Walt. How well a pregnant woman is able to cope with the major psychological concerns of pregnancy informs her psychological well-being postpartum. For example, a common fear for pregnant women is that something will be wrong with the baby. For Skyler, this fear must be intensified, as she and Walt already have a child with a birth defect, cerebral palsy, and their chances of having a child with another defect are dramatically increased. This is not just a fear for Skyler; it is her reality and her only experience with pregnancy and childbirth so far. A woman may experience the awareness that she cannot stop the pregnancy or avoid the delivery. She cannot stop the growth of her baby or control what may or may not be wrong with it. She also becomes aware that she cannot control when and where she goes into labor or how much pain she will experience. These realizations result in an increasing sense of loss of control over her own body. This makes a woman more dependent on and demanding of her support system, because paramount is the fear of being abandoned. To monitor her own psychological and physical safety, women in their third trimesters report a marked increase in sensitivity to their own feelings and what feelings they sense from others. To intensify matters, Skyler, like most pregnant women, is facing the possibility of her own mortality, as the fear of dying in labor is something with which the gravid woman must come to terms. At the same time, Skyler is staring down the barrel of her own husband's mortality.

"All you have to do is be there." This is my advice for nervous fathers who want to know what they are supposed to do while their wife is in labor with their child. "You don't have to know any fancy massage techniques. All you are required to do is protect your wife by staying physically and emotionally present so that she can surrender to the power of birth and become a mother to this baby." I give this recommendation to every father during my prenatal appointments and during childbirth classes. I know that what happens at this birth is forever. It has been demonstrated by psychological studies of postpartum women that the negative events that happen during the course of childbirth become exaggerated in the mind of the mother. Feeling abandoned and feeling out of control are the two biggest emotional triggers for a woman in labor. Being abandoned by a partner during labor and birth sets the stage for postpartum relationship issues.

It has been suggested that the postpartum period is two years long. In my experience, this is just about right. There are predictable psychological signposts along these 24 months that show an unmistakable pattern that confirms the "two year" postpartum estimate for most women. Although each woman is different, this estimate is the same for women who have some form of postpartum depression and those who do not.

Very little has been written on the topic of postpartum psychology. Basically, there's information on postpartum depression, which can be screened for using the Edinburgh Scale (a series of questions, e.g., "in the past two weeks: have you been having fun? Crying?" Etc.) Beyond that, there is the very different postpartum psychosis, which is your basic hallucinatory/suicidal/homicidal mom who is dutifully reported by the news along with the all-caps subtext of "HOW COULD SHE?" These problems, according to the *Diagnostic and Statistical Manual of Mental Disorders* or DSM-V, are to be classified as any other depressive/psychotic/anxious state, only differentiating by the use of the modifier, "with postpartum onset," and even that is only to be used within the first six months postpartum. This, even though the two most harrowing tales of postpartum psychosis, Andrea Yates drowning her five children at seven months postpartum, and Susan Smith driving her car into a lake, killing her two children at 14 months postpartum, beg to differ. What this means is that there is still only incidental recognition that psychological maladies in the postpartum period have anything to do with a woman actually being postpartum. The lack of research on the exclusively feminine experience of the postpartum period points directly to the overwhelmingly still gendered concerns and preconceptions of the medical field.

Laura Tropp argues that "narrative television favors the most extreme representations of [postpartum depression (PPD)] in order to generate excitement and entertainment."[1] The postpartum psychological state is consistently limited by the "depression" tag. Skyler White offers a fresh take on the postpartum experience; she is not extreme, and it is not a stereotypical depression that she is feeling. The other narrative use of postpartum in television often appears with the previous extreme behavior—namely it is the subplot of an episode, often comic relief. And the narrative structure is invariably the process of "getting back to normal," achieved always by episode's end. Tropp cites these and the Mommy Myth, that a woman's value correlates to her abilities as a mother, as the major reasons that the postpartum period is neglected: "The powerful ideology of the Mommy Myth, the limitations of commercial media, and the disagreement among the medical community over how to label and treat PPD all conspire to reinforce problematic representations of the disorder. Without an active resistance against these influences, the sad mommy will continue to be labeled the bad mommy."[2] *Breaking Bad*'s characterization of Skyler White will hopefully raise awareness of the unique postpartum time.

It should hardly be surprising then that the character of Skyler has not been understood in the context of pregnancy and postpartum. Nevertheless, I did find it surprising that so many *Breaking Bad* fans, to put it mildly, don't like Skyler's character. This sentiment was so widely and sometimes so wildly held by such a large portion of viewers that the actress who brilliantly plays Skyler, Anna Gunn, felt compelled to write a defense of her character and herself in the *New York Times*. Her conclusion seems to be that the public at large hates this character because she acts as an antagonist for the character of Walter White. "[She is] the one character who consistently opposes Walter and calls him on his lies," Ms. Gunn says in her piece, "[Skyler-hating] has become a flash point for many people's feelings about strong, nonsubmissive, ill-treated women."[3] Many feminist blogs, too, have taken on Skyler-haters. Many discuss the rape/near rape of Skyler in the second season premiere, "Seven Thirty-Seven," and in the fifth season's episode "Madrigal," and there is plenty of talk about whether or not Skyler is in an abusive relationship with Walt. On and on go the reasons we should hate/not hate Skyler, but none among them refer to her pregnancy or postpartum, even though, according to the Holmes and Rahe Stress Scale, pregnancy and childbirth is one of the most stressful life events, being a major predictor of stress-related health-problems within the following year. I found it amazing that, even though so many women have experienced this time in their lives, there is no compassion for that unique time. It apparently wasn't even worth mentioning in relation to Skyler. Perhaps if the writers had written her character in a more stereotypical way, viewers could have made the connection, but Skyler is neither the sweetheart pregnant woman nor the psycho prego. What she is, though, is subtle and dead-on for a pregnant/postpartum woman in her position.

In *Holistic Midwifery*, Anne Frye states, "In order to have the emotional resources to nurture her newborn, the mother needs to feel supported and nurtured herself. She needs to be able to feel dependent on those around her for support."[4] In the second season's eleventh and twelfth episodes, "Mandala" and "Phoenix," Skyler goes into labor while at work. She calls her husband and the viewer sees him look at his phone, see that it is Skyler calling, and choose to ignore her call twice. After seeing her text that the baby is coming, Walt makes the choice to prioritize a major meth deal over being present for Skyler and the birth of their daughter. Instead, Skyler was supported by literally every other character in her life: her employer, her sister, her brother-in-law, and her teenage son. When Walt enters the room with an apology, he is instantly forgiven with a smile and a nod. Make no mistake, though, Skyler was abandoned by her partner. She begins her postpartum vulnerable and saddled with the reality that while she has a baby depending on her completely, she herself is completely dependent on Walt who has just proved exactly how undependable he has become.

At the time of the birth of Holly, Skyler has already been feeling the chaos from Walt's choices creeping into her own sphere. She senses that her husband's world, to which she does not have access, is much more chaotic than she knows. Once Walt inadvertently reveals the presence of his second cell phone, Skyler knows that something is wrong—strongly enough that she tries to uncover an affair. What she finds, though, is a terrifying chasm between whom she has thought Walt was and the vast unknown that he is now.

Skyler draws her hand back and attempts to create her own stability by removing Walt from the environment in lieu of uncovering any more about the new him. This grasp for stability is so important for a postpartum woman. In "No Más," Skyler half-heartedly guesses at drugs being the source of Walt's behavior, and she is physically shaking when this guess is confirmed by Walt. This physical shaking is a symptom of emotional shock. All of the abandonment, both physical and emotional becomes too obvious to ignore. In the months that pass, Walt's behavior and revelations push Skyler deeper and deeper into her postpartum dysphoria. Every chemical process in Skyler's body is telling her to protect her baby, and every obvious sign is that she is powerless to do so.

The third season's "I.F.T." is possibly the most important episode of *Breaking Bad* for the arc of Skyler's character. At this point in her postpartum, Skyler is bringing Holly to work with her, and she is standing up to her boss' dishonesty. She is strong when Walt visits for family dinner, and she does not let him in because Skyler knows that he is dangerous. She thinks she has everything under control, but when Walt forces himself back into the family home, Skyler realizes that there is no one who is powerful enough to keep her baby safe except Walt who is ironically the very cause of her vulnerability. There is a scene in particular wherein the audience sees this fact fully dawn on Skyler. She threatens Walt with calling the police if he doesn't leave. Walt calls her on the bluff; he knows she won't tell because it would endanger their family. It is clear that she doesn't really want to call the police; she just wants him to leave. Walt keeps his poker face, and Skyler calls the police. Before they arrive, Walt Jr. arrives home from school and expresses great joy that his father is back at home. Skyler has to make a choice: does she choose to strip herself of the stability she has known and that she craves by turning Walt into the police (which would include destroying her son and, in her mind, possibly getting her baby removed from her), or does she make the choice to protect? Who is she protecting with her decision to keep Walt's secret? Everyone.

"I.F.T." also marks the real beginning of a drastic change in the Walt-Skyler dynamic. Walt strips Skyler's support system away from her, while at the same time, making her responsible for all of them. Skyler noticeably begins to deteriorate during this episode. She starts smoking again, the irony, of course, being that her husband is dying of lung cancer. A method to cope with her stressful life and a rebuke to her husband, but at the same time smoking endangers their young daughter. She is still nursing and co-sleeping with Holly, who is even in the room with her as she smokes out the window.

This is highlighted again in "I.F.T." as Skyler talks to her attorney. The attorney offers to protect her, but Skyler decides to "wait for him to die" instead being the one responsible for the pain and humiliation of her entire family. It is my opinion that this is exactly why so many *Breaking Bad* fans hate Skyler. Walt put her in the position of being responsible for all of *his* actions: she must actively take care of their family while Walt is away or repeating his predictable refrain that everything *he* is doing is for the family. In this very episode, he says that if Skyler leaves him, it invalidates everything he has done. Skyler repeatedly protects the family, worries about their appearance, creates the subterfuge about Walt gambling, comes up with the best solution to money laundering with the car wash, and pays off Ted's delinquent IRS bills which emasculates Walt but really protects everyone. Of course, her job is thankless, continually distancing herself from her son; Walt buys him a car, but Skyler insists that they return it. She takes the blame in Walt Jr.'s eyes for her separation from Walt. Skyler sacrifices her own reputation in the eyes of her son, becoming as she says a "bitch," in order to protect their whole family.

"I.F.T.," an acronym that stands for "I fucked Ted," is also the episode in which Skyler begins her affair with Ted Beneke, her boss. Affairs or at least attractions are common in the postpartum period, whether a woman's husband cooks meth or not. Ted becomes all the support she has left, with Walt gone and Walt Jr.'s affection gone. He is someone removed from "Skyler as mother," "Skyler as powerless," "Skyler as accomplice." Most importantly though, an affair with Ted means that Skyler has some control. This affair sends a very clear message to Walt that, even though she didn't turn him into the police, she is not his. Likewise, the extramarital attraction that many women feel between four and nine months postpartum has to do with similar things. A woman, just after her baby is born, is obsessed with the baby to the exclusion of almost everything else. Usually, women are not feeling very sexual because the body is producing hormones that suppress these urges. Soon, a husband can begin to accept his wife in this role; she is an excellent mother, but part of her is lost to him. Around three to four months postpartum, this sexual suppression fades, and as the baby is more independent, a woman can begin to wonder who she has become. She may not even recognize herself in the mirror or in the faces of her friends and family. A "postpartum crush," a term coined by one postpartum support group leader, has to do with a woman looking outward to be validated as a grown-up woman separate from her baby. Most women will never act upon their desires, but sometimes they do. In Skyler's case, she needed someone to validate who she is on many levels.

Shortly, however, Skyler has to realize that Ted is not outside of Walt's reach, and because of her revealing the affair to Walt, she will be humiliated indiscriminately in front of her coworkers. Now, Skyler's only psychological haven and her means of supporting her family is a humiliating place to be. In this episode, "Green Light," Ted asks Skyler to move in. Despite Skyler saying that the time she is with Ted is the only time in her day where she doesn't feel like she's drowning, she chooses to take care of the things she feels are her responsibility and not to abandon her family. Skyler must protect Walt to protect her children. Her affair, by proxy, becomes a danger to her children. The slope becomes more slippery; if Walt is found out, everyone will suffer just the same as if she had turned him in herself.

Things only get deeper for Skyler when Hank gets shot. In the episode "I See You," Skyler knows she has betrayed both Hank and Marie by choosing to not turn in Walt. The stakes are much higher for Skyler now; she had been making her choices in order to protect her whole family. She feels responsible for Hank; she knows that the choices she has so far made, to protect her nuclear family by not turning her husband in to the DEA, has now hurt her extended family. Skyler has fallen into a world for which she was wholly unprepared, and she has done so at the worst time psychologically for herself. Skyler has no frame of reference for decision-making in the scenarios where she constantly finds herself. "Are we safe? Are you safe?" are the driving forces behind every decision Skyler makes during the course of the series.

Skyler operates almost entirely on reflex-response as she desperately tries to understand who she is now. She makes an attempt to atone for her poor judgment by offering to pay Hank's medical bills. Walt's "business" is what allows her to do this. Skyler attempts to integrate her relationships into her new reality by concocting a story to explain her sudden wealth. Skyler insists on buying a car wash, because she thinks this will offer her a way to turn this dishonest venture into an honest business. At this point, she's still buying Walt's story that he is doing all of this to provide the family financial protection. This allows Skyler some measure of control over her situation by allowing her to be at least partially honest with her sister and brother-in-law.

Walt goes along with the story, but in the episode, "Shot Gun," he is willing to blow it because of his pride. Skyler sits next to her husband as he tells Hank, who thinks he has solved the meth case, that he thinks the meth cook is still out there. Just before this, Skyler has let her wall down with Walt and made love with him for the first time since finding out about his dealings. This sets up the events for another pivotal episode for Skyler, "Cornered," or alternatively, "Wherein Skyler Gets Left Holding the Bag." Because of Walt's comments to Hank the night before, Skyler researches the death of Gale. Of course, the audience knows that Walt had Jesse murder Gale, but Skyler assumed that Gale was murdered by a "bad guy." She wakes up Walt and tries to convince him to leave the business and go to the police; maybe together they can protect the family and protect Walt. Unfortunately, she has forgotten or perhaps has never let herself admit that Walt is the bad guy. This point is unforgettably impressed upon Skyler in one of Walt's most compelling scenes. The Walt mask falls down to reveal Heisenberg. Walt says, "Who are you talking to right now? Who is it that you think you see? I am not in danger; I *am* the danger." What happens here to Skyler in terms of her postpartum psyche is that she realizes that, not only does she not know who she is, but also she doesn't know who her husband is. In this scene, he reveals a part of himself, which is startling. The audience has already seen the mask slip on and off between scenes, but Skyler doesn't know about any of that. She only gets glimpses of Heisenberg, and it's terrifying to her. Here, Skyler leaves. She takes Holly and goes to the Four Corners and flips a coin, presumably to decide where she'll go. Her coin lands on Colorado twice, and she looks at Holly and moves the coin back to New Mexico. Skyler feels that she has been pulled down too far to swim back up without Walt.

When she arrives home, Skyler finds that Walt has bought Walt Jr. a new flashy car. Walt tries to make amends for what he said earlier. When Skyler doesn't accept this and she instead insists that he return the car to protect their story, Walt hits her where it hurts. He says that Walt Jr. will blame her for having to return the car, reminding her that she is ultimately responsible. Skyler already knows this. She is responsible for all of Walt's actions. She is responsible for protecting everyone, and sometimes protecting everyone makes one the bad guy. Skyler then says out loud what the audience has only suspected until then, "Someone has to protect this family from the man who protects this family."

This shifting of responsibility spreads even further when Ted Beneke shows back up to ask for Skyler's help with the IRS. While Skyler worked as bookkeeper for Ted, she was responsible for covering up his embezzlement from the company. Now, she becomes responsible for getting him out of it. This is a task she must perform because to protect Ted is to protect Walt, and to protect Walt is to protect her family. Skyler anonymously gives Ted over half a million dollars to pay his back taxes which he refuses to do. Just like Walt, Ted will not allow Skyler to protect her family. Just like Walt, this person who was once her shelter and protection is her biggest threat. Skyler gains control over the situation by having two thugs come and force Ted to pay his taxes and penalties. During the course of this, Ted is injured and paralyzed. Skyler visits Ted in the hospital in the episode "Live Free or Die." Seeing Ted in his hospital bed, Skyler must keenly feel her impotence in her efforts to protect. She must understand on some level that she has no control over her life or who she is becoming. Ted is afraid of Skyler, and Skyler is afraid of the person who causes such fear in Ted's eyes.

As Walt becomes more comfortable with his Heisenberg persona, Skyler becomes increasingly fearful of her new role. Still in shock from visiting Ted,

Skyler returns home and Walt gives her a hug and says, "I forgive you." With his magnanimous line, Walt proves that even he has placed upon Skyler the responsibility to care for and protect the family. This is where Skyler falls into her darkest depression. She has no ability to make sound choices anymore. She has to continue what she is doing, knowing it's wrong, because she's in too far. She knows she has no control over the situation, and it is not fate, but Walt who holds the reigns. In the next two episodes, "Madrigal" and "Hazard Pay," Walt takes full control of Skyler and his home life. In "Madrigal," he has non-consensual sex with Skyler as she lies in bed in a depression. Then in the next episode, he moves back into the family home without request or invitation. This all becomes too much for Skyler, and she has a psychological breakdown in front of Marie. Marie again tries to protect her sister from the unknown problem that has her so unrecognizable, and she puts her foot down with Walt, telling him she will not leave until she knows what is happening to her sister. Walt throws Skyler right under the bus and tells Marie about Skyler's affair with Ted. Marie leaves with no more questions. Skyler's days spent in bed are a psychological moratorium. She is trying to wake up and define who she is now and who she was before all of this.

The next pivotal point in Skyler's postpartum evolution happens in the episode "Fifty One." Walt's reckless dominance over Skyler continues as he re-purchases the flashy car for Walt Jr. and then one for himself. Of course, this flies in the face of all Skyler's attempts to protect. Finally, Walt reveals he is cooking meth again. She comes to the conclusion that her children are not safe, and she has no real power to protect them. She decides the children are better off without her as their mother, and she attempts to get Walt's permission to send Walt Jr. to a boarding school. He refuses, and Skyler gets desperate. At Walt's fifty-first birthday dinner, she walks into the pool in front of Hank and Marie, thus forcing Walt's hand. What follows is a power struggle between Walt and Skyler wherein Skyler makes it clear that she will go to any lengths to protect her children, and Walt demonstrates the same resolve to remain in control of Skyler and their children. Walt reveals that he knows Skyler's deepest fears, that her children will be emotionally harmed or that she will be removed as their mother, and he subtly threatens her to subdue her and to force her to submit to his control.

I find this scene so deeply moving because, though the series is focused on Walt's descent, everyone around him is also descending. It's a process of people making unfortunate but reasonable choices. Walt chooses crime as a way to ensure the financial stability of his family, to confront his masculinity and mortality, to feel the thrill of having power. Meanwhile, Skyler chooses to enable Walt because she feels she has no other choice; it is what she must do to protect those around her.

Both of them invest in these bad decisions and mistakes respectively. Then when the stakes get higher, they must invest just a little bit more, then a little bit more. By the time the situation has become clearly wrong instead of justifiable, the investment is too much, and there is no way out. This scene is the end of the road for Skyler. She has so much at stake that she decides this is the moment she must exert her authority and stand her ground with Walt. In a brutally efficient takedown, Walt demonstrates that any power Skyler thinks she has is imaginary. Walt threatens to put her in a mental hospital. If she is removed from her home, she can no longer protect her children. Skyler's out of options, but she finds the words to remind Walt that, though she may be Walt's unwilling pawn, he is not in control over his own life and death. Skyler says, "I'm not like you. I'm a coward. I can't go to the police, I can't stop laundering your money, I can't keep you out of my house, I can't even keep you out of my bed. I can only wait." Walt asks what she's waiting for, and she says, "I can only wait for you to die."

Skyler's children stay at Hank and Marie's for three months. The pain of Skyler's separation from her children is only overshadowed by her drive to keep them safe. In the episode "Dead Freight," Walt Jr. comes home against his mother's wishes and refuses to leave in a circumstance similar to Walt's break-in earlier in the series. This must be incredible for Skyler. The audience has already begun to see Walt's boundaries in his relationship with Walter Jr. become increasingly blurred and glorifying a dangerous lifestyle such as was the case with the physical altercation at the department store, the sports cars, and most recently, the two of them watching *Scarface* together. Here, a new danger emerges; where Skyler once feared Walter Jr. losing Walt, she now fears her son is becoming like Heisenberg. Not surprisingly, Skyler deteriorates into self-destructive behavior including heavy drinking and smoking. Every move she makes has its own horrible complications. She is resigned to her life as it has become, but not without significant consequences to herself. Skyler clearly needs psychotherapy, and she lies about receiving it in an effort to continue covering her story. It is ironic that Skyler knows to lie about receiving counseling. She is aware enough to know that other people probably think she needs psychological help, but at the same time, it doesn't occur to her to seek it to heal herself. She has clearly sunk into a hopeless depression compounded with an increasingly hopeless situation, and she sees no way out as every turn she has taken has brought her to a darker place.

After the children have been at Hank and Marie's for three full months with no change in her situation except that Walt continues to cut her out of the loop more and more, and she can see that Walt is engaging in increasingly risky and hard-to-control behavior, Skyler comes back around in an attempt to solve the situation by revealing to Walt that she has a giant storage unit full of money. He can stop cooking, and her children can come home. Walt tells her he's getting out, and we see Skyler's shoulder's drop in a sign of relief.

Just as things are coming back to a new normal, Hank deciphers that Walt is Heisenberg. Hank calls a meeting with Skyler. It seems that Skyler is relieved and thinks, as painful as it might be, that Hank can protect her, and that her ordeal can be over. Through the course of their conversation, Skyler gradually realizes that Hank's case against Walt is not air-tight. Skyler quickly decides that siding with Hank is choosing a side that cannot fully protect her or her children. This is not in solidarity with Walt. This is self-preservation. Skyler has seen the things her husband in capable of, and she is terrified of being on the losing side of this.

When Skyler gets home, she must face Marie and tell the horrible truth about what she knows. This is another absolutely punishing thing for her to do, as Marie has been her closest advocate, and besides that, Skyler knows full well what she has done and has allowed Walt to continue to do is wrong. Marie attempts to remove Holly. This is the moment when Skyler psychologically goes all-in with Walt. Marie's implication that the children aren't safe with Skyler as their mother is a far more painful slap in the face than the physical one that Marie inflicted on her just moments before. From this point forward, Skyler shows no allegiance to her sister. In the episode "Confessions," Skyler aids Walt in making a blackmail video, which targets Hank. Although this may seem like she is betraying her sister and brother-in-law to help her husband, Hank has shown that he cares about nothing more than beating Walt, and Marie stands firmly with Hank on this. To Skyler, this is a huge threat, and it is the very thing she has been struggling with throughout the entirety of the series: no one comes before the children, not even her own sister. If Walt can help her protect them, then he's who she's going with.

At this point, the relationship between Walt and Skyler is a mutualistic one. Demonstrated during the infamous guacamole restaurant scene Walt, who seems to care about little else besides emasculating Hank, plays right to Skyler's desire to leave the children unaffected, although the viewer hopefully knows by this point that Walt takes a devil-may-care attitude regarding his own safety and that of his family. He just knows better than Hank how to manipulate Skyler, as she's become a very important player on both sides. Later on, sadly, Skyler must come to terms with the futility of all the choices and risks she took. She was never in control of anything.

Ironically, in a way, it is Marie who took down Walt, or at least started the ball rolling. In the times of greatest stress, it becomes clear how competitive Hank and Marie are with Walt and Skyler. It is never clearer then when Marie walks into the car wash to inform Skyler that Hank has Walt in custody. She is absolutely smug, and Skyler is barely hanging on to her composure. Marie has the power and wields it ruthlessly over Skyler in this scene. Marie rubs Skyler's nose in the choices she has made, giving no compassion to the reasons behind those choices. She forces Skyler to do the opposite of what she wants to do: destroy Walt Jr.'s image of his father. An extension of this shows us that Skyler too had the power to bring down Walt at any time. Once the secret is out, like Dorothy clicking the heels of her ruby slippers, it is all over. So Skyler thinks. In what is one of the most triggering events so far, Skyler realizes that Hank has been killed. Walt tries to explain that it was not his fault and that he had no control over it, but this was not what Skyler wanted to hear. If Hank is dead and Walt could not stop it, then they are not safe either; Walt can't protect them either. Skyler sees clearly that Walt was never any protection and certainly is none now. The full rotten underbelly of the marriage of Skyler and Walt is fully revealed to Walter Jr., and ends with Skyler brandishing a knife for protection, Walter Jr. jumping in front of his mother to protect her, and the kidnapping of Holly by Walt. Skyler's terrified, mournful wails as she runs futilely after the car containing her daughter, show the viewer a real postpartum woman. This act is supposedly Walt's ruse to give Skyler plausible deniability. Walt seems to think that it would be unbelievable for Skyler to think that he would ever hurt Holly, but this possibility is not at all unbelievable to Skyler. She is terrified enough of Walt to threaten his life with a knife to protect her children from him.

This scene in particular is one that should evoke compassion for Skyler from *Breaking Bad* viewers. By the time Walt kidnaps Holly, he has done enough erratic things that, though the viewer may be confused by Walt's actions, the thought that he could actually kidnap Holly to maintain control of his wife and family is not out of the realm of possibilities. Imagine then how Skyler must feel and how out of control her situation must seem. Remember, the major task of the postpartum woman is to integrate herself into her new circumstances and at the same time preserve her former self. To aid the woman in achieving these tasks, the psyche remains open and vulnerable. This time of self-discovery for so many women has turned into a house of mirrors for Skyler as her husband manipulates her in scarcely different ways than he manipulates Jesse, Gale, Hank, or any other character in his life.

I often wondered how things would have been different if Skyler were not postpartum and if she were not so psychologically vulnerable. She could have made different, stronger choices, which could have protected her children much better. Ultimately, if she had taken better care of herself and cared more for her own protection, she may have had some perspective from which to see the situation as it was and to have not been so ruled by anxiety. This is a very common theme in the postpartum period. It comes from a hormonally-driven instinct to protect the young and propagate the survival of the species. It would have been comparatively simple for Skyler to take some of the money in the storage unit and start over with a new identity and her children, but, again, herein lies the rub; the postpartum woman needs stability. This is all Skyler was striving to create for her children and for herself. Cash-grabbing and running away is the opposite of that.

Even when Walt is absolutely depraved in the lengths to which he goes to achieve his own dreams, which included becoming as powerful as possible NO MATTER WHAT, viewers never "hate" him. In contrast, Skyler, despite never directly harming anyone during the course of the series (beside herself) is actively despised. To write this essay, I went back and rewatched *Breaking Bad*, but only the scenes with Skyler. As an initial viewer of the show, I didn't particularly like Skyler, but felt compassion for her being postpartum. After watching the show from Skyler's perspective, Walt is disgusting, and with very few exceptions, ALL of Skyler's actions and reactions are completely understandable.

My original, traditional view of Skyler's last scene was one in which Skyler was redeemed by her tenderness for Walt. My second, Skyler view, was one in which Skyler is in control of her situation for the first time since Walt's revelation. Skyler alone made a home for her children. As the camera pans into the small apartment, the scene is confusing because it looks so similar to the old home. Skyler is in one sense defeated and left with the repercussions of her own decisions, yet she is victorious because she has achieved her postpartum tasks and integrated herself into her new reality. She finally realizes that there are worse things than being a single mother in a small apartment in a bad neighborhood. After all, something often discussed in the postpartum support group is this: "The only thing worse than having help is thinking you have help and not really having it."

Skyler White is the most complex depiction of a pregnant and postpartum mother, one not marked by the media's two major stereotypes of pregnancy. The media's depiction of postpartum hardly exists beyond "unreasonably sad." Postpartum psychological stresses and demands are experienced by all women; all women must achieve the integration, stability, safety, etc. Nevertheless, portrayals of postpartum women are either right back to normal after birth or on the crazy-sad divide. What is worse than media stereotypes is the far worse reality that the postpartum period itself is hardly recognized at large. There exists, of course, the common idea of "postpartum depression," but that terminology classifies as a psychological malady only the extreme end of a spectrum of behaviors and feelings experienced by all women. It has been suggested that the behaviors of postpartum women, except in the extreme, are not psychological disorders at all, but instead a normal female existence following the birth of one's child. This is threatening to the common ideal for women and mothers, and historically, television producers haven't seemed to think it made for very good entertainment. The writers of *Breaking Bad* have achieved this feminist goal of normalizing postpartum so seamlessly that it has slipped past almost every blogger, viewer, and critic without notice.

One might hope that *Breaking Bad*'s depiction of Skyler could remedy characterizations of women that are still rigidly stereotypical. The widespread viewer dislike of the character though seems to arrest this possibility. The audience's capacity to sympathize with Walter White despite his consistent abuse of Skyler is testament to the strength of the series. Its narrative demonstrates the seductive power of Walt's perspective. Skyler's reaction to Walt's kidnapping of Holly, foreshadowed for both the audience and for Skyler by Marie's attempted kidnapping of her, is the most powerful and realistic depiction of the postpartum woman that exists in any media.

Notes

1. Laura Tropp, "Off Their Rockers: Representation of Postpartum Depression," in *Mental Illness in Popular Media: Essays on the Representation of Disorders*, ed. Lawrence C. Rubin, 77–91 (Jefferson, NC: McFarland, 2012), 80.

2. Ibid., 89.

3. Anna Gunn, "I Have a Character Issue," *The New York Times*, August 23, 2013, http://www.nytimes.com/2013/08/24/opinion/i-have-a-character-issue.html?_r=0.

4. Anne Frye, *Holistic Midwifery, vol. I: Care During Pregnancy* (Portland, OR: Labrys Press, 1998), 791.

Breaking Health Care

MATTHEW A. BUTKUS

A fifty-year-old man has had a nagging cough for weeks, but just can't seem to shake it. His chest hurts, he gets bronchitis easily, his voice changes, and sometimes when he coughs he sees blood. This worries him, but he's optimistic—there are a lot of illnesses that can cause a cough. A persistent sinus infection can make you cough for weeks, and some bugs are just harder to shake than others—that takes a toll on your throat. The stress from working two jobs to support his wife and son doesn't help (with another baby on the way)—stress and anxiety, especially over money worries, can make illnesses worse by compromising immune function. He's been burning the candle at both ends for a long time now, so it's no wonder that he's been worn down, and getting sick is just part of that. He decides to hope for the best—he'll take some inexpensive over the counter medication, add some herbal supplements his wife thinks will boost his immune system, and hope it works itself out. There really isn't any need to see a doctor right now—people get sick all the time and he doesn't really have the disposable income if it turns into something serious. Maybe if things get worse he'll get checked out if, say, he collapses at work. Maybe.

The case presented above is Walter White, but he could just as easily be any number of contemporary Americans. Prior to the Patient Protection and Affordable Care Act (ACA), an estimated 48 million Americans were uninsured.[1] The impact of the ACA is still being determined—more time will be needed to see exactly how these numbers have changed, and the framework of health care regulation is, as of this writing, still in flux. Health care for Walter White, however, is defined by the pre–ACA framework (he is diagnosed in 2009), and demonstrates the precariousness of his position, and by extension, the precariousness of many Americans.

Walter delayed his health care because of money concerns, as many Americans do. Money routinely serves as a modifier of the voluntary—a philosophical concept that introduces internally and externally coercive influences in the decision-making process. Decisions that are heavily influenced by these modifiers of the voluntary are generally not seen as authentic expressions of the agent's will. In the context of health care, a visit to the emergency room or primary care physician can easily run into hundreds or thousands of dollars. With a family to support and another baby on the way, it is no wonder that Walter sought to avoid seeing a doctor. The doctor is expensive, tests are expensive, and herbal supplements and over the counter (OTC) medications were significantly cheaper.

This decision, however, profoundly compromised his health care—he is well into stage III lung cancer before he finally gets his diagnosis. Initially, he refuses treatment—his "insurance isn't that great" and he knows that chemotherapy will be expensive. As a matter of pride he turns down multiple offers of assistance, which is common in patients who are seeking to avoid accruing medical debt.[2] Ultimately, however, he decides to try chemotherapy and live longer, which sets in motion the events of the rest of the series.[3] It is no secret that Walter's cancer diagnosis serves as the catalyst for his transmutation from high school chemistry teacher to methamphetamine cook and would be drug lord. It makes for a great story; unfortunately, this fiction speaks to a larger truth.

Walter White is indicative of the experience of many Americans not merely because of the circumstances of his illness, but the illness itself. After heart disease, cancer is the leading cause of death for Americans, with one death in four due to a form of cancer. There are at least 13.7 million Americans now who have experienced cancer, and we expect to see over 1.6 million new cases in 2014.[4] Of this population, we expect almost 600,000 to die this year— over 1600 people per day. We expect to see nearly 225,000 new cases of lung cancer, which is the leading cause of cancer-related death in both men and women. Socioeconomic status directly impacts cancer care—the uninsured are significantly more likely to delay screening and care, at which point their treatment becomes more expensive and complex as well as potentially less likely to succeed.[5] Access to better and earlier screening technology directly impacts lung cancer mortality,[6] as only 15 percent of lung cancers are diagnosed while still localized.[7]

Justice and the Right to Health Care

Framing this discussion is the issue of what, if any, obligation exists for the state to provide for the health and well-being of its citizens. There is, at present, no *legal* basis for a claim to comprehensive health care—we allow for emergency coverage, and we have social programs to assist those who no longer have the means or ability to provide for their own care, but there is nothing that applies to the general population as a whole. But should there be? Is there a right to health care, and if so, what are its justification and scope? These questions have produced a flurry of arguments from philosophers, economists, and political theorists, asking whether there is any essential element of justice or beneficence that requires such a right, as well as how a society can afford to provide for it in light of its pluralistic duties to provide other goods like security, education, regulation of commerce, and law enforcement.

The question of distributive justice—how resources are allocated within society—is quite contentious. At heart, there is a question of fairness and giving each their due, but these have proven to mean different things at different times. The ancient Greeks, for instance, believed that what one was due was dependent on being male or female, citizen or slave, etc., and to treat one as the other would be inherently unjust. Karl Marx proposed a radical redistribution of social resources, eliminating social classes and providing for collective ownership of the means of production, all in the name of fairness and justice. There seems to be an essential plasticity to the concept, serving both as a transcendent ideal as well as a mirror of our own subjective concepts of right and wrong. Two strong traditions emerged in the latter 20th century, however, which have served as rallying points—the contractarian model of distributive justice as developed by John Rawls[8] and the libertarian model developed by Robert Nozick.[9]

Contractarian Distributive Justice

Rawls's contractarian model requires a moral agent to imagine that she is building the rules of society from the ground up—she will be responsible for setting up the political and economic rights of the citizenry. Most theorists agree that there is a natural tendency towards egoism—we look out for our own interests and well-being when we make decisions. Rawls accounts for this by stripping the moral agent of all self-referential knowledge—she does not know her sex, race, socioeconomic status, skills or talents, or any other piece of information that would potentially bias her towards a particular population. She becomes a being of pure, self-interested rationality with no idea where she fits into society. Because of this ignorance, it is in her best interest to arrange social resources in such a way that no matter where she ends up, she will not have disadvantaged herself. This gives rise to a number of essential principles; the most germane of which to the present discussion are the requirement that any inequality that results within a society is to everyone's benefit, and the requirement that goods or positions of power not be tied to any particular socioeconomic status (what Rawls calls the Difference Principle). In light of these requirements, if we are going to have rich and poor in our potential society, we must have programs that level the playing field for the economically disadvantaged, e.g., assistance in securing goods like education, housing, and health care.

The litmus test for any just society per Rawls's model is whether a rational moral agent would agree to be bound by the rules and obligations in the society considered—would she "contract" with that society. If a society were established that agents would not agree to contract with, then there are indications that there are some rather significant shortcomings or injustices. If, for instance, a society were to be structured in such a way that those who lacked financial resources could not secure access to health care, we would rightly call it unjust, and require steps to correct this shortcoming. This is, obviously, the system Walter White finds himself in—he puts off needed health screening and care because he can't afford it. The social system has failed him, with profound consequences for him, his family, friends, business partners, and ultimately, his direct and indirect victims. Because Walter serves as a proxy for many Americans, we can justifiably say that the social system has failed them, too, whenever they must defer health care for other concerns.

Libertarian Economic Justice

Libertarian models of economic justice raise a different set of issues. Nozick argued quite strenuously against the concept of distributive justice as explained by Rawls. He argued that all that mattered in determining the economic justice of a particular society was whether a person came by her property justly (i.e., not obtained through theft or coercion, or if it was received as compensation for past damages). Nozick rejects Rawls's distributive justice (and, in fact, all models of "distributive" justice) because the only model that matters in his analysis is individual choice—no matter how we might structure a theoretical distribution of rights and goods, individual choices can and do alter our social arrangements. If these choices produce resource inequality (even gross inequality), there is no reason to call it unjust—some people have simply made advantageous choices and others have made disadvantageous choices. We see further parallels to Walter's life—he chose to leave the company he helped to found, and in the process he cut himself off from excellent health benefits and a chance at an extremely lucrative career, just as he later chose to put off seeing a doctor when he first fell ill.[10]

While his condition would seem to be a case of personal irresponsibility and the consequences of his disadvantageous health choices, it is still possible to make a libertarian critique of the health care system. Essential to the concept of libertarianism is personal freedom, and a just society is one that allows individuals to act upon their liberties and freedoms.[11] Citing Nozick, Michelle Chandler notes that included within this scope of individual liberty and rights is "the right not to be deprived of life"—very clearly it is hard to reconcile this right with a system that puts barriers into place which prevent people from having access to the care that they need. When we look at the context of Walter's decisions, the apparent irresponsibility of his choices fades and they become understandable. He chose to leave the previous company well before falling ill (or even imagining falling ill), he chose to try to treat himself with OTC medications (as many Americans do), he chose not to seek expensive screening and treatment until he experienced an acute health crisis (again, as many Americans do), and he declined assistance with his health care costs well after he thought his condition was terminal. His recollection of his father's dying process was a powerful motivator for his decision and he wanted to die with dignity. Walter is not an irresponsible man undone by his own hand— he was working two jobs to support his family and attempting to build a good life for them. Even after he decides to cook methamphetamine, he is motivated by a desire to provide a nest egg for his family, calculating how much they would need for their future expenses and education. Walter may be acting badly, but he is doing so for very rational reasons. If we accept the libertarian idea of a just society including the right not to be deprived of life, then we can condemn a health care system that prevents him from being able to afford the treatment he needs.

Practical Justification for a Right to Health Care

Both of these theoretical models are compelling, and they offer a strong philosophical basis for questioning how health care is delivered in the United

States as well as justifying the idea of a right to health care. Philosophical objections, however, are not the only grounds for a basic concept of a right to health care—there are also strong practical reasons for advocating this position. Paul Menzel makes a cogent argument that Americans have already accepted a right to health care using our existing market and health care features.[12] The feature of the current system most salient here is the right to emergency care (we will return to Menzel's argument in the discussion of health care poverty and market failure later).

In the course of making his argument, Menzel points out that Americans have had a form of universal access to health care through the Emergency Medical Treatment and Active Labor Act (EMTALA). Under this legislation, hospitals have an obligation to treat medically unstable individuals who present to their emergency rooms, regardless of their ability to pay for it. This legislation enjoys widespread support—as Menzel rightly points out, people across the entire political spectrum reject the idea of patients bleeding out or women delivering in hospital driveways because they've been turned away. As a result, society as a whole has endorsed the idea that there is some degree of expected care to which we are entitled.

This endorsement carries with it some additional practical consequences that must at least be implicitly endorsed by everyone. First, because we recognize that some individuals receiving care will be unable to pay for it, we have accepted the idea that there is some obligation to the poor and indigent, discussions of this obligation's scope notwithstanding. Second, Menzel points out that frequently this emergency care requires admission to the hospital— if someone is simply "treated and streeted," there is a high degree of probability that they will have to be seen again when they decompensate or their health deteriorates. Because of this, we recognize that we will likely have to share the burden of their costs, either through cost shifting (in which people who have insurance bear higher costs because of the uninsured) or through social welfare programs like Medicare and Medicaid. Cost shifting is perceived as unjust by many, as it is adding unfairly to an existing economic burden—citing research by Stoll,[13] Menzel notes that cost shifting raises the premium the average family pays by almost $1,000 per year and the costs of individuals obtaining insurance through their employers by nearly $350. Stoll further projected that these costs would rise to $1,500/family and $530/individual by 2010. Very clearly, cost shifting can have significant impacts and has drawn criticism from a number of philosophical and political positions, but it does seem to be a logical consequence of requiring hospitals to treat people without insurance. Medicare and Medicaid offer further examples of generally accepted social programs—despite some occasional partisan bickering, there is a general social consensus that some people are simply too old or physically unable to work. As such, as a society we are willing to provide for their medical needs.

All of this combines to offer justification for a right to health care. Admitting this right, however, raises additional questions about its scope. The concept of a medical want versus a medical need has proven to be difficult, and medical scarcity raises a pragmatic barrier to the underlying philosophical concern. To paraphrase Immanual Kant's *Critique of Pure Reason*, "ought" implies "can"—if we are going to place a moral duty upon someone (or a state) to provide a good or resource, we must make sure that it is, in fact, possible for her to meet this duty.[14] It is unreasonable for us to ask for the impossible, and if a society does not possess the resources necessary to provide a good, it is unreasonable for us to call it a moral failing when it cannot. This is not an all-or-nothing principle, however; the scarcity and resultant obligations discussion may be answerable at a more limited scale, and will be a topic we revisit later.

As we have seen, resource scarcity is a multi-level problem; people like Walter make health care decisions based on what they have available to them and in light of the pressures facing them. As of this writing, the debate about health care reform is ongoing, with some advocating a repeal of the ACA. This will undo the benefits gained by increased insurance coverage and the removal of spending caps, returning millions to the inherent uncertainty found in less regulated markets. This weakening of regulation will exacerbate two problems identified with pre–ACA healthcare: underinsurance and market failure.

Health Care Poverty and Market Failure

In the run-up to the passage of the ACA, significant debate centered around the number of uninsured Americans. As noted above, it is estimated that there were 48 million uninsured Americans in 2012, but the number of people impacted by health care costs is significantly higher. When we consider the health care resource scarcity issue, we must include not only those who completely lack insurance coverage, but also those who have too little of it to be effective or be able to take care of their health care needs. In essence, we have people who have too much coverage to count as uninsured, but too little to be adequately covered. Some recent estimates place this population as high as 25 million,[15] translating into over 73 million Americans without adequate access to health care—a condition referred to as health care poverty, which encapsulates a number of medico-economic stressors like yearly and lifetime benefit limits, coverage gaps for medication or adjuvant care, costly premiums, deductibles, copayments, and coinsurance.[16]

There is a necessary caution here, however—it is difficult for us to quantify this population precisely because of some uncertainty inherent to the concept (Ward, 2006). In order for us to understand and define what constitutes "inadequate" health care coverage, we need to have a clearer understanding of what adequate health care coverage entails, which is notoriously difficult to define. A number of theoretical elements have been proposed as definitions of "underinsurance" with varying degrees of success; several studies have clustered around four elements: inadequate service or general coverage, excessive out-of-pocket health care expenditure (identified as either 5 percent or 10 percent of a person's income relative to the Federal Poverty Level), a perception of inadequate insurance, or a combination of these.[17] Some of these have drawn criticism, however; basing a concept of underinsurance on a person's subjective perception of adequacy is not a reliable metric—it is entirely possible for someone to have unrealistic expectations of "adequate" coverage and costs.[18] As such, it is better to rely on metrics that are quantifiable, such as out-of-pocket expenses, premiums relative to income, high deductibles, copayments/coinsurance, and lifetime or annual coverage caps.[19] Despite these questions, there is still an underlying and undeniable reality: it is entirely possible for someone to be paying premiums for an insurance policy that ultimately does not cover their legitimate medical needs, causing them to postpone health care.

Complicating this question further are related issues like existing debts and expenses. Some argue that medical debt is also a relevant factor, as medical debt frequently carries with it a number of direct and indirect costs to the patient, her family, and friends.[20] Medical debt may easily serve as an additional barrier to treatment—people with medical debt can be averse to seek further care because of restrictions on access (like health care providers requiring a deposit or advance payment from patients with outstanding medical bills, or refusing to treat the patient or the patient's family until existing debts are discharged) and aggressive debt collection. Further, patients and their families can exhaust their medical savings, borrow from their friends and family, have their wages garnished, their houses foreclosed upon, and suffer from bad credit for years following their medical emergency.[21] There is, consequently, a strong impetus to avoid important aspects of their health care like outpatient monitoring, follow-up appointments, and fulfilling prescriptions.[22] While working in behavioral health, I routinely encountered this problem—the hospital was a revolving door of patients whose thought and mood disorders would be pharmacologically stabilized to the point where they were ready for discharge, but who would then present back to our emergency room after decompensating within weeks because they could not afford the prescriptions that we gave them. This expensive and inefficient care wasn't tenable, and was exacerbated by the socioeconomics of the health care delivery system—two psychiatric hospitals at which I worked shut down or repurposed themselves into other types of care facilities, which meant a loss of needed mental health beds.

The realities of health care poverty are that it is widespread and invidious. Health care poverty exists within a larger framework, and market factors can exacerbate it. When health care payment is treated as a for-profit commodity (e.g., when health care payment occurs through third party insurers), the underlying motive is return on investment. Quite obviously, a business must at least break even to stay open and must show profits to endure. Health insurance companies are in the business of risk—they make their profits by receiving monthly premiums and avoiding unnecessary payouts. The ideal patient in this model is young and healthy, who routinely pays premiums for decades and never gets sick until the day he or she suddenly dies. While there certainly are some individuals like this, quite clearly the majority of people are not. From the patient's perspective, insurance represents an investment—it is building health care resources for periods of illness when one is well. This has been a source of tension—the company has a strong incentive not to pay for the health care for which their customers are paying premiums. This means that there is a disincentive to pay out on both illegitimate *and* legitimate claims, deny coverage to individuals considered to be high risk, and drop patients from coverage when they accrue too much health care costs (either annually or over the course of a lifetime). This, however, is not a tenable model—in a system of voluntary insurance (i.e., where insurance is not compulsory), if there is dissatisfaction with a company's performance, the individual is ostensibly free to seek coverage elsewhere. In light of this, insurance companies do take on patients who are considered higher risk, but require them to pay higher premiums to off-set that increased risk. In principle, this appears to be a simple case of supply and demand where market forces get individuals the coverage that they need, rewarding both the risks taken on by the insurer as well as the financial foresight of the customer. In practice, however, we do not see such a simple relationship.

Because insurance is voluntary, we see people who forgo paying for it, which increases the costs experienced by those who do pay, as noted in the discussion of justice and cost-shifting above.[23] This cost shift occurs without regard to the individual's personal degree of risk and without their consent—every level of tiered payments from low- to high-risk sees an increase in average premiums, deductibles, or copayments. This provides a disincentive to individuals who are healthy with low health care costs—many private customers have found it simpler and more cost-effective to gamble and not carry insurance (i.e., those who do not get their health care through their employer). Since they are not participating in the risk pool which keeps costs relatively low, the burden shifts disproportionately onto those who must stay in because they cannot afford to go without insurance due to their existing medical conditions. Their health care costs go even higher, which directly impacts both their willingness and ability to pay for their care, exacerbating their overall health burden. In short, these market forces make securing health care access and delivery difficult or impossible for the individuals who most need it—a situation referred to as market failure.[24]

Health care poverty and cost sharing exacerbate market failure, and one does not have to look far for practical examples of their impact. In 2005, Families USA calculated the budget for a family of four at the Federal poverty level.[25] Once essentials have been paid for (housing, utilities, transportation, food, and child care), their yearly budget leaves $215 available for health care ($18/month). In 2005, I was working at a psychiatric hospital, and was injured in the course of caring for a patient (losing some skin to the patient's fingernails). This required a 15 minute trip to the ER downstairs to have the wound irrigated and bandaged (saline, a 2x2 gauze pad, and some tape), for which the hospital charged me $256. Had I been the breadwinner for that family of four, we would have owed 2.5 months of labor to cover the costs above and beyond what we had been able to budget for health care. It is important to note that the Families USA calculation did not figure in any expenses like toiletries, school supplies, clothing, holiday or birthday gifts, life insurance, saving for future education, or, most saliently, medical emergencies. Consequently, the estimated 2.5 months of labor would have likely been extended indefinitely.

Cost sharing via higher deductibles, copayments, and coinsurance was theorized to be a mechanism of controlling health care costs by making people more selective about when they would choose health care—it would appear, however, that instead it simply increases the risk of incurring medical debt.[26] As many people with health care poverty treat the emergency room as their primary care physician, we see a simple mechanism by which health care costs increase, feeding into an escalating pattern of higher costs and burdens to society as a whole. Health care poverty is not limited to low income populations—it is a very real risk to many Americans.[27] The average person who earns a modest income and is ill is probably underinsured,[28] and millions of Americans are no more than one major illness away from financial ruin.[29]

Rising health care costs are multifactorial—there is no single "silver bullet" that will allow us to contain them,[30] and health care coverage and access is only part of a solution. Taken as a whole, the health care system of the United States is not as cost-effective as other industrialized nations. The Organization for Economic Cooperation and Development (OECD) tracks the health care costs for countries across the globe.[31] They have found that the total expenditure on health in the United States consistently ranks the highest among member countries—17.7 percent of GDP, nearly twice the OECD average (9.3 percent), and spending $8,508 per capita, nearly twice as much as France, for instance. In light of this expenditure, do we get the best return on our investment? It would seem that we don't—we have fewer physicians (2.5/1000 people; OECD average: 3.2/1000), fewer hospital beds (3.1/1000; OECD average: 4.8/1000), and a lower life expectancy (78.7 years; OECD average: 80.1 years). When we compare our 2011 infant mortality rate (6.1 deaths for 1000 live births) with 33 other countries, we rank 32nd—only better than Turkey (7.2/1000) and Mexico (13.6/1000). Salient to the discussion of Walter White, in 2010 the United States experienced more deaths from cancer (193.6/100,000 people) than Mexico (121.0/100,000), Switzerland (181.5/100,000), Finland (182.5/100,000), Japan (186.1/100,000), Sweden (189.1/100,000), and Israel (189.2/100,000), and was barely better than Korea (193.7/100,000). Very clearly there is room for improvement.

Health Care Reform and the Affordable Care Act

The Patient Protection and Affordable Care Act (ACA) was a compromise measure passed by Congress in 2010. It was a continuation of a larger effort to modify health care delivery in the United States (dating back to Medicare's enactment in 1965), and has proven to be a polarizing law. It is important to note that this essay is being written after the passage of the ACA, but within a volatile political framework. Since the legislation was ruled constitutional in 2012, there have been 50 votes in the United States House of Representatives to repeal, defund, or dismantle the Affordable Care Act (as of this writing in May 2014). It is uncertain what the immediate future holds—it is entirely possible that a shift in Congressional or White House administration could put the law in peril, potentially revoking part or all of it. Further, the implementation timeline initially proposed by the law has been altered several times, making it unclear exactly how much of the law will be implemented by what date. Given this uncertainty, it is useful to consider the framework existing before the ACA was approved, as it could potentially be the framework to which the United States returns.

The philosophical goals of the ACA are two-fold: the law aims to extend coverage to the millions of Americans who are currently without insurance, and it aims to slow the increasing costs of health care delivery. While the law contains many elements that have not created significant social controversy (e.g., elimination of lifetime coverage caps, increased funding of children's health insurance programs, preventing new insurance policies from discriminating against those with pre-existing medical conditions, and creating a mechanism that rewards quality over quantity of care for Medicare patients), the biggest touchstone issue is the mandate for citizens to obtain health care insurance. There is strong political and social opposition to the mandate, typically from more socially conservative or libertarian Americans, who argue that it is fundamentally unfair to require them to purchase a good that they feel should be voluntary. A compelling argument against this position is found in Menzel, who notes that market failure requires health insurance mandates to make the privatized system tenable. We have known for decades that people get the extended social and medical benefits of living in a healthier society even if they elect not to purchase health care.[32] To avoid this social leeching—a principle that ought to appeal to libertarian theorists of social justice—we remove the voluntary element of paying for health care. By forcing "freeloaders" back into the risk-pool, we can avoid cost-shifting, remove lifetime caps on coverage, and make health care more affordable for those who need it most.[33] This will reduce overall health care poverty as a result. Further a compelling philosophical case can be made that following personal preferences is not always the best course of action, and that circumstances can arise when personal choices can be overridden when they conflict with other personal long-term goals—it may be the case that we have an obligation *not* to let people do what they want in order to help them to reach their goals.[34] Since people normally would not want to be crippled by health care costs, we might require them to act against their short term interests.

There is some question as to whether these benefits will really obtain, however—some studies have suggested that while the ACA will reduce the number of uninsured, it may leave many without insurance or simply be shifting some people into underinsurance.[35] Part of the ACA's plan is an expansion of Medicaid, and states have been cutting benefits and exploring options to increase cost-sharing by Medicaid recipients. This is especially problematic in the southern United States, whose states generally have refused the Medicaid expansion and are less generous with its benefits.[36] It remains to be seen how the ACA will change the medical and social landscapes in the next few years, but it is reasonable to expect these trends to continue. Despite these concerns, there is compelling reason to believe that the ACA represents a positive step towards universal coverage, as it is the first significant effort to alleviate health care poverty in decades. While health care in the United States is better now than in the pre–ACA era, there are some who argue that it does not go far enough in providing universal coverage.

Providing Universal Coverage

Calling back to the discussion of a right to health care, there is clearly legitimate basis for the claim that societies have an obligation to meet the health care needs of their citizens. How it goes about doing so, however, allows for variation. Broadly speaking, there are three main mechanisms by which most industrialized nations have provided for the health and well-being of their citizens: single payer systems, two-tier systems, and insurance mandates.

Single-payer systems have a central source of government funding for health care, but may require their citizens to make copayments or carry coinsurance for particular services. Examples of single-payer systems include Canada, Finland, Iceland, Italy, Japan, Norway, Portugal, Slovenia, Spain, and the UK. With the money coming from a single source, there tends to be significantly less administrative costs involved. A major contributor to the cost of health care in the United States is due to excessive administration—it is estimated that at least one-quarter of our current spending is due to the paperwork needed by public and private insurance providers.[37] Health care costs in the United States are expected to surpass $3 trillion, which translates into $750 billion spent solely on paperwork instead of actual patient care. Single-payer advocates in the United States argue that much of this money could be saved by modeling our overall health care after other federal programs like Medicare, which has a significantly lower administrative cost. Single-payer systems seem to offer other strengths that are not present in the U.S.'s mandated system, namely greater horizontal and vertical equity (horizontal equity refers to idea that people with the same medical needs should receive the same level of health care resources; vertical equity refers to prioritizing the people who need it most (e.g., those with significantly greater disadvantages)).[38] There are some concerns about delays in care in some single-payer systems,[39] and it will be important to see how care might be streamlined if it is eventually implemented in the United States. There is some experimentation with alternative strategies of paying for health care (such as Vermont's functional single-payer plan), but these are isolated cases and not yet indicative of a new trend.

Two-tier systems are those in which a basic level of care (for instance, catastrophic care) is provided, but citizens are encouraged or required to purchase additional supplemental insurance. Countries with two-tier systems of health care delivery include Australia, Denmark, France, Ireland, Israel, the Netherlands, and New Zealand. Two-tier systems seem to offer some competitive advantages—they encourage some level of cost-sharing (and hence, the possibility of prudent health resource utilization), while providing for individuals' basic needs. The two-tier system would seem to draw from the strengths of both single-payer and competitive health care systems, allowing individuals greater freedom to tailor their health care delivery. This does seem to allow for individuals to receive different levels of care, which would call into question whether there is true horizontal or vertical equity—supplemental insurance may open up particular health care resources to population A that might not be available to population B, which could undermine health care equity and opportunity.[40]

Health care mandates refer to a system in which the government requires its citizens to purchase health care from private companies, as we currently have in the United States. The list of private insurers is not necessarily set—that will vary internationally with some being more restrictive than others. Some countries simply require citizens to have insurance and confine the federal role to one of regulation and enforcement. Countries with mandated insurance include Austria, Belgium, Germany, Greece, Korea, and Luxembourg. Insurers are barred from refusing to cover individuals with pre-existing conditions, but their risks are minimized by requiring everyone to take part in it. This level of universal coverage seems to place the largest onus on the patient, in that it explicitly maintains and relies upon a system of health care financing that is explicitly adversarial (as noted above in the discussion of market failure).

It is possible to compare across systems—for instance, at least one major study has explored horizontal equity in Manhattan, Paris, and London (representing insurance mandates, two-tiered, and single-payer systems, respectively).[41] Overall, Manhattan fared the worst of the three, while Paris achieved the best horizontal equity in terms of primary and specialty health care service use. Thus, it would seem that there is reason to believe that we could be doing better—both France and the UK spend less than we do, but achieve better health equity. Simply put, it isn't enough to make sure that people have insurance—we must ensure that we are addressing the underlying socioeconomic health inequities by providing a safety net as well.[42]

This evidence suggests that health care reform like the Affordable Care Act is necessary, but that we are not yet where we need to be. Mandated insurance as a delivery mechanism for universal coverage is better than the market failure we endured before, but clearly there are better solutions. Every OECD country with a single-payer or two-tier system experiences longer lives and spends less money than we do. Our system is not where we need it to be, medically or morally. We have too much inequity in our care.

Whether our goal ought to be some variation on a single-payer system or a two-tier system will be the question for the next phase of health care reform, but the lesson is clear: we don't get the best return on our health care dollar, and we should look at other delivery systems if we want our health care system to be stronger. The United States health care system failed Walter White and his family, as it fails tens of millions of people every year. This cannot be the best the United States can hope for, and if we do not recognize this failing and take the necessary steps to correct it, we are morally complicit in these deaths. *Breaking Bad* was an amazing television show, and it would be better for us all if it were only fiction.

Notes

1. Carmen, DeNavas-Walt, Bernadette D. Proctor, Jessica C. Smith, and U.S. Census Bureau, "Income, Poverty, and Health Insurance Coverage in the United States: 2012," in *Current Population Reports*, 60–245 (Washington, D.C.: U.S. Government Printing Office, 2013).

2. Robert W. Seifert and Mark Rukavina, "Bankruptcy is the tip of a medical-debt iceberg," *Health Affairs* 25 (2006): w89-w92.

3. It's important to note that Walter is not the only character who suffers with financial problems due to medical care. In the third season, his brother-in-law Hank is grievously injured and in need of care above and beyond what his insurance provides. Like Walter, he is underinsured, as the level of care to which he has access initially will address his medical issues but not at a level that will reliably return him to function. The best outcomes will cost tens of thousands of dollars out-of-pocket, well beyond the means of Hank and his immediate family. His long and arduous rehabilitation only happens as a result of Skyler offering to pay for the additional care using the money

Walter earns through cooking methamphetamines. Hank's injury and recovery are integral to the plot in Season Four, when he uses this down time to look over evidence that leads him to discover the local methamphetamine distribution ring (ultimately leading him to Walter himself).

4. American Cancer Society, *Cancer Facts & Figures 2014* (Atlanta: American Cancer Society, 2014).

5. American Cancer Society, *Cancer Facts & Figures 2014*; Winson Y. Cheung, et al., "Analysis of Wait Times and Costs During the Peri-Diagnostic Period for Non-Small Cell Lung Cancer," *Lung Cancer* 72 (2011): 125–131.

6. Jiemin, Ma, Elizabeth M. Ward, Robert Smith, and Ahmedin Jemal, "Annual Number of Lung Cancer Deaths Potentially Avertable by Screening in the United States," *Cancer* 119 (April 2013): 1381–1385.

7. American Cancer Society, *Cancer Facts & Figures 2014*.

8. John Rawls, *A Theory of Justice* (Cambridge: Harvard University Press, 1971).

9. Robert Nozick, *Anarchy, State, and Utopia* (New York: Basic Books, 1977).

10. It is important to remember that after Walter disclosed his cancer diagnosis, he received offers of assistance both from his brother-in-law Hank as well as his former business partner (who offered to rehire him with both a higher salary and better insurance benefits to help with the costs of chemotherapy). These were clearly disadvantageous choices per the libertarian model.

11. Michelle Chandler, "The Rights of the Medically Uninsured: An Analysis of Social Justice and Disparate Health Outcomes," *Journal of Health & Social Policy* 21, no. 3 (2006): 17–36.

12. Paul T. Menzel, "The Cultural Moral Right to a Basic Minimum of Accessible Health Care," *Kennedy Institute of Ethics Journal* 21, no. 1 (2011): 79–119.

13. Kathleen Stoll, *Paying a Premium: The Added Cost of Care for the Uninsured* (Washington, D.C.: Families USA, 2005).

14. Immanuel Kant, *Critique of Pure Reason* trans. by Norman Kemp Smith (London: Macmillan, 1983).

15. Hema Magge, Howard J. Cabral, Lewis E. Kazis, and Benjamin D. Sommers "Prevalence and Predictors of Underinsurance Among Low-Income Adults," *Journal of General Internal Medicine* 28, no. 9 (2013): 1136–1142.

16. Lisa Raiz, "Health Care Poverty," *Journal of Sociology and Social Welfare* 33, no. 4 (2006): 87–104.

17. Magge et al., "Prevalence and Predictors of Underinsurance Among Low-Income Adults," 2013; Raiz, "Health Care Poverty."

18. Andrew Ward, "The Concept of Underinsurance: A General Topology," *Journal of Medicine and Philosophy* 31 (2006): 499–531.

19. Shana Alex Lavarreda, E. Richard Brown, and Claudie Dandurand Bolduc, "Underinsurance in the United States: An Interaction of Costs to Consumers, Benefit Design, and Access to Care," *Annual Review of Public Health* 32 (2011): 471–482.

20. Robert W. Seifert and Mark Rukavina, "Bankruptcy Is the Tip of a Medical-Debt Iceberg," *Health Affairs* 25 (2006): w89-w92.

21. Seifert and Rukavina, "Bankruptcy Is the Tip of a Medical-Debt Iceberg."

22. Cathy Schoen, Sara R. Collins, Jennifer L. Kriss, and Michelle M. Doty, "How Many Are Underinsured? Trends Among U.S. Adults, 2003 and 2007," *Health Affairs* 102 (2008): w298-w309.

23. Quite obviously this reflects the framework before the ACA and mandated coverage. We do see, however, a large number of individuals expressing a preference to pay the annual fine for not carrying insurance rather than signing on to a plan (1 in 3, according to a Gallup poll, http://www.gallup.com/poll/165500/uninsured-americans-unfamiliar-health-exchanges.aspx, accessed February 27, 2014), which is comparable in both spirit and practice.

24. J. Michael McWilliams, "Health Consequences of Uninsurance Among Adults in the United States: Recent Evidence and Implications," *The Milbank Quarterly* 87, no. 2 (2009): 443–494; Paul T. Menzel, "The Cultural Moral Right to a Basic Minimum of Accessible Health Care," *Kennedy Institute of Ethics Journal* 21, no. 1 (2011): 79–119; Paul T. Menzel, "Justice and Fairness: A Critical Element in U.S. Health System Reform," *Journal of Law, Medicine, & Ethics* 40, no. 3 (2012): 582–597.

25. Families USA, *Cost-Sharing in Medicaid: It's Not about "Skin in the Game"—It's about Lives on the Line* (Washington, D.C.: Families USA, 2005).

26. Schoen et al., "How many are underinsured? Trends among U.S. Adults, 2003 and 2007."

27. J. Michael McWilliams, "Health Consequences of Uninsurance Among Adults in the United States: Recent Evidence and Implications."

28. Jon R. Gabel, Roland McDevitt, Ryan Lore, Jeremy Pickreign, Heidi Whitmore, and Tina Ding, "Trends in Underinsurance and the Affordability of Employer Coverage, 2004–2007," *Health Affairs* 28, no. 4 (2009): w595-w606.

29. Keziah Cook, David Dranove, and Andrew Sfekas, "Does Major Illness Cause Financial Catastrophe?" *Health Services Research* 45, no. 2 (2010): 418–436.

30. Thomas Bodenheimer, "High and Rising Health Care Costs. Part 1: Seeking an Explanation," *Annals of Internal Medicine* 142 (2005): 847–854; Thomas Bodenheimer, "High and Rising Health Care Costs. Part 2: Technologic Innovation," *Annals of Internal Medicine* 142 (2005): 932–937.

31. Accessed February 27, 2014, from the OECD Health Data website (http://www.oecd.org/health/health-systems/oecdhealthdata.htm).

32. Michael Marmot, *The Status Syndrome: How Social Standing Affects Our Health and Longevity* (New York: Holt Paperbacks, 2005); Richard G. Wilkinson, *Unhealthy Societies: The Afflictions of Inequality* (New York: Routledge, 1996).

33. McWilliams, "Health Consequences of Uninsurance Among Adults in the United States: Recent Evidence and Implications;" Menzel, "The Cultural Moral

Right to a Basic Minimum of Accessible Health Care;" Menzel, "Justice and Fairness: A Critical Element in U.S. Health System Reform."

34. Sarah Conly, *Against Autonomy: Justifying Coercive Paternalism* (Cambridge: Cambridge University Press, 2013).

35. Kevin M. Gorey, et al., "Better Colon Cancer Care for Extremely Poor Canadian Women Compared with American Women," *Health & Social Work* 38, no. 4 (2013): 240–248; Steffie Woolhandler and David U. Himmelstein, "Life or Debt: Underinsurance in America," *Journal of General Internal Medicine* 28, no. 9 (2013): 1122–1124.

36. Magge, et al., "Prevalence and Predictors of Underinsurance Among Low-Income Adults."

37. Bodenheimer, "High and Rising Health Care Costs. Part 2: Technologic Innovation."

38. Ahmed M. Bayoumi, "Equity and Health Services," *Journal of Public Health Policy* 30 (2009): 176–182; Kevin M. Gorey, et al. "Better Colon Cancer Care for Extremely Poor Canadian Women Compared with American Women," *Health & Social Work* 38, no. 4 (2013): 240–248; Rajan Ragupathy, Katri Aaltonen, June Tordoff, Pauline Norris, and David Reith, "A 3-Dimensional View of Access to Licensed and Subsidized Medicines Under Single-Payer Systems in the U.S., the UK, Australia, and New Zealand," *Pharmacoeconomics* 30, no. 11 (2012): 1051–1065.

39. Cheung, "Analysis of Wait Times and Costs During the Peri-Diagnostic Period for Non-Small Cell Lung Cancer."

40. Lynn A. Blewett, "Persistent Disparities in Access to Care Across Health Care Systems," *Journal of Health Politics, Policy and Law* 34, no. 4 (2009): 635–647.

41. Michael K. Gusmano, Daniel Weisz, and Victor G. Rodwin, "Achieving Horizontal Equity: Must We Have a Single-Payer Health System?" *Journal of Health Politics, Policy and Law* (2009): 617–633.

42. American Cancer Society, *Cancer Facts and Figures 2014*; Bayoumi, "Equity and Health Services;" Blewett, "Persistent Disparities in Access to Care Across Health Care Systems;" Gusmano, Weisz and Rodwin, "Achieving Horizontal Equity: Must We Have a Single-Payer Health System?"

Scientific Ethics and *Breaking Bad*

RON W. DARBEAU

It does not require much of a stretch to argue that a society devoid of laws, bereft of some framework signaling that which is allowed and that which is not, will eventually crumble—imploding upon itself, as the strong make prey of the weak, until only a savage, twisted few remain. Unchecked, lawlessness is a cancer that can feed upon the fabric of a society, disintegrating it into a warped, shadowy form in which the weak are fearful and the strong, entitled. Lawlessness dissolves the bonds of society until it decomposes into something that can no longer be considered a *civil*ization. Laws, however, are anthropogenic constructs—they are ideas made words, agreed upon by those placed in authority, written upon paper and enforced by a system charged with keeping anarchy at bay. Ethics though, are different. Rather than defined, communal lines—crossed at the peril of one's resources, freedom, or life—ethics are arbitrary, malleable ... nebulous. Laws are like electrons orbiting the nucleus in well-defined, Bohrian radii[1] with well-defined energies that are allowed (as Walt, a chemist, would say "quantized"). Ethics, in contrast, are electron clouds— vague, poorly-defined regions of electron density that cannot be contained in nice, neat convenient packages. They are but principles—beliefs that guide the individual or a group of like-minded individuals assembled for a common, mutually beneficial purpose.

Ethics are also the pulse of a society, they are its temperature, they mirror its values and reflect those qualities that a society and its members hold precious. But herein lies a problem—one that exists at the heart of this discussion—because society is comprised of individuals, all of whom are fundamentally flawed, the ethics of a society must, by definition, be flawed as well. For the servant cannot be greater than the master, nor can the image be more beautiful than the object. As a species, we knowingly poison the planet, yet for the sake of convenience, we refuse to take the careful, deliberate steps to repair and reverse our actions. In the face of overwhelming evidence, for naught but the inconvenience of facing an indicting truth, we still debate the validity of climate change and, in utter hubris, we tend to measure time in the scope of our lifespan and often mark as "real" only those things we can observe. Thus, we relegate an event not seen or felt in our lifetime almost as a non-event. In short, as a species, humanity is often conflicted, fickle, and myopic and as a consequence, so too are the ethics we embrace.

A society's ethics are malleable. They may be molded, shaped and reshaped by such agents as geography, time, experiences, and fears. Was it not ethical to keep slaves in ancient Rome? And, until approximately 1825, was it not ethical to do so in the southern United States but not in the north? Has not the fear of "undermining the fabric of our society" made marijuana use, alcohol consumption and pornography "unethical" at various times and places? Yet, as we move along the space-time continuum, we see the ethics of one society differ from those of another, separated by just a few hundred miles even in the very same timeframe and we see the ethics of a given society differ over the course of mere decades. Societal ethics, then, as a compass, are, at best, unreliable. They can be, and often are, mutated by great upsurges of conscience and great moments of desperation and despair. They are inconstant and fickle and, as such, can offer little by way of direction or even rationale because there is no fixed point—the North Star moves and all stars are likely to point north if you give them enough time and space.

Yet, while the broader society is accustomed to, and apparently comfortable with this quagmire of contradiction and uncertainty, there exist segments of the populace to which such disarray does not apply. Among these oases is the scientific profession. Science deals with facts—their acquisition, synthesis, dissemination and use in explaining and predicting natural phenomena. Science owes allegiance just to facts and this central tenet is unaffected by decade, culture, or geography. The Ethos of science is, oddly enough, based upon faith, or perhaps, for those who see a contradiction here, where none exists—scientific ethics are based upon trust. This "trust" exists in a dynamic, linear, bidirectional relationship between end users of science and the tools of science. For example, the scientist slogging away in his lab, *trusts* that the instruments he uses to measure mass or volume or temperature or some other physico-chemical properties are accurate. The supervisor to whom he reports his data *trusts* that her student or employee is using sound principles of chemical analysis and is reporting all of the data honestly. When the data are submitted for publishing, the editor *trusts* that the work is original and conducted in keeping with the strictest codes of scientific conduct and, further, *trusts* that the reviewers he calls upon to examine the work will do so with due diligence. When the work is finally available to the public at large, society *trusts* that the results reflect a vetted, honest, rigorous attempt by qualified professionals using appropriate methodologies to describe the system under study. And yet, while all this assumption of "trust" might make the uninitiated nervous or skeptical, the process inspires a great level of confidence in scientists, employers, funding agencies, etc. For at the heart of this confidence is the understanding that science and its practitioners owe allegiance to no one.

The ethos of science is straightforward and beautiful in its simplicity. Science describes, explains, and predicts natural phenomena. Whether these events and processes are interstellar, atmospheric, biological, mechanical, or chemical, scientists seek to catalog, contextualize, describe, and explain why the world does what it does. In some ways we are puppeteers—placing matter (inanimate or animate) under a wide range of experimental conditions, carefully manipulating variables and taking careful measurements of its behavior. In many ways, though, we are also journalists reporting on natural phenomena from the subatomic levels of quarks[2] and gluons,[3] through the macroscopic level of greenhouse gases and DNA, to the level of billiard balls and the behavior of galaxies. In the search for the truth of the universe, we use the best materials we can, employ the best practices we can, and then use these to stretch the boundaries of our knowledge. We do so recognizing that all knowledge improves our lot and shines a light, however feeble, compelling the darkness of ignorance to retreat before us. One of the most deeply ingrained weaknesses of our species is the fear of the unknown. Science, in the pursuit of truth, simultaneously banishes our fears and brings us closer to being masters of our world rather than slaves to its whims. To be trite, knowledge is power ... to know and understand a thing is to be able to manipulate that thing—whether that thing is DNA, triggers for cancer and Alzheimer's disease, the movement of current in metals and semiconductors, the ozone layer or climate change. Further, it is every scientist's hope that their work—or if the Gods of Science smile down upon them—their contributions and discoveries will influence our quality of life. Chemistry, for example, is the *Science of Change* and like all scientists, chemists harbor hope that our efforts will have an effect on society ... that they will change society. Yet, while we would much prefer that our efforts positively impact society, we recognize and accept that not all change is positive—sometimes change is negative and sometimes, it is both. We also recognize that often, the anticipated value of our work is not always realized and that our results are not used the way we may have imagined. Our contributions are sometimes employed in related applications but, quite often, they manifest in areas well outside the intended sphere of influence. Scientists additionally, are mortal and so not without human vanities. Secretly, or not, we all hope to gain the recognition and respect of our peers for our efforts and perhaps ... just perhaps, to achieve immortality through our contributions— witness the Doppler effect,[4] Newton's laws of motion, Einstein's theory of relativity, the Corey-Posner-Whitesides-House reaction,[5] the Rutherford gold foil experiment,[6] the Watson-Crick model,[7] the Hubble telescope, and yes, even the *Heisenberg* Uncertainty Principle![8]

It is noteworthy too, that for the pursuit of science to be effective in terms of its precision, accuracy and acceptability, the *Scientific Method* is employed. Few aspects of science are as vilified and misrepresented as this simple code. Many express it as a rigorous, restrictive methodology that, in effect, reduces scientists to automatons who plug an idea into one end of the method and collect a result from the other. Nothing could be further from the truth. This narrow, misunderstood, vision ignores the simple fact that scientists bring their own personalities, their own biases, their own passions, their own backgrounds and training into an endeavor and, as such, no two scientists would approach the same problem in exactly the same way. This is why science is enriched by engagement across a broad sociocultural and experiential spectrum. Scientists ask questions and figure out repeatable, rigorous ways to answer them. We raise questions based upon our observations, research what others have done on the topic and learn from their findings. We conceive a tentative idea as to the system's behavior and conduct multiplicate experiments to test our idea—gathering and analyzing data and using the results to reshape and refine our hypotheses. The rigor of this method, of this code, is such that it allows us to pursue the truth to the best of our abilities with diligence, persistence and with no pre-conceived end-point in mind. We pursue this truth wherever it leads us, unencumbered by anything but the honesty of the method and the honesty of the data—its acquisition, its verification, its manipulation, and reporting.

Enter Walter White. In the slow, inexorable demise of our leading character, Walter White transforms from a desperate, well-intentioned father to a ruthless drug kingpin. As he slides, with increasing fervor and decreasing guilt, down the slippery slope from sympathetic protagonist to (insert adjective here) villain, we witness, among other things, the stark distinction between the nebulous ethos embraced by society and the immutable one that defines science. Others in this compendium will, no doubt, discuss the unethical nature of the manufacture and distribution of drugs, the violence associated with establishing and protecting a drug empire, the DEA's attempt to cripple Heisenberg's network, and the meth-heads' attempts to obtain funds to secure their next fix. Yet others will, no doubt, lament the corruption of a scientist unethically using his skills for the demise of society rather than for its benefit. Some will bemoan the treachery of a high school teacher, entrusted with the sacred and honorable duty of engaging and stimulating young minds instead laying them to waste with the very tool meant to enrich them. Walt will be demonized as a shallow, myopic, hypocrite who churns forth poison by the gigagram[9]—all to corrupt the youth of Albuquerque, and far, far beyond, while trying to protect his own children. He will be cast as a social vampire who unapologetically, almost joyfully, sucks the lifeblood of society—its youth and its resources—leaving in its wake the dead and those who are, one way or the other, slaves to him (repeat customers, law enforcement obsessed with him, etc.). I leave all of the self-righteous, self-indulgent, psychobabble to the pundits to attempt to tag a moving target with independently mobile crosshairs ... to pinpoint a man standing on shifting sand, to judge the actions of a man by a code as constant as a tide, and I wish them all good luck. Instead, my attempt will be to view Walt's actions through the lens of science, to examine neither his reasons nor his decisions, not even the contexts in which they were made, but his actions concerned with the synthesis of his "product." The intent is to focus solely upon his actions inside of the lab—from the RV to Gus Fring's immaculate sub–Laundromat haven, to homes in suburban Albuquerque. Stripping away all of the extraneous sociocultural matters then, and drilling down to the central matter at hand, the questions to be asked and answered in this context, then are: "Did Walt exhibit good scientific ethics?" and "Was Walt's conduct in keeping with the traditions of scientific investigation?"

So ... what do we do when an unknown pathogen with a short incubation period and a 100 percent fatality rate springs up in our midst? What do we do when we need new, effective sources of energy, or clean air and water? What do we do when we want plants to grow in arid areas, or grow out of season or resist pests? Or, perhaps, closer to the topic at hand, what do we do when trapped in the middle of the Arizona desert, in blistering heat, with no water, no communication and hundreds of miles away from help? The answer to each and all of these questions ... call a scientist (or hope you have one with you). In the episode "4 Days Out,"[10] Jesse and Walt after a prolonged cook, produce more than $1.3 million worth of product. But, in typical Jesse style, he has run down the battery by leaving the keys in the ignition for days. Ok, this is bad, but it is not a major problem. Walt (like the average person would have done) pulls out the generator and tries to jump start the battery in the RV. Unfortunately, the battery catches fire and Jesse douses it with the only water they have. Ok, this is worse, but have no fear, the scientist is here. Walt (unlike what the average person would have done) isolates the commutator unit[11] from the generator and begins cranking away and he and Jesse take turns building enough power for a trickle charge to the battery. The ignition turns over but doesn't catch, and desperation sinks in ... they lie down in failure and contemplate their mortality. Ok, so, at this point, the situation is the worst case scenario—this is when hope is lost and panic and despair set in. Eventually, Jesse turns to Walt "...think of something scientific!" he pleads. "How 'bout you take some of these chemicals and mix up some rocket fuel, that way you can send up a signal flare, or make some kind of robot to get us help, or, a homing device or build a new battery. Or what if we take some of the stuff off the RV and build it into something completely different, like a dune buggy?" Jesse, of course, has no idea if any of these things is feasible and he generously and unwittingly mixes ideas that are possible with those that are improbable and impossible. But Walt identifies a path forward and pursues it—building a simple battery complete with a cathode of mercuric oxide and graphite, an anode of zinc and an electrolyte of potassium hydroxide. He tries to engage Jesse in the process but his apprentice looks on in complete ignorance missing even the simple prompt "...and what particular element comes to mind ... [that we] would ... use to conduct this beautiful electricity?" he asks waving the copper wire as a hint. "Ahh..." begins Jesse "...wire." Walt ignores the fact that wire is not an element, informs Jesse that the correct response is copper, and forges ahead to answer the need and save their lives. The situation in this episode is a microcosm of the role of science and scientists in our lives. For, regardless of whether it is fundamental or applied, science provides a vector by which its practitioners are empowered to answer the call to improve our lives. In many, many tangible ways they stand between society and discomfort, disease, and despair, recognizing that while all of society are end users of our labor, the vast majority doesn't fathom how we do what we do. "Build a battery" they plead, then close their eyes or blankly leave them open and disengage, while the magic happens and we pull the rabbit out of the hat, again and again.

One of my favorite movies is *Jurassic Park* ... the first one. The story is rich and endearing and the special effects are stunning even by today's standard. Yet the one peeve I harbor with this movie is in the scene where the mathematician played by Jeff Goldblum berates the park's creator for pursuing the dinosaur-making technology (the whole bit about extracting DNA from blood consumed by mosquitoes and splicing in frog DNA to cover the missing pieces.) He says something to the effect that "the problem is that the Park's scientists didn't earn the knowledge themselves. They read what others had done and stood on their shoulders, taking their knowledge to the next level. They were too busy asking themselves if they *could* do it and too little asking themselves if they *should*." What drivel! What utter nonsense! Ever so often, science will advance in huge leaps because of a major contribution, observation or finding—a falling apple, elements being lined up by atomic numbers,[12] finches on the Galapagos Islands,[13] red-shifting of light from distant galaxies.[14] But, what the public still does not fathom is that far more commonly, science inches forward, pushed and pulled by the plebeians slogging away in little nondescript laboratories (in RVs, under Laundromats and in suburban houses in Albuquerque, for example). Those small gains are made possible by standing on the shoulders of predecessors and peers—for we are a family, supporting each other and moving forward together to expand our knowledge.

A scientist cannot afford to question what a society does or will do with his or her findings. That is neither in the job description nor in the zip code of their pay grade. Should we never have effected *l*ight *a*mplification by the *s*timulated *e*mission of *r*adiation (laser) because of its credible use as a weapon? Tell that to all those who now have 20/20 vision and freedom from cataracts or whose recovery from more effective, non-scalpel surgery is faster and more pain-free. Should we have abandoned nuclear fission or stem cell research because of the risk of their use as weapons? Tell that to those states whose energy costs are low or to those families having loved ones returned to them from death's doorstep from some disease affecting one in every million. It is not the responsibility of a single scientist or even of a group of scientists to decide the course of human civilization. We discover things, we discover newer, better ways of making things and in the process, we add arrows to the quiver, we add ammunition to the weapons used to battle those things that afflict us. The first and only duty of a scientist is to the truth ... to the relentless pursuit of that truth wherever it might lead us. Our duty as scientists is not to guess at the influence of our work on society. It is to offer our work to humanity and leave mankind to decide what to do with it—leave them free to use our findings to destroy, to build or, quite frankly, to do both. Knowing that civilization could benefit tremendously from our discoveries, from our improvements, from our efforts, we toil away in fervent hope that our species will use our gifts for the greater good. For we recognize that neither we, nor mankind, would benefit from the cessation of our efforts or from our own self-imposed censure. Simply put: would we as a society have benefitted more from a German "watchmaker"-*cum*-patent clerk, rather than from the unbridled genius of Albert Einstein?[15]

In *Breaking Bad*, Walt uses his considerable chemical expertise to design and execute a novel synthetic scheme to produce methamphetamine. Now, having not seen Walt's "process" (and as an organic chemist myself, I must confess to having sketched out quite a few potential options on napkins now conveniently hidden away for safe keeping just in case my circumstances change catastrophically and *Breaking Bad* becomes *Breaking Real*) I can only guess at the approach. But, there are several points to be made here. First, a novel synthetic process was developed. Perhaps it used different chemical reagents than the classical schemes or, perhaps, the same reagents were used, but the solvents were different. Or maybe, even with the same reagents and solvents, the sequence, temperatures, pressures and lengths of times in which the classical chemicals were combined, differed. Perhaps Walt used the same reagents and solvents but different catalysts were placed in strategic points along the reaction pathway. Who knows? (Though it does lead one to speculate that perhaps the series creator, Vince Gilligan, might well have his own napkins squirreled away for any Bad Times, and the program we so dearly love was really a roadmap, a foreshadowing ... a virtual mulligan).[16] The net result is that Walt's novel efforts gave rise to the coveted "Blue Sky or Big Blue" at a staggering 99.1 percent purity, beating out absolutely everything else on the market (both here and especially abroad) by miles. The show does a good job of impressing upon its audience that what Walt did was absolutely stunning. That his competitors sought to remove his product from the market and him from the business were indicators of both Blue Sky's appeal and Walt's perceived lack of respect (su falta de respeto). That Declan, an accomplished meth trafficker himself, agreed to suspend his own lucrative operation, to "give up [his] cook" just to become a distributor in Walt's empire for 35 percent of the take, speaks volumes. For when 35 percent of the profit from the sale of x is better than 100 percent of the profit from the sale of Y, then x must be vastly superior. And, indeed it was: 99.1 percent purity ("The New York Yankees") vs. 70 percent purity ("grade school tee-ball") or perhaps the better analogy: "classic Coke" vs "just some tepid, off-brand, generic cola."[17] Walt's process was of such quality and novelty that the Mexican cartel, rather than extinguishing Fring for his disobedience and unwillingness to yield, chose instead to corner him into providing them with a "cook" of their own—for even they didn't "really wanna live in a world without Coca Cola." Let's not even get started on how Lydia's export of Blue Sky to Europe affected consumers there. Surely the need for a separate storage facility just to house a humongous pile of cash, a pile big enough to dwarf even Huell Babineaux (and upon which he could take a weird, orgasmic-looking power nap)[18] is confirmation that Walt's process and the product it yielded was in Tuco Salamanca's words "tight, tight, tight!"[19]

So what is the lesson so far? It is that the scientist in Walt, recognized that the methamphetamine being bandied about by Jesse, *et al*, in Season One was of poor quality. It was laced with crap like talc and chili powder. So, having identified the problem, he set about the meticulous task of creating a superior process that would produce a purer material. Granted, many of the original cooks took place in the infamous RV, but, truly the venue was beyond his control. Fortunately, however, good science can occur anywhere. What Walt did not do, was compromise the integrity of the chemistry being conducted by using either sub-standard reagents or inappropriate equipment and glassware. He procured the materials and apparatus that his process required, ensuring that his work would be of good quality. Without the infrastructure, ventilation and personal protective equipment that was required, Walt obtained and used respirators and aprons to be employed during the cooks. He took on Jesse as an apprentice, elevating him to the status of arguably the second best meth cook in the world, in much the same way as a Ph.D. mentor lifts and molds a fledgling, bumbling, first year graduate student to the level of "doctor." Consider the fact that Walt successfully transferred his knowledge and expertise to a junkie who could likely not even spell "chemistry." Indeed, he should be commended for imparting such expertise and alacrity to Pinkman that his young apprentice was able to duplicate the process independently and with such skill and bravado as to dress down and humble that stuck-up chemist, south of the border, giving him a convincing tongue lashing for the poor state in which he kept the lab. In one of my many favorite scenes, when the chemist in question, (played by Carlo Rota) dressed in his pristine, buttoned, white lab coat asks Jesse, "Who do you think you are?" Jesse, now with months of experience behind him making product in the ultra–90 percent range, replies with bluster: "I'm the guy your boss brought here to teach you how it's done. You're lucky he hasn't fired your ass. Now, if you don't want that to happen, I suggest you stop whining like a little bitch and do as I say!"[20] And, more importantly, all bluster aside, Walt taught Jesse well enough that under even trying conditions, with his safety in doubt, his ability to return to the U.S. in question, in an unfamiliar lab, and with many watching his every move and some, no doubt, secretly wishing him to fail, he was able to produce "Heisenberg-level" product—even though the phenylacetic acid was not to be found in the familiar "barrel with the B on it." I would submit then that, at least through the lens of science, Walt's search for a better synthetic process and a purer product, unadulterated with additives and diluents, was in keeping with the highest code of scientific ethics. I also submit that his insistence upon using the very best materials and appropriate glassware and apparatus was, likewise a check in the "good scientist" column. Additionally, his effective mentoring of his young student ought to earn Mr. White earnest kudos as a scientist for communicating the information and propagating the skill set.

The episode "Fly"[21] used to be one of my least favorites. I thought it uncharacteristically pedantic and, at some points, even bordering on the ridiculous. And yet, as I revisited the episodes (only for the purpose of writing this essay, you understand) I realized, on more mature reflection, that I had missed a great deal of nuance the first time around. I realized too, that this single episode, perhaps beyond all the others, highlighted two central arguments regarding Walt's adherence to the principles of scientific ethics. Firstly, in keeping with the purity of the pursuit of excellence, a good scientist is required to identify, control and manipulate any and all variables that affect the outcome of the endeavor; they must adhere carefully to established protocols to ensure consistently high quality control. And secondly, scientists are required to identify any and all inconsistencies in their data and to vigorously and thoroughly pursue their elimination until the data show the reproducibility demanded at the highest level. And, really, "Fly" brilliantly demonstrates Walt's commitment to both these guiding principles.

After every cook, Walt and Jesse meticulously cleaned and scrubbed the lab equipment removing all impurities and prepping the equipment for the next day's cook. The intent here is clearly to ensure clean workspaces and equipment so that the risk of contamination of the next batch is low. I won't dwell on this matter much except to say that this activity illustrates Walt's pursuit of excellence and his intimate involvement in even the gritty, less romantic parts of chemistry—that of keeping the work area and equipment in pristine condition. In fact, it is this training that empowers Jesse to confront Carlo Rota's character later on and insist that all of the equipment and surfaces in the lab be cleaned *before* the cook. Indeed, had that group lived past Fring's treachery, the experience would have cemented the value of eliminating contaminants (= variables) from the exercise, in the quest for perfection. As "Fly" progressed, Walt discovers a fly in the sub-laundromat superlab and much of the rest of the episode revolves around his comical, somewhat disturbing obsession with the creature's demise. He spends the entire night pursuing the demon-bug and upon Jesse's return the next day, even insists upon halting the process mid-cook and resorts to locking the frustrated Jesse out of the lab shouting, "If you're not gonna help me, stay out of my way!" Now, I grant you that this behavior is a bit extreme. Walt's over-zealous passion for the consistency of his product was, no doubt, fuelled by the stress he was feeling in his personal life at the time and the confluence of the two matters took a somewhat toxic turn. Nonetheless, the central idea here is Walt's relentless pursuit of quality control by eliminating the fly variable.

This episode also shows Walt's intimate familiarity with his process and its idiosyncrasies, its ebbs and flows. When he discovers that the yields are consistently short, he leaves no stone unturned in trying to identify why that is the case. He shrugs off Jesse's suggestions of "spillage," "evaporation" and "condensation" and briefly entertains, albeit reluctantly, the possibility of "vestiges" (essentially leftovers) being responsible for it. But, in reality, he secretly concludes that they could not be accountable for the discrepancy. This is a scientist who understands his system well enough to recognize when a problem is extraneous to the system, when it is not endemic to the system. He determines then, that the fault does not lie in the methodology, but in the human element … in Jesse, and gives his protégé the chilling warning about the consequences that would arise if Gus found out that Jesse was skimming product.

So, where are we now on Walter White's scientific ethics? Could we agree to the following elements? Indictment #1: That recognizing a need and a problem, he developed a superior process for the production of a material with exceedingly superior quality to replace the poor predecessor already being marketed. Indictment #2: That he employed the best materials and the best equipment at his disposal to produce his product. Indictment #3: That he ensured reproducible quality and quantity by diligently controlling all experimental variables (including abiotic ones like dirty glassware, workspaces and vats, and biotic ones like Jesse and hell spawn flies). Indictment #4: That he successfully communicated his methodology—training two protégés and raising at least one of them to international prominence. Indictment #5: That, overall, he demonstrated passion and respect for his chemistry—the product and the process by which it was manufactured.

I am a *Star Trek*[22] fan. I have loved everything *Star Trek* since I was six years old. And, as I have matured, both as an individual and as a scientist, I have grown to recognize that my affinity with the series lies especially with the philosophy and science of Roddenberry's masterpiece and not so much with the soap operas in space. As such, I make the clear distinction between being a "trekker" and a "trekkie"—largely because I neither salivate at the prospect of attending a SciFi convention, nor go to work in full dress uniform, pips and all, armed with a phaser on the chance encounter with a treacherous Romulan[23] or one of those freakishly annoying Tribbles![24] My point here, is that I recognize that no matter how compelling and engaging a TV show is, it is just that—a TV show. There exists a clear line of demarcation between fiction and reality. That being said, however, some of the finer nuances of the dichotomy between scientific ethics and societal ethics that played out in *Breaking Bad* are not without parallel in real world situations.

In 1933, Leo Szilard, who had conceived the idea of a nuclear chain reaction a few years before, patented the concept of a nuclear reactor with Enrico Fermi. Six years later, news had reached Szilard that Nazi Germany had made significant progress in harnessing the awesome power of his concept into a weapon of mass destruction. Szilard penned a correspondence to President Franklin Roosevelt warning him of the disastrous global consequences if Germany was to succeed in this endeavor and convinced the preeminent scientist of the day, none other than Albert Einstein, to cosign the now infamous Einstein-Szilard letter. In it, they urged the President to accelerate U.S. research toward production of their own atomic weapon. Roosevelt recognizing the danger, commissioned the Manhattan Project under General Leslie Groves. The brilliant and multi-talented, J. Robert Oppenheimer, a gifted teacher and an equally gifted research physicist and administrator, was charged with leading the Project which began in earnest in June 1942. By July 1945 a small prototype of the bomb was successfully detonated and, less than a month later, its much bigger brothers were dropped on Hiroshima and Nagasaki. The rest, as they say ... is history.

Many of the scientists involved in any phase of the Manhattan Project were never the same after 1945. Szilard and Einstein harbored deep regret at their involvement in its catalysis. Oppenheimer himself struggled with his role and lamented his myopia—he blamed himself for being so focused on creating something new and winning the race against the Nazis, that the human collateral had never entered his mind, not until that collateral was evaporated and poisoned on a scale unparalleled in human history. But, what would have happened if Szilard had not gone to Einstein, or if Einstein had not lent the weight of his reputation to the letter? Would Roosevelt have acted so quickly, or at all? What if Oppenheimer and the hundreds of scientists had the benefit of foresight and chose to remove themselves from the equation, deciding that the conflict of conscience was too weighty to bear? How would the fate of the world have been shaped? There can be little doubt that the Nazis would have found a way to weaponize nuclear fission, and it is also almost certain that they would have deployed the bomb to demonstrate their superiority and might. In so doing they surely would have completed their subjugation of Europe and who knows if their appetite would have been satisfied there? So what of Szilard, Einstein, Oppenheimer et al., then? These men are considered reluctant heroes, moral casualties of World War II. Had they not acted as they did ... how would they have been viewed? What's the phrase? "All that is needed for evil to triumph, is that good men do nothing."

Let us focus for a minute on Oppenheimer and his league of physicists and engineers working diligently at Los Alamos. Let us agree to stipulate, for the record, that their pursuit of nuclear fission as an effective energy source satisfies most, if not all, of the indictments we leveled four paragraphs earlier at good ol' Walt. Thus, let us accept that they exhibited good scientific ethics. With respect to societal ethics, however, this was a "damned if you do, damned if you don't" scenario. For either way, they are monsters—those who by their actions facilitated butchery, or those who by their inactions allowed butchery to occur. Had the scientists at Los Alamos refused to pursue the technology and to do so under the best scientific codes to ensure its effectiveness, we would have demonized them, one and all, as those SOB's who had the ability to do something, to actually save the world from tyranny—but stood by and did nothing. And now, we secretly wonder on whose hands does all that blood lie, whose souls have to answer for the lost dreams, the lost loves, the lost lives? That much blood cannot be washed away, and the ghosts of those many lost dreams and shattered lives cannot be banished. Does the impossibility of their situation resonate with the reader yet? If so, be very clear, that such impossibility is far too often the case for scientists. Consider stem cell research, genetic manipulation, the pursuit of nuclear fusion, the pursuit of AI (artificial intelligence) and the list goes on, and on, and on. Work in all of these fields and many, many more, stands to revolutionize our world, but they can do so for good or for ill. The world needs scientists to do the things that we do ... science is the engine that drives society—but it is not our task to steer the car, just to power it. And, while we are the only ones who give birth to new technologies, new processes and new products, we cannot also be their caretaker. Once the Pandora's box is open, our stewardship of our discoveries ceases ... it must. We are torn then, between the impulse to pursue discovery to the farthest reaches possible, and the impulse to be good citizens of society.

To which impulse then, should scientists hearken? Whose lead should they follow? To which label should we adhere ... hero or monster, butcher or butcher? The answer then is as simple, as it is inevitable ... we follow no leads but the ones the data suggest. We listen to no voice, save the one that pushes us towards scientific truth. We do not choose the label "hero" or "monster," instead, we choose door number three ... "scientist." Our labors are neither moral, nor immoral ... they are amoral. We do not scrutinize our actions through the lens of societal ethics, but through those of scientific ethics. Our toil cannot be subject to the whims of a society that cannot make up its mind, that is fickle, that cannot understand us or what we do, that craves and depends upon our offerings, but is quick to turn around to sit in judgment of us and our contributions when it is this very society that uses our efforts destructively. This is the equivalent of someone buying an iPhone, hurtling it at their new iMac, destroying all of their saved files and contacts then turning around and suing Apple for pain and suffering ... and winning! But, scientists recognize that we serve two masters—the one that drives us to create, and the one to whom our creations ultimately belong. The one is constant and faithful like a lighthouse in a raging tempest, and the other *is* the tempest. We follow the one and accept, as occupational hazard, the buffets and howls of the other ... and we stay the course, guided by the ethics of our field, by the one compass point that is fixed and true ... the only one we can trust.

Before we return to Walt, there is a caveat that must be addressed at this juncture. The perspective of giving license to men and women of science, *carte blanche,* guided only by the scientific code, with no repercussions, is neither one I share, nor promote. But there lies a vast chasm between the science "practiced" by Walt and Oppenheimer and that of, say Mengele at Auschwitz,[25] or Heim at Mauthasen.[26] At the heart of this difference lies two issues. The first is the manipulation of inanimate objects, animate matter, and sentient subjects, and the second is the sanctity of, and respect for, all aspects of the scientific endeavor. Although a case can be made that life, itself, is a scientific experiment, random or otherwise, it is not difficult to agree that it is precious, if not for its wonderfully complex simplicity, then for its apparent rarity. And, in the face of such rarity, the value of sentience becomes astronomically fathomless. It is one thing to have society, outside the lab, use science for evil. That sin is upon society ... that blood is on their hands. But, it is not for the scientists in the lab to engage in actions that defile sentience. To be clear, the direct abuse of sentience as part of the scientific investigation is an abomination that is fundamentally contrary to the ethos of science. For, at its very heart, science seeks to understand, to be aware—and that is the very quality that defines sentience. Sentience destroying itself in the search for itself is unnatural, inharmonic and contradictory—and none of these are terms consistent with science. To conduct science, however, to create a product or a technology that *may* be dangerous and *may* even threaten sentient life, is a guiltless endeavor. For the power of that which destroys, can build; and the power of that which builds, can destroy. The tool is the weapon, and the weapon the tool, they have always been and will ever be blameless. It is the user who, based upon his use of the technology, must take the accolades or suffer the blame.

And so, finally, let us return to Walter Hartwell White—husband, father, teacher, carwash attendant, cancer patient, drug kingpin, scientist. Whatever bag of emotions this character summons in fans of the show, can the reader at least agree to separate Walt, the scientist, from his other alter egos? This would only seem fair. The woman who is a CEO of a Fortune–500 company by day, and who bakes cookies for her toddlers by night, would not be promoted at work for the tastiness of her snickerdoodles, nor would she score any points at home for landing that billion dollar contract with Beijing, if the pralines she conjures are dry. In like manner, surely Walt the scientist, in the arena of the RV, or Fring's superlab—the only arena this contribution examines—should be judged only as a scientist. And, if we agree on that issue, then surely we can agree to judge Walt, the scientist, using the laws by which scientists conduct their trade, to judge Walt's actions only by those ethics, only by those tenets. Divorcing all other concerns, all other peeves then, can we not agree that, throughout the series, Walt demonstrated a passion for, and loyalty to science? And if so, then we are in agreement that with respect to scientific ethics, Walt's actions in the arena of science were, in a word, exemplary.

Like Walt, my stock in trade is chemistry. Whether he was perfecting his product, or building a battery, or dissolving the dead Emilio,[27] I will confess openly, that on several occasions, I was tickled pink to be a chemist. It reminded me of the value I, and so many, many others place upon the central science and upon the training of the next generation to take our place.

The *MacGyver* series[28] sparked creativity and interest in science in the late 80's and early 90's and *CSI*[29] and *NCIS*[30] have done the same to science aficionados in the last decade. What they had done, Gilligan's *Breaking Bad* has also done—brilliantly reengineered with a sublime twist. Whichever side the reader takes in the issue of Walter White's ethics, let us agree to tip our hats to a wonderfully conceived and brilliantly executed series. *Yo, yo, yo, straight up man ... that shit was the bomb, yo!*

Notes

1. One of the older models of the atom is attributed to Niels Bohr who suggested that the electrons were negative particles that orbited the nucleus in fixed, unchanging orbits with well-defined radii. The radii of the orbits were related to the energies of the electrons. Because the radii were fixed, the energies of the electrons were fixed—meaning that the electrons could possess certain energies, but not others. This is the concept of quantization.

2. Quarks are elementary particles and are one of two classes of the basic building blocks of matter. They combine to form, among other things, such particles as protons and neutrons.

3. Gluons are elementary particles that serve as the exchange particles for the force between quarks.

4. Named for Austrian physicist Christian Doppler, this refers to the change in frequency (pitch for sound, color for light) of a wave for an observer moving relative to the wavesource.

5. Named for Nobel Laureate E.J. Corey, Gary H. Posner (one of my mentors at Johns Hopkins), George M. Whitesides and Herbert O. House, the reaction refers to a sequence by which carbon chains in certain organic molecules are coupled to produce large hydrocarbons.

6. Named for Nobel Laureate Ernest Rutherford who, after sanctioning the bombarding of a thin strip of gold foil with alpha particles and seeing some of them bounce back, postulated the nucleocentric model of the atom in which the atom is largely empty with a dense positive nucleus.

7. Named for joint Nobel Laureates James Watson and Francis H.C. Crick, this model was the first to propose the double helical structure of DNA.

8. Named for Werner Heisenberg, it is a quantum mechanical principle that limits the precision with which complimentary variables (like position and energy) of a subatomic particle (like an electron) can be known simultaneously. The more certain you are about one variable the fuzzier you are about the other.

9. One billion grams

10. "4 Days Out," *Breaking Bad,* Season 2, Episode 9.

11. The moving part in many rotary electrical switches in electric generators.

12. The atomic number is the number of protons in an atom. When the elements

are lined up based upon their atomic numbers the Periodic Table of Elements results: elements fall into columns called groups with other elements of like properties, and rows called periods in which physicochemical properties change gradually.

13. While studying finches on the Galapagos islands, Darwin noticing that the birds showed wide variations in beak shape and size from island to island concluded that they adapted to take advantage of the different food sources on the islands. This was a prelude to his Theory of Natural Selection and the concept of evolution.

14. As per the Doppler effect, light from stars and galaxies moving away from us is shifted to lower wavelengths and appears redder. Since this happens wherever we look then the whole universe is moving away from itself ... i.e., it is expanding and must have been compacted some time ago. By extrapolating the expansion to a single point, the "Big Bang Theory" was born and we can also approximate the age of the universe.

15. "The release of atomic power has changed everything except our way of thinking ... the solution to the problem lies in the heart of mankind. If only I had known, I should have become a watchmaker." Albert Einstein, 1945.

16. Gilligan originally conceived of the show in a joke about if making it in television doesn't work out, they could cook meth.

17. "Say My Name," *Breaking Bad,* Season 5, Episode 7.

18. "Buried," *Breaking Bad,* Season 5, Episode 10.

19. "A No-Rough-Stuff-Type-Deal," *Breaking Bad,* Season 1, Episode 7.

20. "Salud," *Breaking Bad,* Season 4, Episode 10.

21. "Fly," *Breaking Bad,* Season 3, Episode 10.

22. The *Star Trek* science fiction entertainment franchise was created by Gene Roddenberry and first aired in 1966 and ran for 3 seasons. It includes *Star Trek: The Original Series* and its live action TV spin-off shows, *Star Trek: The Next Generation, Star Trek: Deep Space Nine, Star Trek: Voyager* and *Star Trek: Enterprise* as well as the *Star Trek* film series. Less "canonical" are *Star Trek: The Animated Series* and an extensive array of *Star Trek* novels and comics.

23. Romulans are a manipulative, deceptive, warlike race of humanoids (evolutionary cousins of the more peaceful, logical Vulcans) that have appeared as villains throughout the *Star Trek* franchise.

24. Tribbles are small, furry, slow-moving fictional animals in the *Star Trek* universe. They purr when coddled and reproduce very quickly, consuming massive amounts of food in the process. Starfleet forbids their transportation aboard Federation vessels.

25. Josef Mengele was a German SS officer and physician in the Auschwitz concentration camp who was infamous for performing gruesome and often deadly human experiments on prisoners during World War II and for the selection of victims to be killed in the gas chambers.

26. Aribert Ferdinand Heim (aka Dr. Death) was an Austrian SS doctor in the Mauthausen concentration camp. He was accused of killing and torturing many

inmates by various methods including direct injections of toxic compounds into his victims' hearts.

27. "Cat's in the Bag," *Breaking Bad,* Season 1, Episode 2.

28. *MacGyver* is an action-adventure television series which followed the ultra-resourceful secret agent Angus MacGyver, played by Richard Dean Anderson, who worked as a troubleshooter for the Phoenix Foundation The show ran for seven seasons from 1985 to 1992.

29. *CSI: Crime Scene Investigation* is a crime drama television series whose original installment followed Crime Scene Investigators working for the Las Vegas Police Department using science, physical evidence, and deductive reasoning to solve murders. The original spawned two spin-offs *CSI: Miami* and *CSI: NY* and plans are underway to launch another spin-off based in Quantico, Virginia, called *CSI: Cyber.*

30. *NCIS* is a television drama series featuring a team of special agents from the Naval Criminal Investigative Service investigating crimes perpetrated by and on the U.S. Navy and Marine Corps. The show has led to two spin-off series, *NCIS: Los Angeles* and *NCIS: New Orleans;* the latter has not yet aired.

Talking 'bout
Some Heisenberg
Experimenting with
the Mad Scientist

CHERYL D. EDELSON

At the risk of oversimplification, we might suggest that the success of many recent cable television series can be attributed at least in part to these shows' defamiliarization of popular cliché. Programs such as *The Sopranos*, *Big Love*, and even the recent *True Blood* operate by infusing stereotypes with psychological realism.[1] This formula also holds true for Vince Gilligan's *Breaking Bad*, which debuted on AMC in January of 2008. While other series attempt to breathe new life into clichéd figures such as the gangster, the Mormon polygamist, and the vampire, *Breaking Bad* experiments not only with the drug-dealer, but also, more subtly, with the iconic character of the mad scientist. Although *Breaking Bad* conserves many aspects of the mad scientist, this series reconstitutes this familiar parody of Enlightenment rationalism by incorporating elements of psychological realism as well as conventions common to superhero comics. Like almost all mad scientist narratives, *Breaking Bad* has Luddite tendencies; but whereas most literary mad scientists are static, Gilligan allows us to see a gradual transformation of his protagonist from mild mannered high-school chemistry teacher Walter White into the formidable and unstable persona of "Heisenberg"—a cancer patient-cum-meth dealer who unleashes the terrors of everyday science onto Albuquerque's underworld.

While a thorough review of scholarship on the mad scientist is beyond the scope of this essay, a few background ideas enable our discussion of *Breaking Bad*. Peter H. Goodrich offers a useful review of the mad scientist's lineage, delineating the way in which this figure owes its existence to roots in Prometheus, Merlin, and Faust:

> [T]he mad scientist is in one sense a technologized Merlin as well as a Prometheus, a Faust, a Prospero. Metaphorically and historically speaking, the mutating figure of Merlin has come to include these three traditional models of the type, thus becoming master trope or icon.... These conventions are attributed to the mad scientist by a populace which does not share his special expertise, and which therefore views it alternately with admiration and suspicion. His genius has been individually determined as a natural gift of heredity, grace or study—Merlin's abilities in Medieval romance come from both the devil, who gives him his knowledge of what has been, and from God who gives him knowledge of what is and is to come; in modern treatments they are often the product of hard work and study to develop his innate talent. However, his "madness" is socially determined because all extraordinary genius provoked doubt in ordinary mortals—a doubt confirmed in the literature by events.[2]

In 1957, cultural critic Dwight MacDonald suggested that horror films reveal modern anxieties about the destructive potential of Enlightenment technological advances. As MacDonald suggests, "[S]cience gives man mastery over his environment" but

> science itself is not understood, therefore not mastered, therefore terrifying because of its very power. Taken this way, as the supreme mystery, science becomes the stock in trade of the "horror" pulp magazines and comics and movies. It has got to the point, indeed, that if one sees a laboratory in a movie, one shudders, and the white coat of the scientist is as blood-chilling a sight as Count Dracula's black cloak.[3]

MacDonald goes on to argue that this technophobic anxiety finds its way into *Frankenstein*, *King Kong*, and other mass cultural texts in which "the scientist's laboratory has acquired ... a ghastly atmosphere."[4] Christopher P. Toumey takes exception to this technophobia, arguing that the relative complexity with which scientists are treated in Victorian fiction becomes degraded in drama and film. According to Toumey, the last two centuries are marked by an increasing Gothic antirationalism that gives rise to a flat mad scientist stereotype.[5] Each of these interpretations of the evil scientist is useful in reading the gravitation of Walter White toward the volatile figure of meth-cook Heisenberg.

Throughout its many iterations, however, the mad scientist tends to be a static figure who is usually well on his way to Faustian damnation before the narrative in question begins. A parodic exaggeration of this convention may be found in Professor Hubert W. Farnsworth (Billy West) in *Futurama* (1999–present) as well as the Bugs Bunny cartoons "Hare Raising Hare"(1946) and "Water, Water Every Hare" (1952). In their very simplicity, these clarify the basic pattern of this narrative: in each short episode, the protagonist runs afoul of an "evil scientist" (as the Gothic castle's neon sign makes clear) who is already fully formed and ready to menace the hero with an insane experiment—in the latter case, a Karloff-inspired geek who wants to harvest Bugs's brain. More complex variations on this theme appear in H.G. Wells's *The Island of Dr. Moreau* (1896), Ernest B. Schoedsack's *Dr. Cyclops* (1940), and Fred M. Wilcox's *Forbidden Planet* (1956). Perhaps these examples lend some credence to Christopher P. Toumey's contention that cinematic mad scientists lack the moral complexity of their fictional counterparts, which have the luxury of developing well-rounded characters.[6] But even the mad scientists of Victorian fiction—Mary Shelley's Victor Frankenstein, Nathaniel Hawthorne's Aylmer (in "The Birth-Mark"[1843]), and R. L. Stevenson's Dr. Jekyll, for example—immediately impress the reader as obsessive researchers whose excesses will be their undoing. Glossing these figures, Roslynn Haynes argues, "Alchemists and scientists are typically presented in literature as having different allegiances from other people. Like religious and political extremists, they are ruthless in their idealism, prepared to sacrifice people or animals in the cause of their experiments."[7] Following David Skal, Alberto Brodescu argues that Walter White develops a variation on the "mad doctor syndrome": "As prescribed by mad science tradition, hubris goes beyond control and begins to act against the interest of the individual."[8] Gilligan's *Breaking Bad* enters into the mad scientist canon by rehearsing the full arc of Walter White's metamorphosis from Walter White to Heisenberg. Ensuing seasons dramatize the mad scientist's struggle to quite literally attain his "rightful place" in the world.

When we are introduced to White in the first episode of *Breaking Bad*, he is an altogether sane scientist—more a victim than a symbol of Enlightenment rationalism. Having turned away from a career in research (this disclosed a few episodes later), Walter supports himself and his family—pregnant wife Skyler (Anna Gunn) and disabled son Walt Jr. (R.J. Mitte)—as a high-school chemistry teacher. Lecturing bored teens cannot cover the cost of living, so Walter works part-time as a cashier in a local car-wash. If the mad scientist represents Enlightenment autonomy taken to an unhealthy extreme, Walter's life represents the devolution of the rational subject into an alienated piece-worker. Working for a moment on the line of the car wash, Walter collapses amid the machinery only to wake up in the hospital to devastating news: he suffers the advanced stages of lung cancer. This diagnosis propels Walter further into the heartless world of rational technocracy. At Skyler's insistence, he agrees to undergo experimental radiation treatments that fall outside his skimpy insurance plan. And once he begins the treatments, Walter endures the dehumanization that often accompanies modern western medicine—in an important scene, he is painted with a red-dot target and subjected to doses of radiation intended to kill the cancer; here the scientist has become the object of science. *Breaking Bad* therefore begins with Prufrock rather than Prometheus, an average "Joe the Teacher" who experiences various levels of alienation and disempowerment. And matters are only made worse by Walter's blowhard brother-in-law Hank Schrader (Dean Norris); he's a DEA agent whose adventurous tales render Walter even more emasculated and irrelevant. But Hank's obtrusive presence ironically opens the door for Walter's transition to Heisenberg.

When Hank unwittingly introduces Walter to the drug underworld, the downtrodden chemistry teacher takes his first steps toward mad science. Riding along during one of Hank's drug-busts, Walter glimpses his former student Jesse Pinkman (Aaron Paul) fleeing the scene. And so begins Walter's "breaking bad"—a street euphemism for deviation from the path of conventional respectability. Desperate to finance his treatments without bankrupting the family, Walter looks up Jesse, known as "Captain Cook" because of his innovative crystal-meth recipe (spiced up with a dash of chile powder). Explaining the relationship between chemistry and meth production, Walter cajoles "F" student Jesse into taking him on as a silent partner. The unlikely pair set off into the New Mexico desert in an RV-cum-lab, and it is here that Walter begins to look a bit more like the mad scientist that we all know and love. Surrounded by beakers, flasks, and other iconic "laboratory paraphernalia"[9] filched from Walt's classroom, the methodical Walter at one point throws out a serviceable batch of crystal, much to Jesse's chagrin; this is the kind of perfectionism conventionally associated with obsessive researchers and a tendency that accrues throughout the first season of *Breaking Bad*. Another predictive moment occurs when Walter and Jesse run afoul of local drug dealers who want to take over their small but emerging operation. Holding off the murderous thugs by promising to reveal his secrets, Walter hurls together a caustic blend of chemicals and then seals his victims in the Winnebago; although they perforate the RV with bullets, Emilio (John Koyama) and Krazy–8 (Max Arciniega) succumb to the noxious fumes, setting the stage for yet more grisly scenarios. The Winnebago sequences are significant in a number of ways. Although Walter starts to shape up as a recognizable mad scientist, he is remarkable in his Luddite aspect. Exchanging the chilling white lab-coat for white briefs and an apron—and working in a ramshackle RV instead of a secret fortress—Walter possesses a populist aspect that has always been the source of anxiety about the mad scientist rather than one of his hallmarks. Working on his own recipes and coming up with solutions on the fly, Walter is a hero of Certeauvian "space" as opposed to a villain of Foucauldian "place."

The sense of an idiosyncratic, fluid space continues as Walt and Jesse set up operations at the latter's suburban home. In contrast to the sterile laboratories of evil scientists such Ian Fleming's Dr. No or Dr. Morbius of *Forbidden Planet* (Fred M. Wilcox, 1956), Jesse's two-story mission style property becomes a porous and dynamic Gothic mansion—a decided counterpoint to Walt's own modest ranch home. Walt and Jesse return to this site with the lifeless bodies of Emilio and Krazy–8. Jesse attempts to dissolve Emilio's corpse with acid in his upstairs bathroom—this contrary to Walt's explicit instructions to conduct this horrifying business only in a plastic container. The acid eats through the tub to deposit Emilio's liquefied remains all over the first floor hallway; after this incident, Jesse opts to sell the house. Meanwhile, Krazy–8 survives and is confined in the basement by means of a u-lock collar around his neck. Balking at cold-blooded murder, Walt nurses him back to health only to later strangle him with the u-lock during a desperate hand-to-hand fight. After these grim developments, Walt and Jesse relocate their meth lab to the basement, a decision that comically curtails the realtor's open-house. All of these movements represent creative reinterpretations of Gothic conventions. As Walt evolves in the direction of the evil genius, Jesse assumes the role of bumbling assistant—a conflation of the youthful "threatened innocent" and the "visibly crippled assistant" that Andrew Tudor identifies as two common motifs of the mad scientist narrative.[10] As suggested above, Jesse's home gets revamped as a Gothic mansion—which, in Toumey's paradigm, would be interpreted as the antirationalist expression of popular fears about the destructive power of science, in whatever form. And yet the decision to resituate the narrative away from the foreclosed place of the formal laboratory and into this impromptu house of horrors suggests something of the open-endedness with which Gilligan treats identity in *Breaking Bad*.

Although Walt is deeply disturbed by the killings of Emilio and Krazy–8, he is at the same time reinvigorated by his descent into the criminal underworld and his arc toward the mad scientist persona of Heisenberg. Despite the debilitating effects of chemotherapy, he becomes more virile in his sexual relations with Skyler and more aggressive in everyday life. When a trio of bullies razz his crippled son in a retail store, Walt physically assaults the most formidable of them and faces down the others. At another point, he deftly uses his technical acumen to destroy a loudmouth's BMW at a gas station. At the same time, he aspires to expand his production and distribution of crystal-meth, a venture that involves stealing large quantities of methylamine from a chemical supply facility. Explaining his strategy with a brief lecture on World War II demolitions, much to the astonishment of Jesse, Walt makes a small thermite bomb (derived from an Etch-a-Sketch) to breach the locks of the industrial complex. In such moments, Walt gravitates between the moral intentions that Toumey assigns to literary mad scientists. While some of these figures act out of altruism gone wrong, others seek vengeance on a world that has wronged them. If Walt began with a reluctant intention to produce small quantities of meth in order to underwrite his treatment—and thereby protect his family—he is at this point seduced by the power of his enterprise as well as a desire to wreak havoc on a world that has devalued him.[11] He therefore resembles characters such as the conundrum-laden Dr. Victor von Doom in Stan Lee's *Fantastic Four* comics; an orphaned gypsy, Dr. Doom combines sorcery and science as well as medievalism and modernity in his feud with Reed Richards's Fantastic Four and the status quo that they champion. As Andrew Terjesen points out, Doom is also "a complex megalomaniac with noble qualities."[12] And this complexity certainly looks forward to the ways in which the character of Walter White evolves throughout *Breaking Bad*.

In keeping with mad scientist pretexts such as Dr. Doom, Gilligan and his writers coordinate Walt's physical appearance so as to underscore their anti-hero's "alchemical" transformation.[13] Given the hair-loss that accompanies radiation treatments, Walt shaves his head, prompting his son Walt Jr. to exclaim, "Wow! Bad ass dad!" Walt's baldness may be a sign of his debilitation, but it is also an essential part of mad scientist iconography and therefore a symbol of empowerment. The glistening bald cranium—an emblem of mind over matter— has become entrenched as a synecdoche of the mad scientist, most notably in Superman's nemeses Ultra-Humanite and Lex Luthor (to whom Jesse explicitly compares Walt)[14] but also in successive figures such as Thorkel (Albert Dekker) in *Dr. Cyclops*, Dr. Ernst Blofeld (Donald Pleasance) in the James Bond film *You Only Live Twice* (Lewis Gilbert, 1967), and his knockoff Dr. Evil (Mike Myers) in the *Austin Powers* films (Jay Roach, 1997–2002).

All of these threads come together in the climactic sequence of *Breaking Bad*'s Season One finale, "A No-Rough-Stuff-Type Deal." In need of an additional $90,000 for cancer treatments, Walt compels Jesse to negotiate a distribution deal with drug kingpin Tuco (Raymond Cruz), a decision he regrets when the crime-boss viciously beats Jesse and steals their product. Walt then penetrates Tuco's headquarters under the pretense of offering even more of his now famous ice. Of course joking on the word "tweak," Walt punctuates the climax of the first season with his own big bang. In the final episode, he and Jesse reencounter Tuco to work out an even grander scheme.

Walt's assumption of the moniker "Heisenberg" is obviously quite meaningful. In one sense, the allusion speaks to the ways in which Walt attempts to push back the Naturalistic forces that confront him. Although he may feel like a tiny, insignificant particle in a vast and uncaring universe, he cannot be definitively located and is therefore capable of more possibilities than statistically certain death and poverty. In other words, he is unpredictable, even to himself—a fact highlighted by the climactic scene in which he takes on Tuco with a bag of homemade explosive. The Heisenberg handle also points out Walt's course of transformation throughout the first season. He may have begun his adventure as a reluctant, part-time meth cook, hoping for a controlled experiment in supplemental income. However, as the show carries on, Walt, true to the Uncertainty Principle, becomes deeply involved in his own experiment. And this is where the conventions of the mad scientist come into play: once he starts to cook, Walt becomes possessed by the motives of perfectionism, vengeance, and will-to-power that mark evil the Promethean evil genius of the last two hundred years. With this conclusion, Season 1 of *Breaking Bad* accomplishes a remarkable degree of narrative unity.

The early narrative movements of *Breaking Bad* court the mad scientist subtext, as the marginalized Walt strikes back by taking on the volatile persona of meth chemist Heisenberg. While the dominant genre of the series as a whole is the gangster film—in that Seasons 2–5 follow Walt's rise and fall as a crime mogul—the mad scientist motif interestingly perseveres through setting. Of all popular iconic figures, the mad scientist is the character most intimately associated with its setting: the laboratory, which, in turn, remains ensconced in other remote spaces such as a castle, island, or subterranean complex. Some mad scientists, such as Stevenson's Dr. Jekyll or Fritz Lang's Rotwang (Rudolf Klein-Rogge) in *Metropolis* (Fritz Lang, 1927) seclude themselves in the midst of a populous city. The former experimenter occupies a thatched cottage that brings together speculative technology with arcane medieval imagery. More common and memorable, however, is the scientist's lair that is far removed from the mainstream of humanity. Like Rotwang's domicile, the lonely castle of Dr. Frankenstein (Colin Clive) in James Whale's adaptation of Mary Shelley's novel, juxtaposes modernity with the Middle Ages, underscoring the relationship of the scientist with alchemy and wizardry.[15] In *Dr. Cyclops*, Thorkel sets up his lab at the mouth of a pitchblende mine in the jungles of Peru; here Aztec ruins replace the medieval castle in the binary opposition between ancient and modern.

As declared in the title of H.G. Wells's *The Island of Dr. Moreau* (1896), the mad scientist presides over an even more distant domain, enabling the construction of a compound and conversion of the jungle into proving grounds. The island setting corroborates Goodrich's association of the mad scientist with Shakespeare's Prospero. In the science fiction adaptation of *The Tempest*, Fred M. Wilcox's *Forbidden Planet* (1956), the island is rendered as an even more cut-off locale: a planet bereft of all inhabitants except for Dr. Morbius (Walter Pigeon), his daughter Altaira (Anne Francis), and Ariel-like servant Robby the Robot. James Bond's nemesis Dr. No (Joseph Wiseman), in the 1962 film of that name, takes advantage of Crab Key for an imposing base of operations that encompasses land and sea. As Daniel Ferraras Savoye argues, Dr. No's island compound

> is also metonymically related to one of the main terms of the basic conflict— that is, the Villain—for Dr. No defines himself as the Enemy through the reality he has created for himself and from which he intends to disrupt the Order. Being the unquestioned master of a micro-structural society, he represents a valid threat since his very existence demonstrates the possibility of an alternate Order, which is naturally inadmissible. The lair of Dr. No reflects the dual semiotic value of the island in the relationship to the natural elements, for it is both land and sea. Consequently, the first climactic confrontation between Bond and Dr. No takes place in a hybrid space that cominces Earth and Water.[16]

This reading of Dr. No's complex as a "micro-structural society," one that posits an "alternative Order," reveals the mad scientist's "rightful place." The latter concept takes on added significance in light of Michel de Certeau's theories of the built environment. In *The Practice of Everyday Life*, Certeau delivers a theoretical counterpoint to Michel Foucault's arguments about spatial hegemony:

> If it is true that the grid of "discipline" is everywhere becoming clearer and more extensive, it is all the more urgent to discover how an entire society

resists being reduced to it, what popular procedures (also "minuscule" and "quotidian") manipulate the mechanisms of discipline and conform to them only in order to evade them, and finally, what 'ways of operating' form the counterpart, on the consumer's (or "dominee's") side, of the mute processes that organize the establishment of socioeconomic order.[17]

Panopticism (and heterotopia) are in Certeau's theory "strategic" uses of space, "the calculus of force- relationships which becomes possible when a subject of will and power (a proprietor, an enterprise, a city, a scientific institution) can be isolated from an 'environment.'" Whereas a strategy is "the victory of space over time, a tactic depends on time—it is always on the watch for opportunities that must be seized 'on the wing.'" For Certeau, "The place of the tactic belongs to the other."[18] At another point in *The Practice of Everyday Life*, Certeau describes an analogous opposition between "place" and "space": while the former means that "the elements taken into consideration are beside one another, each situated in its own 'proper' and distinct location it defines. A place is thus an instantaneous configuration of positions. It implies an indication of stability." And, along with tactics, "*space is a practiced place*. Thus the street geometrically defined by urban planning is transformed into a space by walkers."[19] Following Certeau, as well as critics such as MacDonald and Savoye, I would argue that the conventional mad scientist represents popular anxieties about the way in which "scientific institutions" attempt mastery over the environment and everyone in it. With far-removed demesnes such as Dr. No's Crab Key, the mad scientist comes across as an antagonist who first and foremost conquers physical terrain in order to create a thoroughly conquered and regulated "place." Although the mad scientist figure is alienated from mainstream society, his lair—whether it be castle, island, or planet— represents an exaggeration of the "grid of discipline" that permeates modern life. *Breaking Bad* reinterprets the mad scientist as a master of space, in the Certeauvian sense of the term.

In the course of its five seasons, *Breaking Bad* not only describes an arc of the protagonist's transformation from Walter to Heisenberg; the series also narrates this mad scientist's contention for space over place. Early episodes of *Breaking Bad* find Walt a "dominee" within the "grid of discipline." Having been excluded from the Gray Matter enterprise that he founded with the Schwartz's (the equivalent of the conventional mad scientist's exclusion from mainstream academia), Walt becomes subject to the disciplinary operations of three industrial complexes: education, business, and medicine.

Having experienced a career transition from researcher/entrepreneur to high-school classroom teacher, Walt finds himself lecturing on the wonders of chemistry to bored and inattentive teenagers. The hum-drum character of Walt's teaching may constitute a critique of contemporary education; if so, however, this critique has to do with the fact that Walt has allowed himself to be scripted, along with his students, into oppositional subject-positions determined largely by classroom design: the tired scenario of standing lecturer before seated students. Although educational theorists—most notably Paolo Freire[20]—focus primarily upon the objectification of students within this traditional pedagogy, there is also a sense in which the lecturer is simultaneously empowered and limited by the spatially determined role as "sage on the stage." Walt does indulge in an enthusiastic proclamation that "chemistry is the study ... of change": "Electrons change their energy levels. Molecules change their bonds. Elements combine and change into compounds. But that's all of life, right? It's the constant, it's the cycle. It's solution, dissolution. Just over and over and over. It is growth, then decay, then transformation. It's fascinating really." These observations, which prefigure Walt's own experience as Heisenberg, have come to be recognized as some of the most significant lines in *Breaking Bad*. Pyrotechnics and poetry notwithstanding, however, the lecture itself dissolves into an episode of awkward classroom management situation and an uninspired resort to the textbook: "Ionic Bonds, Chapter 6." Despite his enthusiasm for the wonders of chemistry, high school chemistry teacher Walt falls into the "banking method" of teaching at its worst, with both teacher and pupils stultified. An inveterate lecturer, Walt finds it very difficult to break out of this routinized pedagogy.[21]

Walt's pedagogy echoes factory piece-work; "Is it surprising," queries Michel Foucault, "that prisons resemble factories, schools, barracks, hospitals, which all resemble prisons?"[22] After completing his teaching day, Walt moves on to his part-time job at the A1A Car Wash, where he is deployed as a "gopher" for boss Bogdan Wolynetz (Marius Stan). Mechanically reciting the A1A mantra ("Just hand this claiming disk to your car wash professional. Thank you; come again.") behind the cash register, Walt must also detail cars in the aftercare area. In a poignant moment, Walt encounters two disrespectful students while scrubbing the young man's Corvette. As Chad (Evan Bobrick) photographs Walt at work, admonishing him to "make those tires shine," his girlfriend immediately calls a friend to spread the news of Walt's demeaning after-hours job. Although it is tempting to suggest that the teens function as part of some disciplinary panopticon, what really transpires here is the opposite. Walt's humiliation proves to be the last straw, contributing to Walt's ultimate rebellion against the places that dominate him. Having been pushed too far by these demeaning conditions, Walt grabs his crotch and explodes, "Fuck you, Bogdan! Fuck you and your eyebrows... Wipe down this!"

Walt proves no less outraged at the disciplinary mechanisms of the medical-industrial complex. Ben Wetherbee and Stephanie Weaver have speculated that Foucauldian theories may prove quite relevant for interpreting "Walt's marginalized positions as a cancer patient in the hospital...." *Breaking Bad's* medical sequences find Walt a "doctor's specimen"[23] or a patient whose prone body is subject to the various contortions of radiology, radiotherapy, chemotherapy, and surgery. These textual moments conform to the Foucauldian reading that modern medicine deploys surveillance and other disciplinary techniques that "create a context for a 'docile' state to emerge. This is typified in the caricature of a submissive patient, lying silently (for fear of interrupting) during a ward round, while physicians conduct their observations and discuss the nature of the disease and treatment."[24] In keeping with the pre-text of the A1A Carwash, however, this disempowerment provokes Walt's outrage and rebellion. He delivers impassioned speeches against medical establishment prognoses that will surely diminish his autonomy and quality of life: "These doctors ... talking about surviving, one year, two years, like it's the only thing that matters. But what good is it, to just survive if I am too sick to work, to enjoy a meal, to make love?" Walt goes on to declare, "What I want, what I need, is a choice. Sometimes I feel like I never make any of my own.... My entire life it just seems I never ... had a real say about any of it. Now this last one, cancer ... all I have left is how I choose to approach this." Waiting in hospital gown and sock-feet for an imaging procedure, Walt blasts a fellow patient:

> "To hell with your cancer. I've been living with cancer for the better part of a year. Right from the start, it's a death sentence. That's what they keep telling me. Well, guess what? Every life comes with a death sentence, so every few months I come in here for my regular scan, knowing full well that one of these times—hell, maybe even today—I'm gonna hear some bad news. But until then, who's in charge? Me. That's how I live my life."

According to Mark A. Lewis, these scenes contribute to a conversion narrative within which Walt undergoes a transformation common among metastatic cancer patients, a sense of liberation brought about by the prospect of impending death.[25] Subject to a series of disempowering places, Walt feels disempowered and yet goaded into rebellious action. Tempered by literary realism, Walt's character recalls another of Stan Lee's scientists—Dr. Bruce Banner of *The Incredible Hulk* (1962-). While conducting research in New

Mexico, Dr. Banner receives a huge dose of gamma radiation. The neurotic (not to say "mad") physicist then transforms into the Hulk, a gargantuan inspired by Frankenstein's monster and Mr. Hyde. After his initial metamorphosis, Banner/Hulk smashes through the walls of a hospital; it is not too much to suggest that this variation on the mad scientist character represents popular anxieties about the medical establishment as well as science in general. Like Banner/Hulk, Walt/Heisenberg both develops from and opposes disciplinary places such as laboratories and hospitals.

Walt embarks on a career as the drug kingpin Heisenberg. But he also wages a campaign of space against place, one that drives both setting and narrative structure of *Breaking Bad*. After Hank accidentally introduces Walt to the drug underworld, the downtrodden chemistry teacher takes his first steps toward Certeauvian mad scientist. Walt and Jesse strike out into the New Mexico desert in the RV-cum-lab that Jesse later dubs "The Crystal Ship." As Ensley F. Guffey contends, this 1986 Fleetwood Bounder is "perhaps the most iconic symbol of the series, and for the first three seasons, takes on such a central role that it can be considered a character in its own right."[26] As we see in its brand name, the "Fleetwood Bounder" represents Walt's first true departure from the disciplinary grid that has come to define his existence. Remoteness notwithstanding, this ramshackle camper stands in stark contrast to the fixed installations of the conventional mad scientist. Unlike the places that represent "the victory of space over time," the RV exemplifies Walt's propensity to realize "opportunities that must be seized 'on the wing.'" Jesse assures Walt, "[A] mobile meth lab'd be the bomb.... You can drive way out in the boonies. Be all evasive." This is Walt's training ground as a mad scientist, the site in which he outwits Krazy–8 and Emilio by trapping them in the RV with poisonous vapors. Walt's tactics proves more redemptive in "Four Days Out," when he repairs the Bounder with a DIY battery. More importantly, Walt here perfects his signature blue meth. In the end, the Fleetwood Bounder serves as a muse to inspire the evolving mad scientist toward unconventional tactics such as bricolage, all of which confute the disciplinary grid.[27]

Thus empowered, Walt goes on to exact his revenge against the disciplinary places that would confine or configure him. *Breaking Bad*'s decisive battle between place and space, unfolds in seasons two through four as Walt and Gustavo Fring (Giancarlo Esposito) contend for Albuquerque's meth business. Gus at first seduces Walt by constructing a "superlab" in the basement of his inconspicuous commercial laundry plant. Walt is initially taken in by the lab equipment and his new expert assistant Gale Boetticher (David Costabile). It would seem that the mad scientist Heisenberg has found an ideal setting amidst the shining equipment of this secret bunker. Like the subterranean base of Dr. No, the superlab promises a hidden "micro-structural society" that will usher in an "alternative Order." But the honeymoon ends as Walt realizes that the superlab is just another disciplinary place characterized by panoptic surveillance and violent spectacle.[28] This secret lair belongs to another mad scientist, though one whose science is management rather than chemistry.

This reality dawns upon Walt when he notices that Gus has installed motion-activated cameras in the superlab. Recalling the series "Pilot," Walt flips off the camera and begins deep-laid plans to eliminate his rival. This will involve "smashing" a hospital, if not through the brute strength of the Hulk. After two prosaic attempts on Gus's life, Walt defeats his rival; and he does so on the premises of another disciplinary place—the rest-home. Perhaps taking a page from Gus's playbook, Walt succeeds in recruiting Hector Salamanca (Mark Margolis), who passionately hates both Walt and Gus. Walt makes it appear that Hector will cooperate with the DEA. This tactic lures Gus to the Casa Tranquila convalescent home, where Hector has been living following the death of his nephew Tuco. The appropriately named "House of Tranquility" highlights the ways in which a rest-home operates as a disciplinary place. Foucault of course names the rest-home, along with the psychiatric hospital and the prison, as "heterotopias of deviation ... in which individuals whose behavior is deviant in relation to the required mean or norm are placed" (see above). Heisenberg flourishes in scenarios that allow him to exert tactics (Certeau's "opportunities that must be seized 'on the wing'") against those, like Gus, who strategize through the built environment. Walt resumes his "cooking," this time to manufacture a pipe bomb that he plants in Hector's wheelchair. When Gus and his henchman visit Hector in order to murder him with an injection, the old man favors Gus with a malicious expression and explodes the pipe bomb with his bell, which Walt has fashioned into a trigger. In a macabre scene appropriate to the Gothic origins of the mad scientist (one might even recall the opening of the film *Dr. Cyclops*), Gus walks out into the hallway to reveal that the explosion has exposed half of his skull. "I won," declares Walt, in the wake of the blast. The Casa Tranquila explosion represents the climactic moment of Walt's battle against his rival mad scientist and "the grid of discipline" in general. Unlike Gus, Walt has used time-bound tactics against the strategy of place to destroy an antagonist that stands for disciplinary control.

Walt celebrates the Casa Tranquila triumph by burning down the superlab; he goes one step further by using a giant magnet to wreck the Albuquerque

PD evidence locker that holds evidence of his work in the lab. As the series concludes, Walt engages in two additional movements that highlight his commitment to championing space over place and his revision of the mad scientist figure. Following a brief hiatus, Walt gathers Jesse and Mike Ehrmantraut (Jonathan Banks) in order to carry on Gus's distribution of meth both locally and in central Europe (this market developed by Lydia Rodarte-Quayle [Laura Fraser]). In a bold daylight raid, Walt and his crew stop a freight train and siphon the methylamine. But this caper serves an even greater operation—Vamanos Pest Control. Walt, Jesse, and Mike acquire this shady business as a means of housing a new roving, self-contained lab that is itself housed within a different tented residence. Of all the workspaces presented in *Breaking Bad*, this arrangement, in Certeau's language, most clearly "transforms another person's property into a space borrowed for a moment by a transient."[29] Declaring the motto "Let's go," Vamanos symbolizes the spirit of provisionality initiated with the Fleetwood Bounder in Season 1. Although he will never enjoy the fixed installation of castle or island, Heisenberg may at least revel in the fact that this facility, unlike superlab, has no fixed place to be detected or destroyed. In short, the Vamanos lab should be understood as a major iconic and philosophical revision to the conventional mad scientist figure.

Breaking Bad's spatial thematics come together in the concluding episode "Felina." It is fitting that the smug pronouncements of the Schwartz's kindle Walt's ire enough to derail his plans for surrender. After watching the Schwartz interview on a barroom TV, Walt hatches his intricate scheme to take revenge on his remaining enemies. While Elliott (Adam Godley) and Gretchen (Jessica Hecht) have used their technocratic capital to build a nice place, a sumptuous McMansion, Walt once again deploys brilliant tactics, fooling them with a few dollars worth of clerical supplies (laser pointers) into thinking that they are covered by hit-men. Timing comes together with bricolage in the final showdown with Jack Welker's (Michael Bowen) gang. After shooting down Hank (Dean Norris) and Gomez (Steven Michael Quezada) in the desert, the neo–Nazis enslave Jesse in the reassembled Vamanos meth lab. In addition to recalling the slave-labor of Third Reich factories such as the Dora-Nordhausen, this set-up undoes the tactical nature of Walt's Vamanos operation and represents a crude regression to the discipline of Gus's superlab. Here Jesse is compelled through torture, terrorism, and outright muscle memory to shuffle mindlessly, on a track, through the procedures of the meth cook. He has been debased into what Foucault would call a "machine-man" robbed of agency and identity through "disciplinary mechanization."[30]

But Walt frees this "robot" by means of another: a remote-controlled M-60 machine gun hidden in the trunk of a 1977 Cadillac Sedan de Ville. The operation hinges on Walt's ability to momentarily park the Cadillac near Welker's club-house. Walt pretends to attack Jesse only to activate the remote M-60 for a devastating hail of gunfire. The mad scientist's deadly robot punctuates Walt's long list of improvised weapons, ad hoc devices that work in concert with Walt's sense of "scheduling" to subvert enemies who attempt to dominate through space rather than time. He expires amidst his reconstituted laboratory, the space in which he feels most at home.

While the gangster and domestic melodrama genres predominate, *Breaking Bad* subtly and yet undeniably weaves the sf/horror conventions of the mad scientist into its five-year run. In the anti-hero Walter White/Heisenberg, the series stirs up memories of mad scientist pre-texts. Like Bruce Banner and Victor Von Doom, Walt is a scientist who faces a long history of vocational and psychological challenges that culminate in a life-threatening crisis. He responds to the cancer diagnosis in a way that carries on the tradition of these characters— by assuming a larger-than-life persona complete with a moniker that alludes to one of the historical researchers who contributed to the real-life technological horrors of modernity.[31] As Heisenberg, Walt is clothed in the iconography of famous cinematic mad scientists such as Dr. Thorkel of *Dr. Cyclops* and Dr. Morbius of *Forbidden Planet*. Heisenberg's exploits match his diabolical appearance; Walt cooks up not only a revolutionary street drug, but also weapons that include poisons such as ricin, which we associate with global terrorism, all kinds of explosives and incendiaries, giant magnets, and even robotic gunners. When Walt's comparatively mundane killing of Jane (Krysten Ritter) sets in motion a chain of events that results in an air disaster, this mad scientist edges toward the apocalyptic destruction of his comic book and film counterparts. These are the dark deeds that lead Walt to announce, "I am the one who knocks"— an outraged rejoinder to Skyler's dismissal of her husband as "A *school teacher? Cancer?* Desperate for money? Roped into working for—unable to even *quit*?"

In terms of methodology, Heisenberg does become consumed with the single-mindedness and obsession that alienates the literary mad scientist from his family and community. Like Shelley's Frankenstein and Hawthorne's Aylmer, this fanatical pursuit endangers the family; the Whites are drawn into a chaotic and dangerous world that makes them vulnerable to the authorities as well as the terrors of the criminal underworld. But methodology also represents *Breaking Bad*'s major point of departure from mad scientist convention.

In contrast to Dr. No and other rogue researchers, Walt/Heisenberg cannot establish an isolated lab or base from which to launch his projects; he must instead make use of available spaces and resources in order to accomplish his nefarious ends. This variation of the mad scientist schema is not simply comic relief, as might be inferred from the highly publicized image of Walt standing in apron and "tightie-whities" outside his Fleetwood Bounder. But the question of Walt's methodology brings up an important political/philosophical issue: the interplay of what Certeau describes as "space and place," of the disciplinary panopticon versus transient, resilient human uses of space. This subtext adds depth and complexity to the existentialist drama that many see in *Breaking Bad*.[32]

Notes

1. R. Colin Tait, "The HBO-ification of Genre," *Cinephile* 4, no. 1 (Summer 2008), 50–57.

2. Peter H. Goodrich, "The Lineage of Mad Scientist: Anti-types of Merlin," in *Dionysus in Literature: Essays on Literary Madness*, ed. Branimer M. Rieger (Bowling Green, OH: Bowling Green State University Popular Press, 1994), 82.

3. Dwight MacDonald, "A Theory of Mass Culture," in *Cultural Theory and Popular Culture: A Reader*, ed. John Storey (Athens: University of Georgia Press, 1998), 32.

4. Ibid.

5. Christopher P. Toumey, *Conjuring Science: Scientific Symbols and Cultural Meaning in American Life* (New Brunswick, N.J.: Rutgers University Press, 1996), 134.

6. Ibid., 133–135.

7. Roslynn Haynes, "The Alchemist in Fiction: The Master Narrative," *HYLE: International Journal for Philosophy of Chemistry* 12, no. 1 (2006), 29.

8. Alberto Brodescu, "Heisenberg: Epistemological Implications of a Criminal Pseudonym," *Breaking Bad: Critical Essays on the Contexts, Politics, Style and Reception of the Television Series*, ed. David Pierson (Lanham, MD: Lexington Books, 2013), 58. W. Scott Poole labels Walt a "super-villain" in the DC tradition, but ultimately reads Heisenberg as a crime kingpin figure comparable to the Joker. W. Scott Poole, "Walter White, Super Villain," *Huffington Post*, last modified November 26, 2013, accessed May 6, 2013, http://www.huffingtonpost.com/w-scott-poole/walter-white-super-villai_b_4339912.html.

9. Toumey, 6.

10. Andrew Tudor, *Monsters and Mad Scientists: A Cultural History of the Horror Movie* (Oxford: Basil Blackwell, 1989), 29.

11. See also Kirby Arinder and Joseph Milton's "The Siren Song of Mad Science," in *Supervillains and Philosophy: Sometimes, Evil Is Its Own Reward*, ed. Ben Dyer, Popular Culture and Philosophy Series 42 (Chicago: Open Court, 2009).

12. Andrew Terjesen, "Why Doctor Doom Is Better Than the Authority," in

Supervillains and Philosophy: Sometimes, Evil Is Its Own Reward, ed. Ben Dyer, Popular Culture and Philosophy Series, 42 (Chicago: Open Court, 2009), 82.

13. In the series pilot, Walt describes chemistry in lyrical terms: "Electrons change their energy levels. Molecules change their bonds. Elements combine and change into compounds. But that's all of life, right? It's the constant, it's the cycle. It's solution, dissolution. Just over and over and over. It is growth, then decay, then transformation. It's fascinating really." As Dustin Freeley suggests, these lines describe Walter's character as we find it in the series: "Walt has grown from child to adolescent to adult; *at the age of fifty and upon* his diagnosis, one could say that he has begun to decay; and, the money that he hopes will signify his existence is his transformation." Dustin Freeley, "The Economy of Time and Multiple Existences in *Breaking Bad*," in *Breaking Bad: Critical Essays on the Contexts, Politics, Style and Reception of the Television Series*, ed. David Pierson (Lanham, MD: Lexington Books, 2013), 38.

14. See Poole: "When Jesse Pinkman first sees Walt's shaved head in season two, the first words out of his mouth are: 'You look like Lex Luthor.' Walt's propensity for super-villainy seems to have triggered the rumors that he would actually play Luthor in the upcoming Superman/Batman film from Warner Bros."

15. Goodrich, 72.

16. Daniel Ferraras Savoye, *The Signs of James Bond: Semiotic Explorations in the World of 007* (Jefferson, NC: McFarland, 2013), 95.

17. Michel de Certeau, *The Practice of Everyday Life* (Berkeley: University of California Press, 1984), xiv.

18. Ibid., xix.

19. Ibid., 117.

20. Megan Watkins, *Discipline and Learn: Bodies, Pedagogy and Writing* (Rotterdam: Sense, 2011), 5.

21. Citing the educational theorist Jacques Rancière, Samuel Chambers critiques Walter White's pedagogy, concluding that Walt is a "stultifier." Interestingly, Chambers does not address Walt's formal classroom teaching at J.P. Wynne High School. Samuel Chambers, "Walter White Is a Bad Teacher: Pedagogy, *Partage*, and Politics in Season 4 of *Breaking Bad*," *Theory & Event* 17, no. 1 (2014).

22. Michel Foucault, *Discipline and Punish: The Birth of the Prison* (New York: Vintage, 1979), 215. See also Todd May, *The Philosophy of Foucault* (Montreal: McGill-Queen's University Press, 2006), 74.

23. Stephanie Weaver and Ben Wetherbee, "'You Know the Business and I Know the Chemistry': The Scientific Ethos of *Breaking Bad*," *Excursions* 4, no. 1 (2013): 10.

24. L. Forbat, et al., "The Use of Technology in Cancer Care: Applying Foucault's Ideas to Explore the Changing Dynamics of Power in Health Care," *Journal of Advance Nursing* 65, no. 2 (Feb. 2009), 308.

25. Mark A. Lewis, "From Victim to Victor: *Breaking Bad* and the Dark Potential of the Terminally Empowered," *Culture, Medicine, and Psychiatry* 37, no. 4 (Dec. 2013), 664.

26. Ensley F. Guffey, "Buying the House: Place in *Breaking Bad*," in *Breaking Bad: Critical Essays on the Contexts, Politics, Style and Reception of the Television Series*, ed. David Pierson (Lanham, MD: Lexington Books, 2013), 155–172.

27. Dwelling, moving about, speaking, reading, shopping, and cooking are activities that seem to correspond to the characteristics of tactical *ruses and surprises: clever tricks of the "weak" within the order established by the "strong," an art of putting one over on the adversary on his own turf, hunter's tricks, maneuverable, polymath mobilities, jubilant, poetic, warlike discoveries.* Certeau, 40.

28. Weaver and Wetherbee argue, "Walt ... loses his status as Heisenberg once he enters Gus's lab, and the third and fourth seasons can be read as Walt's quest to reclaim that identity. He becomes increasingly feminised under Gus's watch: viewers often spend more time watching Walt and Jesse clean the lab than actually make meth, while their mistrustful employer's security cameras and henchman look on." They go on to suggest that, in contrast to the RV, both hospital and superlab "see Walt in a vulnerable position, unable to decide matters for himself or express his own interiority, he is either Gus's tool or the doctors' specimen." Stephanie Weaver and Ben Wetherbee, "'You Know the Business and I Know the Chemistry': The Scientific Ethos of *Breaking Bad*," *Excursions* 4, no. 1 (2013).

29. According to Certeau, "Renters make comparable changes in an apartment they furnish with their acts and memories; as do speakers, in the language into which they insert both the messages of their native tongue and, through their accent, through their own "turns of phrase," etc., their own history; as do pedestrians, in the streets they fill with the forests of their desires and goals." Certeau, xxi.

30. Foucault, 242.

31. See Paul L. Rose, *Heisenberg and the Nazi Atomic Bomb Project, 1939–1945: A Study in German Culture* (Berkeley: University of California Press, 1998).

32. Sara Waller, "I Appreciate the Strategy," in *Breaking Bad and Philosophy: Badder Living Through Chemistry*, eds. David. R. Koepsell and Robert Arp (Chicago: Open Court, 2012), 129.

Bibliography

Adorno, Theodor W. "How to Look at Television." In *The Culture Industry: Selected Essays on Mass Culture*, edited by J.M. Bernstein, 158–177. New York: Routledge, 2001.

____. "Television as Ideology." In *Critical Models: Interventions and Catchwords*, translated by Henry W. Pickford, 59–70. New York: Columbia University Press, 2005.

American Cancer Society. *Cancer Facts & Figures 2014*. Atlanta: American Cancer Society, 2014.

Arinder, Kirby, and Joseph Milton. "The Siren Song of Mad Science." In *Supervillains and Philosophy: Sometimes, Evil Is Its Own Reward*, edited by Ben Dyer, 31–39. Popular Culture and Philosophy Series 42. Chicago: Open Court, 2009.

Backhaus, Jürgen G. "The Word of Honour." In *Friedrich Nietzsche (1844–1900): Economy and Society*, edited by Jürgen G. Backhaus and Wolfgang Drechsler, 87–110. New York: Springer, 2006.

Bakhtin, M. M. *The Dialogic Imagination: Four Essays*. Ed. Michael Holquist. Trans. Caryl Emerson and Michael Holquist. Austin: University of Texas Press, 1982.

Bandura, Albert. "Selective Moral Disengagement in the Exercise of Moral Agency." *Journal of Moral Education* 31 (2002): 101–119.

Barrette, Pierre, and Yves Picard. "Breaking the Waves." In Pierson, *"Breaking Bad": Critical Essays*, 121–138.

Baumeister, Roy F. "A Self-Presentational View of Social Phenomena." *Psychological Bulletin* 91 (1982): 3–26.

Bayoumi, Ahmed M. "Equity and Health Services." *Journal of Public Health Policy* 30 (2009): 176–182.

Bernard, Viola W., Perry Ottenberg, and Fritz Redl. "Dehumanization: A Composite Psychological Defense in Relation to Modern War." In *Behavioral Science and Human Survival*, edited by Milton Schwebel, 64–82. Lincoln, NE: iUniverse, 2003.

Blewett, Lynn A. "Persistent Disparities in Access to Care Across Health Care Systems." *Journal of Health Politics, Policy and Law* 34, no. 4 (2009): 635–647.

Bodenheimer, Thomas. "High and Rising Health Care Costs. Part 1: Seeking an Explanation." *Annals of Internal Medicine* 142 (2005): 847–854.

____. "High and Rising Health Care Costs. Part 2: Technologic Innovation." *Annals of Internal Medicine* 142 (2005): 932–937.

_____. "High and Rising Health Care Costs. Part 3: The Role of Health Care Providers." *Annals of Internal Medicine* 142 (2005): 996–1002.

_____. " High and Rising Health Care Costs. Part 4: Can Costs Be Controlled While Preserving Quality?" *Annals of Internal Medicine* 143 (2005): 26–31.

Bolonik, Kera. "Leaves of Glass *Breaking Bad*'s Walt Whitman Fixation." *Poetry Foundation*. August 6, 2013. http:/www. poetryfoundation.org/article/246218#article.

Booth, Wayne C. *The Rhetoric of Fiction*, 2d ed. Chicago: University of Chicago Press, 1983.

Bossert, Ray. "*Macbeth* on Ice." In Koepsell and Arp, "*Breaking Bad*" and *Philosophy*, 65–77.

Bowins, Brad. "Psychological Defense Mechanisms: A New Perspective." *The American Journal of Psychoanalysis* 64 (2004): 1–26.

Bowman, James. "Criminal Elements." *The New Atlantis* 38 (Winter/Spring 2013): 163-173.

Braveman, Paula, Susan Egerter, and David R. Williams. "The Social Determinants of Health: Coming of Age." *Annual Review of Public Health* 32 (2011): 381–398.

Brodescu, Alberto. "Heisenberg: Epistemological Implications of a Criminal Pseudonym." In Pierson, "*Breaking Bad*": *Critical Essays*, 53–70.

Brooks, Peter. *Reading for Plot: Design and Intention in Narrative*. Cambridge: Harvard University Press, 1992.

Buntin, Melinda Beeuwkes, Jose S. Escarce, Kanika Kapur, Jill M. Yegian, and M. Susan Marquis. "Trends and Variability in Individual Insurance Products." *Health Affairs* (2003): w3–449-w3–459.

Burdeau, Emmanuel. "En las entrañas de *Breaking Bad*." *So Film* 1 (2013): 50–58.

Catalano, Ralph, et al. "The Health Effects of Economic Decline." *Annual Review of Public Health* 32 (2011): 431–450.

Certeau, Michel de. *The Practice of Everyday Life*. Translated by Steven F. Rendall. Berkeley: University of California Press, 1984.

Chambers, Samuel. "Walter White Is a Bad Teacher: Pedagogy, Partage, and Politics in Season 4 of *Breaking Bad*." *Theory & Event* 17, no. 1 (2014).

Chandler, Michelle. "The Rights of the Medically Uninsured: An Analysis of Social Justice and Disparate Health Outcomes." *Journal of Health & Social Policy* 21, no. 3 (2006): 17–36.

Cheung, Winson Y., et al. "Analysis of Wait Times and Costs During the Peri-Diagnostic Period for Non-Small Cell Lung Cancer." *Lung Cancer* 72 (2011): 125–131.

Chou, Chiu-Fang, Pamela Jo Johnson, Andrew Ward, and Lynn A. Blewett. "Health Care Coverage and the Health Care Industry." *American Journal of Public Health* 99, no. 12 (2009): 2282–2288.

Conly, Sarah. *Against Autonomy: Justifying Coercive Paternalism*. Cambridge: Cambridge University Press, 2013.

Cook, Keziah, David Dranove, and Andrew Sfekas. "Does Major Illness Cause Financial Catastrophe?" *Health Services Research* 45, no. 2 (2010): 418–436.

Cooke, Alice Lovelace. "Whitman's Indebtedness to the Scientific Thought of His Day." *Studies in English*, no. 14 (July 8, 1934): 89–119. http://www.jstor.org/stable/20779454.

Courtwright, Andrew M. "Justice, Health, and Status." *Theoria* 112 (2007): 1–24.

DeNavas-Walt, Carmen, Bernadette D. Proctor, Jessica C. Smith, and U.S. Census Bureau. "Income, Poverty, and Health Insurance Coverage in the United States: 2012." In *Current Population Reports*, 60–245. Washington, D.C.: U.S. Government Printing Office, 2013.

Di Leo, Jeffrey R. *Corporate Humanities in Higher Education: Moving Beyond the Neoliberal Academy*. New York: Palgrave Macmillan, 2013.

_____. *From Socrates to Cinema: An Introduction to Philosophy*. New York: McGraw-Hill, 2007.

Dubber, Markus Dirk. *The Police Power: Patriarchy and the Foundations of American Government*. New York: Columbia University Press, 2005.

Eaves, Megan. "A Do-It-Yourself *Breaking Bad* Tour of Albuquerque." Lonely Planet, October 17, 2013. http://www.lonelyplanet.com/usa/travel-tips-and-articles/a-do-it-yourself-breaking-bad-tour-of-albuquerque.

Echart, Pablo, and Alberto N. García. "Crime and Punishment: Greed, Pride and Guilt in *Breaking Bad*." In *A Critical Approach to the Apocalypse*, edited by Alexandra Simon-López and Heidi Yeandle, 205–217. Oxford: Inter-Disciplinary Press, 2013.

Eleftheriadis, Pavlos. "A Right to Health Care." *Journal of Law, Medicine, and Ethics* 40, no. 2 (Summer 2012): 268–285.

Emerson, Ralph Waldo. "The Poet." In *The Essential Writings of Ralph Waldo Emerson*, edited by Brooks Atkinson, 287–306. New York: The Modern Library, 2000.

Evans, Dylan. *An Introductory Dictionary of Lacanian Psychoanalysis*. New York: Routledge, 1996.

Families USA. *Cost-Sharing in Medicaid: It's Not about "Skin in the Game"—It's about Lives on the Line*. Washington, D.C.: Families USA, 2005.

FEDREV. "'The Empire Business': *Breaking Bad*, Capitalism, and the Family." *FEDREV*. July 31, 2013. http://fedrev.net/?p=485. Accessed May 14, 2014.

Feldman, Roger. "Quality of Care in Single-Payer and Multipayer Health Systems." *Journal of Health Politics, Policy and Law* 34, no. 4 (2009): 649–670.

Fleck, Leonard M. "Just Caring: Defining a Basic Benefit Package." *Journal of Medicine and Philosophy* 36 (2011): 589–611.

Forbat, L., R. Maguire, L. McCann, N. Illingworth, and N. Kearney. "The Use of Technology in Cancer Care: Applying Foucault's Ideas to Explore the Changing Dynamics of Power in Health Care." *Journal of Advanced Nursing* 65, no. 2 (Feb. 2009): 306–315.

Foucault, Michel. *Discipline and Punish: The Birth of the Prison*. Translated by Alan Sheridan. New York: Vintage, 1979.

____. *Foucault Live: Complete Interviews, 1961–1984*. Edited by Sylvere Lotringer, translated by Lysa Hochroth and John Johnston. New York: Semiotext(e), 1996.

____. *Madness and Civilization: A History of Insanity in the Age of Reason*. Translated by Richard Howard. New York: Vintage, 1979.

____. "Of Other Spaces." In *The Visual Culture Reader*, edited by Nicholas Mirzoeff, 238-244. New York: Routledge, 1998.

Freeley, Dustin. "The Economy of Time and Multiple Existences in *Breaking Bad*." In Pierson, *"Breaking Bad": Critical Essays*, 33–52.

Freire, Paulo. *Pedagogy of the Oppressed*. New York: Continuum, 2000.

Frye, Anne. *Holistic Midwifery, vol. I: Care During Pregnancy*. Portland, OR: Labrys Press, 1998

Gabel, Jon R., Roland McDevitt, Ryan Lore, Jeremy Pickreign, Heidi Whitmore, and Tina Ding. "Trends in Underinsurance and the Affordability of Employer Coverage, 2004–2007." *Health Affairs* 28, no. 4 (2009): w595-w606.

Garland, David. "On the Concept of Moral Panic." *Crime Media Culture* 4 (2008): 15.

Gilligan, Vince. "*Breaking Bad* Insider Podcast, Episode 516." *AMC*. http://www.amctv.com/shows/breaking-bad/insider-podcast-season–5. Accessed May 14, 2014.

Glied, Sherry. "Single Payer as a Financing Mechanism." *Journal of Health Politics, Policy and Law* 34, no. 4 (2009): 593–615.

Goffman, Erving. *The Presentation of Self in Everyday Life*. Garden City, NY: Doubleday, Anchor, 1959.

Goldberg, Steven. *The Inevitability of Patriarchy*. New York: William Morrow, 1973.

Goodrich, Peter H. "The Lineage of the Mad Scientist: Anti-Types of Merlin." In *Dionysus in Literature: Essays on Literary Madness*, edited by Branimer M. Rieger, 71–88. Bowling Green, OH: Bowling Green State University Popular Press, 1994.

Gorey, Kevin M., et al. "Better Colon Cancer Care for Extremely Poor Canadian Women Compared with American Women." *Health & Social Work* 38, no. 4 (2013): 240-248.

Gostin, Lawrence O. "Redressing the Unconscionable Health Gap: A Global

Plan for Justice." *Harvard Law & Policy Review* 4 (2010): 271–294.

Griswold, Charles. *Forgiveness: A Philosophical Exploration*. Cambridge: Cambridge University Press, 2007.

Guffey, Ensley F. "Buying the House: Place in *Breaking Bad*." In Pierson, *"Breaking Bad": Critical Essays*, 155–172.

Guffey, Ensley F., and K. Dale Koontz. *Wanna Cook? The Complete, Unofficial Companion to "Breaking Bad."* Toronto: ECW Press, 2014.

Gunn, Anna. "I Have a Character Issue." *The New York Times*. August 23, 2013. http://www.nytimes.com/2013/08/24/opinion/i-have-a-character-issue.html?_r=0. Accessed May 14, 2014.

Gusmano, Michael K., Daniel Weisz, and Victor G. Rodwin. "Achieving Horizontal Equity: Must We Have a Single-Payer Health System?" *Journal of Health Politics, Policy and Law* (2009): 617–633.

Halpern, Jodi, and Harvey Weinstein. "Rehumanizing the Other: Empathy and Reconciliation." *Human Rights Quarterly* 26 (2004): 561–581.

Hamilton, Roberta. *The Liberation of Women: A Study of Patriarchy and Capitalism*. London: George Allen & Unwin, 1978.

Hausman, Daniel M. "Benevolence, Justice, Well-Being and the Health Gradient." *Public Health Ethics* 2, no. 3 (2009): 235–243.

Haynes, Rosslyn. "The Alchemist in Fiction: The Master Narrative." *HYLE: International Journal for Philosophy of Chemistry* 12, no. 1 (2006): 5–29.

Heitman, Danny. "*Breaking Bad* Brings Walt Whitman Back to the Forefront of Pop Culture." *The Christina Science Monitor*. August 20, 2013. http://www.csmonitor.com/Books/chapter-and-verse/2013/0820/Breaking-Bad-brings-Walt-Whitman-back-to-the-forefront-of-pop-culture. Accessed May 14, 2014.

Heller, Agnes. *The Power of Shame: A Rational Perspective*. London: Routledge & Kegan Paul, 1985.

Himmelstein, David U., Elizabeth Warren, Deborah Thorne, and Steffie Woolhandler. "Illness and Injury as Contributors to Bankruptcy." *Health Affairs* (2005): w5-63-w5-73.

Hsiao, William C., Anna Gosline Knight, Steven Kappel, and Nicolae Done. "What Other States Can Learn from Vermont's Bold Experiment: Embracing a Single-Payer Health Care Financing System." *Health Affairs* 30, no. 7 (2011): 1232–1241.

Hudson, Laura. "Die Like a Man: The Toxic Masculinity of *Breaking Bad*." *Wired*, October 5, 2013. http://www.wired.com/underwire/2013/10/breaking-bad-toxic-masculinity/. Accessed May 14, 2014.

Jacobs, Matthew. "Why I've Struggled to Reconcile the Fate of Jesse Pinkman on *Breaking Bad*." *Huffington Post*. September 29, 2013. http://www.Huffingtonpost.com/jacobs-matthew/the-fate-of-jesse-pinkman-breaking-bad_b_4013526.html. Accessed May 14, 2014.

Jung, C. G. *Nietzsche's Zarathustra: Notes of the Seminar given in 1934–1939*, vol. 1. Edited by C. G. Jung and James L. Jarrett. Princeton: Princeton University Press, 1988.

Kant, Immanuel. *Critique of Pure Reason*. Trans. Norman Kemp Smith. London: The Macmillan, 1983.

Kaufmann, Walter. *Existentialism: From Dostoevsky to Sartre*. Cleveland: World, 1956.

Koepsell, David R., and Robert Arp, eds. *"Breaking Bad" and Philosophy: Badder Living through Chemistry*, Chicago: Open Court, 2012.

Kotsko, Adam. *Why We Love Sociopaths: A Guide to Late Capitalist Television*. Winchester, UK: Zero Books, 2012.

Kucskar, Jonathan M. "Laboratories of Democracy: Why State Health Care Experimentation Offers the Best Chance to Enact Effective Federal Health Care Reform." *Journal of Health Care Law & Policy* 11, no. 2 (2008): 377–405.

Kuo, Michelle, and Albert Wu. "In Hell, 'We Shall Be Free': On *Breaking Bad*." *Los Angeles Review of Books*. July 13, 2012. http://lareviewofbooks.org/article.php?id=761&fulltext=1. Accessed April 5, 2013.

Lammers, Joris, and Diederik A. Stappel. "Power Increases Dehumanization." *Group Processes Intergroup Relations* 14 (2011): 113–126.

Lavarreda, Shana Alex, E. Richard Brown, and Claudie Dandurand Bolduc. "Underinsurance in the United States: an Interaction of Costs to Consumers, Benefit Design, and Access to Care." *Annual Review of Public Health* 32 (2011): 471–482.

Lazzarato, Maurizio. *The Making of the Indebted Man: An Essay on the Neoliberal Condition*. Los Angeles: Semiotext(e), 2012.

Lee, Junghee, and William Donlan. "Health Care for the Poor: Politics, Culture, and Community." *Journal of Poverty* 13 (2009): 196–213.

Levin, Jack, and James A. Fox. "Normalcy in Behavioral Characteristics of the Sadistic Serial Killer." In *Murder and the Psychology of Violent Crimes*, edited by Richard N. Kocsis, 3–14. Totowa, NJ: Humana Press, 2008.

Lewis, Mark. "From Victim to Victor: *Breaking Bad* and the Dark Potential of the Terminally Empowered." *Culture, Medicine, and Psychiatry* 37, no. 4 (Dec. 2013): 656–669.

Lewis, Michael. "Self-Conscious Emotions: Embarrassment, Pride, Shame, and Guilt." In *Handbook of Emotions*, edited by Michael Lewis, Jeannette M. Haviland-Jones, and Lisa Feldman Barrett, 742–756. New York: Guilford Press, 2010.

Lifton, Robert J. *The Nazi Doctors: Medical Killing and the Psychology of Genocide*. New York: Basic Books, 1986.

Lindsay-Hartz, Janice, Joseph de Rivera, and Michael F. Mascolo. "Differentiating Guilt and Shame and Their Effects on Motivation." In *Self-Conscious Emotions. The Psychology of Shame, Guilt, Embarrassment and Pride*, edited by June Price Tangney and Kurt W. Fischer, 274–300. New York: Guilford Press, 1995.

Loving, Jerome. *Walt Whitman: The Song of Himself*. Berkeley: University of California, 1999.

Ma, Jiemin, Elizabeth M. Ward, Robert Smith, and Ahmedin Jemal. "Annual Number of Lung Cancer Deaths Potentially Avertable by Screening in the United States." *Cancer* 119 (April 2013): 1381–1385.

MacDonald, Dwight. "Masscult and Midcult." In *Against the American Grain: Essays on the Effects of Mass Culture*, 3–75. New York: Random House, 1962.

_____. "A Theory of Mass Culture." In *Cultural Theory and Popular Culture: A Reader*, edited by John Storey, 22–36. Athens: University of Georgia Press, 1998.

Magge, Hema, Howard J. Cabral, Lewis E. Kazis, and Benjamin D. Sommers. "Prevalence and Predictors of Underinsurance Among Low-Income Adults." *Journal of General Internal Medicine* 28, no. 9 (2013): 1136–1142.

Marcotte, Amanda. "Breaking Bad Recap: S5E15, 'Granite State.'" *The Raw Story*. September 23, 2013. http://www.raw story.com/rs/2013/09/23/breaking-bad-recap-s5e15-granite-state/. Accessed May 14, 2014.

Marmot, Michael. *The Status Syndrome: How Social Standing Affects Our Health and Longevity*. New York: Holt Paperbacks, 2005.

Martin, Brett. *Difficult Men: Behind the Scenes of a Creative Revolution; From* The Sopranos *and* The Wire *to* Mad Men *and* Breaking Bad. New York: Penguin, 2013.

May, Todd. *The Philosophy of Foucault*. Montreal: McGill-Queen's University Press, 2006.

McGowan, Todd. *The End of Dissatisfaction? Jacques Lacan and the Emerging Society of Enjoyment*. Albany: SUNY Press, 2004.

_____. *Enjoying What We Don't Have: The Political Project of Psychoanalysis*. Lincoln: University of Nebraska Press, 2013.

_____. *Out of Time: Desire in Atemporal Cinema*. Minneapolis: University of Minnesota Press, 2011.

McWilliams, J. Michael. "Health Consequences of Uninsurance Among Adults in the United States: Recent Evidence and Implications." *The Milbank Quarterly* 87, no. 2 (2009): 443–494.

Menzel, Paul T. "Justice and Fairness: A Critical Element in U.S. Health System Reform." *Journal of Law, Medicine, & Ethics* 40, no. 3 (2012): 582–597.

_____. "The Cultural Moral Right to a Basic Minimum of Accessible Health Care." *Kennedy Institute of Ethics Journal* 21, no. 1 (2011): 79–119.

Merton, Robert. *Social Therapy and Social Structure.* New York: Free Press, 1957.

Minow, Newton N. "Television and the Public Interest." Speech, Washington, D.C., May, 9, 1961. American Rhetoric. http://www.americanrhetoric.com/spe eches/newtonminow.htm.

Morrison, Toni. *Beloved.* New York: Vintage, 2004.

Nietzsche, Friedrich. *Thus Spoke Zarathustra: A Book for All and None.* Translated by Graham Parkes. New York: Oxford University Press, 2008.

_____. *Thus Spoke Zarathustra: A Book For Everyone and No One.* Translated by R. J. Hollingdale. New York: Penguin, 1969.

Nozick, Robert. *Anarchy, State, and Utopia.* New York: Basic Books, 1977.

Pagan, Jose A., and Mark V. Pauly. "Community-Level Uninsurance and the Unmet Medical Needs of Insured and Uninsured Adults." *Health Services Research* 41, no. 3pt. 1 (2006): 788–803.

Pierson, David. "Breaking Neoliberal? Contemporary Neoliberal Discourses and Policies in AMC's *Breaking Bad*." In Pierson, *"Breaking Bad": Critical Essays,* 15–32.

Pierson, David, ed. *"Breaking Bad": Critical Essays on the Contexts, Politics, Style, and Reception of the Television Series,* ed. David Pierson. Lanham, MD: Lexington Books, 2014.

Poole, W. Scott. "Walter White, Super Villain." *Huffington Post.* Last modified November 26, 2013. http://www.huffing tonpost.com/w-scott-poole/walter-white -super-villai_b_4339912.html. Accessed May 6, 2013.

Preis, John F. "Witch Doctors and Battleship Stalkers: The Edges of Exculpation in Entrapment Cases." *Vanderbilt Law Review* 52, no. 6 (November 1999): 1869–1909.

Ragupathy, Rajan, Katri Aaltonen, June Tordoff, Pauline Norris, and David Reith. "A 3-Dimensional View of Access to Licensed and Subsidized Medicines Under Single-Payer Systems in the U.S., the UK, Australia, and New Zealand." *Pharmacoeconomics* 30, no. 11 (2012): 1051–1065.

Raiz, Lisa. "Health Care Poverty." *Journal of Sociology and Social Welfare* 33, no. 4 (2006): 87–104.

Ram-Tiktin, Efrat. "The Right to Health Care as a Right to Basic Human Functional Capabilities." *Ethical Theory and Moral Practice* 15, no. 3 (2012): 337–351.

Rawls, John. *A Theory of Justice.* Cambridge: Harvard University Press, 1971.

Rose, Paul L. *Heisenberg and the Nazi Atomic Bomb Project, 1939–1945: A Study in German Culture.* Berkeley: University of California Press, 1998.

Sánchez-Baró, Rossend. "Uncertain Beginnings: *Breaking Bad*'s Episodic Openings." In Pierson, *"Breaking Bad": Critical Essays,* 139–153.

Savoye, Daniel Ferreras. *The Signs of James Bond: Semiotic Explorations in the World of 007.* Jefferson, NC: McFarland, 2013.

Schlenker, Barry R. *Impression Management: The Self-Concept, Social Identity, and Interpersonal Relations.* Belmont, CA: Brooks/Cole 1980.

Schoen, Cathy, Sara R. Collins, Jennifer L. Kriss, and Michelle M. Doty. "How Many Are Underinsured? Trends Among U.S. Adults, 2003 and 2007." *Health Affairs* 102 (2008): w298-w309.

Seifert, Robert W., and Mark Rukavina. "Bankruptcy Is the Tip of a Medical-Debt Iceberg." *Health Affairs* 25 (2006): w89-w92.

Sepinwall, Alan. *The Revolution Was Televised: The Cops, Crooks, Slingers and Slayers Who Changed TV Drama Forever.* New York: Touchstone, 2012.

Shields, Michael. "Walter White v. Walt Whitman," *Across the Margin.* August 4, 2012. http://acrossthemargin.com/walter-white-vs-walt-whitman/. Accessed May 14, 2014.

Shklovsky, Victor. "Art as Device." In *Theory*

of Prose, translated by Benjamin Sher, 1-14. Elmwood Park, IL: Dalkey Archive Press, 1990.

Smith, Jon. *Finding Purple America: The South and the Future of American Cultural Studies.* Athens: University of Georgia Press, 2013.

Stoll, Kathleen. *Paying a Premium: The Added Cost of Care for the Uninsured.* Washington, D.C.: Families USA, 2005.

Tait, R. Colin. "The HBO-ification of Genre." *Cinephile* 4, no. 1 (Summer 2008): 50–57.

Tangney, June Price, and Kurt W. Fischer. "Self-Conscious Emotions and the Affect Revolution: Framework and Overview." In *Self-Conscious Emotions: The Psychology of Shame, Guilt, Embarrassment, and Pride*, edited by June Price Tangney and Kurt W. Fischer, 3–22. New York: Guilford Press, 1995.

Terjesen, Andrew. "Why Doctor Doom Is Better Than the Authority." In *Supervillains and Philosophy: Sometimes, Evil Is Its Own Reward*, edited by Ben Dyer, 81–90. Popular Culture and Philosophy Series 42. Chicago: Open Court, 2009.

Todd, William Mills. "*The Brothers Karamazov* and the Poetics of Serial Publication." *Dostoevsky Studies* 7 (1986). http://www.utoronto.ca/tsq/DS/07/087.shtml.

Toumey, Christopher P. *Conjuring Science: Scientific Symbols and Cultural Meaning in American Life.* New Brunswick, NJ: Rutgers University Press, 1996.

Tropp, Laura. "Off Their Rockers: Representation of Postpartum Depression." In *Mental Illness in Popular Media: Essays on the Representation of Disorders*, edited by Lawrence C. Rubin, 77–91. Jefferson, NC: McFarland, 2012.

Tudor, Andrew. *Monsters and Mad Scientists: A Cultural History of the Horror Movie.* Oxford: Basil Blackwell, 1989.

Waller, Sara. "I Appreciate the Strategy." In Koepsell and Arp, *"Breaking Bad" and Philosophy*, 125–135.

Ward, Andrew. "The Concept of Underinsurance: A General Topology." *Journal of Medicine and Philosophy* 31 (2006): 499–531.

____. "Needs, Medical Necessity, and the Problem of Helping the Uninsured." *Theoria* 112 (2007): 73–98.

Watkins, Megan. *Discipline and Learn: Bodies, Pedagogy, and Writing.* Rotterdam: Sense, 2011.

Weaver, Stephanie, and Ben Wetherbee. "'You Know the Business and I Know the Chemistry': The Scientific Ethos of *Breaking Bad*." *Excursions* 4, no. 1 (2013): 1–17.

Whitman, Walt. *Leaves of Grass.* Edited by Harold W. Blodget and Sculley Bradley. New York: W.W. Norton, 1968.

____. "Preface." *Leaves of Grass*, Inclusive ed. Edited by Emory Holloway. New York, 1926.

____. *Whitman's Works*, Camden ed. Edited by R.M. Bucke, T.B. Harned & H. Traubel. New York, 1902.

Wilkinson, Richard G. *Unhealthy Societies: The Afflictions of Inequality.* New York: Routledge, 1996.

Williams, Lisa A., and David DeSteno. "Pride and Perseverance: The Motivational Role of Pride." *Journal of Personality and Social Psychology* 94, no. 6 (2008): 1007–1017.

Williams, Raymond. *Television.* London: Routledge, 2003.

Wittgenstein, Ludwig. *Philosophical Investigations.* Translated by G. E. M. Anscombe. New York: Macmillan, 1953.

Woolhandler, Steffie, and David U. Himmelstein. "Life or Debt: Underinsurance in America." *Journal of General Internal Medicine* 28, no. 9 (2013): 1122–1124.

The World Bank. *The Decline of the Breadwinner: Men in the 21st Century.* World Development Report 2012: Gender Equity and Development, Spread 2. http://go.worldbank.org/6R2KGVEXP. Accessed May 14, 2014.

Žižek, Slavoj. *The Fragile Absolute, or Why Is the Christian Legacy Worth Fighting For.* New York: Verso, 2000.

____. *Looking Awry: An Introduction to Jacques Lacan Through Popular Culture.* Cambridge: MIT Press, 1991.

____. *The Plague of Fantasies.* London: Verso, 1997.

About the Contributors

Jacob **Blevins**, a professor of English at McNeese State University, is the author or editor of five books and the editor of the comparative literature journal *INTERTEXTS*. His research interests include 16th and 17th century literature, Latin poetry, literacy theory, Shakespeare and Milton.

Matthew A. **Butkus** is an associate professor of philosophy at McNeese State University specializing in medical and scientific ethics. His work in several health care systems has ranged from patient care to ethics cases, critical care research and administration, and he has taught evidence-based practice, research methodology and current issues in health care.

Neil **Connelly** teaches creative writing at Shippensburg University. He has published five books; his *The Pocket Guide to Divorce: A Self Help Work of Fiction* (Gorsky Press, 2014) won the 2014 Molly Ivors Prize.

Ron W. **Darbeau** is a native of Trinidad and Tobago. He has authored dozens of research articles and is a professor of chemistry and head of the Department of Chemistry and Physics at McNeese State University.

Jeffrey R. **Di Leo** is a professor of English and philosophy and the dean of Arts and Sciences at the University of Houston–Victoria. His recent books include *Turning the Page: Book Culture in the Digital Age—Essays, Reflections, Interventions* (Texas Review Press, 2014) and *Corporate Humanities in Higher Education* (Palgrave Macmillan, 2014).

Pablo **Echart** is a lecturer in screenwriting and the academic director of the master's degree in screenwriting at the University of Navarra (Spain). He has published on Hollywood comedy and filmmakers such as Woody Allen, Alexander Payne, David Mamet, Clint Eastwood and Paul Auster.

Cheryl D. **Edelson** is an associate professor of English and the English discipline coordinator at Chaminade University of Honolulu. Her research and teaching interests include American literature, the literary Gothic, film and television studies, indigenous literatures, and popular culture.

Alberto N. **García** is an associate professor of film and television studies at the University of Navarra (Spain). He has been a visiting professor at the University of Stirling (UK), George Washington University (U.S.), and the Universidad de los Andes (Chile). His research interests include emotions, narrative and television series.

Jason **Landrum** is an associate professor of English at Southeastern Louisiana University, where he teaches courses in film studies, critical theory, and American literature. He has recently published on the criminal profiler film in *International Journal of Žižek Studies* and on the films of Joel and Ethan Coen in *No Country for Old Men: From Novel to Film* (Scarecrow, 2009).

Philip **Poe** is an assistant professor of communication at Mississippi State University, where his research interests include media effects and health communication campaigns, and television and the family. His preferred research methods are face-to-face surveys and textual and content analysis.

Rebecca **Price-Wood** is a licensed midwife in Lake Charles, Louisiana. She was clinical director of Peak Midwifery and Birthing Center and the founder of her city's sole postpartum support group. Her fields of study include prenatal and postpartum psychology, feminism and birth.

Miguel E. H. **Santos-Neves** is the director of communications at the Brazil Foundation in New York City. He is writing a book that looks beyond regionalist readings of Faulkner's work, by placing them in context with international trends of the early 20th century.

Meron **Wondemaghen** is a lecturer in criminology at the University of New England. Her research interests include forensic mental health, criminal law and psychiatry, neuro-law, criminology, media coverage of crime, television and film studies, and social constructionism.

Dafydd **Wood** is an assistant professor of English and foreign languages at McNeese State University whose work focuses on interdisciplinary modernism and poetics. A contributor to the latest edition of the *Princeton Encyclopedia of Poetry and Poetics*, he has also published original poetry, scholarly articles and translations from the French.

Index